Digital Destiny

New Media and the Future of Democracy

JEFF CHESTER

THE NEW PRESS

NEW YORK
LONDON

Published in the United States by The New Press, New York, 2007
Distributed by W. W. Norton & Company, Inc., New York

LIBRARY OF CONGRESS CATALOGING-IN-PUBLICATION DATA
Chester, Jeff.
Digital destiny : new media and the future of democracy / Jeff Chester.
p.   cm.
Includes bibliographical references and index.
ISBN-13: 978-1-56584-795-8 (hc.)
ISBN-10: 1-56584-795-4 (hc.)
1. Mass media—Political aspects—United States.   2. Mass media—Technological
innovations.   3. United States—Politics and government—2001–4.
4. Democracy—United States.   I. Title.
P95.82.U6C479 2007
320.973—dc22   2006012053

The New Press was established in 1990 as a not-for-profit alternative to the large,
commercial publishing houses currently dominating the book publishing industry. The
New Press operates in the public interest rather than for private gain, and is committed
to publishing, in innovative ways, works of educational, cultural, and community value
that are often deemed insufficiently profitable.

www.thenewpress.com

Composition by NK Graphics/Group360 Visual Communications
This book was set in Bembo

Printed in the United States of America

2   4   6   8   10   9   7   5   3   1

In memory of the late Erik Barnouw and Greg MacArthur,
and for Kathy and Lucy

We live life in real space, subject to the effects of code. We live ordinary lives, subject to the effects of code. We live social and political lives, subject to the effects of code. Code regulates all these aspects of our lives, more pervasively over time than any other regulator in our life. Should we remain passive about this regulator? Should we let it affect us without doing anything in return?

—Lawrence Lessig, *Code and Other Laws of Cyberspace*, 2000

I don't have to tell you things are bad. . . . We know the air's unfit to breathe and our food is unfit to eat, and we sit and watch our teevees while some local broadcaster tells us today we had fifteen homicides and sixty-three violent crimes, as if that's the way it's supposed to be. . . . All I know is first you have to get mad. You've got to say, "I'm a human being goddammitt. My life has value." So I want you to get up now. I want you to get out of your chairs and go to the window. Right now. I want you to go to the window, open it, and stick your head out and yell. I want you to yell, "I'm mad as hell, and I'm not going to take this any more!"

—Paddy Chayefsky, *Network* screenplay, 1976

Contents

Acknowledgments

For the past twenty-five years, I have been involved in what is known as media policy advocacy. From fighting in the early 1980s to preserve and expand the role independent producers play in public broadcasting to helping challenge recent corporate plans for further media consolidation, I found myself on the front lines. It is ironic that the only way to help ensure that the United States has a communications system that fosters diversity of expression is to engage in a political battle with the very forces that make up our media: newspaper chains; broadcast networks; cable, satellite, and telephone monopolies; and now "new media" behemoths. But that has been necessary to help ensure that an ever-dwindling number of giants don't control almost all the communications outlets in a single town, let alone the nation. Political pressure has also been necessary to help make the electronic media support what little is left of serious journalism and public service. Today, however, instead of "rearguard" efforts to make our "old" media as accountable as possible, the focus of our advocacy must be on ensuring that the digital media system meaningfully serves us all as citizens and other active participants in a democracy.

This book offers a glimpse inside the political apparatus of the media and communications industries. It explores their vision for our media future, which is primarily focused on unleashing the most powerful, personalized, interactive marketing machine the world has ever witnessed. It reveals the media industries and their political lobbies at their most crass. But the book also illustrates how collective outrage over the industries' self-serving objectives recently helped defeat some of their plans. Such activism is necessary if we are to help the United States and indeed the world achieve the kind of just civil society that we deserve. This book will, I hope, serve as a helpful history lesson about past battles and lessons learned, and a guide to some of the issues that now require activism.

This book would never have been written without the encouragement, insight, and great patience of my editor, André Schiffrin, at The New Press. His assistant, Joel Ariaratnam, has also graciously provided insightful editorial advice (and extended deadlines). I was fortunate to first meet André at a meeting organized in Washington, DC, by the Advocacy Institute. I thank the institute co-directors at the time, Michael Pertschuk and David Cohen, for inviting me.

Without the help and unflagging camaraderie of my Center for Digital Democracy colleague Gary O. Larson, and the always-excellent editorial advice from my wife, Kathryn C. Montgomery, I never would have been able to finish this book. I thank my daughter, Lucy, for her support and encouragement, and my longtime friend Janine Martin for her constant support. I am grateful as well to Suzanne Goldberg. I also thank Sarah Fan of The New Press and Cindy Milstein, who copyedited the manuscript.

I have only been able to work on communications policy during the last ten years because of the support of philanthropic foundations. I am grateful to the Angelina Fund of the New World Foundation, the Annie E. Casey Foundation, the Arca Foundation, the Albert A. List Foundation, the Carnegie Corporation of New York, the Ford Foundation, the HKH Foundation, the Nathan Cummings Foundation, the Phoebe Haas Trust, the Open Society Institute, the John D. and Catherine T. MacArthur Foundation, the J. Roderick MacArthur Foundation, the Rockefeller Family Fund, the Stern Family Fund, and the Schumann Center for Media and Democracy. To all my program officers at these institutions, past and present, I express my gratitude.

I salute my colleagues in Washington, DC, and around the world for their dedication to the public interest in communications. I especially wish to thank Angela Campbell, Mark Cooper, Gene Kimmelman, and Andrew J. Schwartzman. I am indebted to both Ralph Nader and his colleague John Richard for helping me start my career as a Washington, DC–based policy advocate. I have also been helped by so many others—friends, colleagues, and allies—too numerous to mention.

Finally, this book would not be possible without the inspiration of investigative reporters and independent producers who have and will continue to offer the public a version of our lives that is essential—but far too often out of view.

Introduction:
Communications at the Crossroads

We are on the eve of the emergence of the most powerful media and communications system ever developed. A flood of compelling video images propelled by the interactivity of the Internet will be delivered through digital TVs, PCs, cell phones, digital video recorders, iPods, and countless mobile devices. These technologies will surround us, immerse us, always be on, wherever we are—at home, work, or play. We will have access, if we can afford it, to an ever-expanding array of news, entertainment, and communications from around the world. Much of the programming will be personalized, selected by us with the help of increasingly sophisticated, but largely invisible, technologies that will "sense" or "know" our interests, dislikes, and habits. Information about our travels—in cyber- and real space—will be collected and stored, most often without our awareness. Such data will be the basis of computerized profiles that generate in a flash commercial pitches honed to precisely fit our psychology and behavior.

The changes we are witnessing in our media system are occurring at a dizzying pace. Each day, there seems to be some new technological innovation or an even bigger industry merger announced. It's hard for anyone to keep up with these developments, let alone have a clear understanding of what they will ultimately mean for our society.

But decisions are being made today about our country's digital future by the biggest media companies, advertisers, technology manufacturers, lobbyists, and politicians. The U.S. public, sadly, has not been invited to participate, even though these decisions will affect everyone here and—since the United States is so dominant—around the rest of the world. The corporate media know where they wish to take us. If they are successful, we are likely to live with a communications system that offers us dazzling entertainment and seeks to fulfill our every consumer desire. Yet it will not meaningfully contribute to improving our lives or our democracy. We run the risk of merely serving as observers while special interests determine America's "digital destiny."

Our electronic media serve as a brilliant mirror that, at best, provides us with critical sources of information, insight, inspiration, creative expression, and commerce. But by its own design as well as through the media industry's collective economic and political power, it's largely become a fun-house mirror that distorts what we see, imagine, know, and understand. And in the digital age, this mirror will be powered by a torrent of microchips, fiber-optic wires, and computers able to instantaneously transport us to worlds we can only now imagine and perhaps even fear.

The dramatic, lightning-fast changes now occurring within communications are one reason why we can't afford to be silent. If we act now to express our collective vision of the kind of communications system that the United States requires in the twenty-first century, we might have a media environment that nurtures free expression, education, social justice, and economic well-being. Missing from what should be intense and well-publicized debates about where our digital society is headed are discussions of how our media can foster civic participation, make government more accountable to the public, address the needs of low-income people, and help ensure that our programming reflects the nation's diversity.

For decades, lawmakers along with other government officials and agencies, including the Federal Communications Commission (FCC), have been the recipients of huge sums of money to help maintain the corporate media status quo. Billions of dollars are spent in campaign contributions and for lobbying to buy control of politicians and the policy process. A gold-plated "revolving door" regularly sends our communications policymakers into high-paying corporate jobs. The largest media companies deploy teams of lobbyists to besiege and beseech lawmakers, constantly asking—and winning—an endless stream of favors. They have been able to compile far-reaching empires through their political operations, including a hold over the country's newspapers, radio and TV stations, cable systems, satellite services, and programming channels.

Now they have their sights on the foremost digital prize: the Internet. A few wish to be lords of the digital domain, able to control—and greatly profit from—what should be our public communications highway. They hope to hijack what should be a public resource and treasure. They want to transform the Internet into a digital tollbooth that will send us gaming, gambling, more movies on demand, and interactive advertising. If they succeed, we will travel over a corporate-run piece of electronic real estate where we are numbered, digitally shadowed, and evaluated based on income, race, and class. All so we can be better around-the-clock consumers in virtual spaces and off-line (the real world). Media and telecommunications industry lobbyists are now using their practically unlimited power and checkbooks to have Congress, the White House, the courts, and the FCC help them transform the Internet from what a federal court termed in a landmark decision "the most participatory form of mass speech yet developed" into a system of corporate-controlled private "pipes."

In the last century, we witnessed the development of some of the most profound instruments for communication. At each stage when so-called new communications technology was introduced—radio, broadcast TV, and cable—pundits and industry supporters promised that it would fundamentally make our media system more democratic. Yet powerful commercial forces worked to undermine the then-new medium's potential. As we know from leading media historians Erik Barnouw and Robert W. McChesney, the country was promised an electronic media system that would seriously address its social, civic, and educational needs. But such assurances from the broadcasting industry during the debate over the 1934 Communications Act was part of a skillful and well-funded lobbying campaign designed to ensure that broadcasters could operate without any specifically mandated public-interest requirements. As McChesney chronicles in his outstanding history of the period, citizens' groups seeking serious policies to safeguard the public interest were overwhelmed by industry. Pledges that documentaries, quality cultural programming, and other public-service efforts would be a core part of radio and TV were quickly forgotten. The preeminent forces that ultimately shaped our communications system were related to how advertisers could best be served.[1]

As a result, a few companies were made fabulously wealthy by being given permission to use public resources, including our airwaves. At every turn, this "media monopoly," as historian and journalist Ben Bagdikian has called it, besieged the Congress and the FCC, seeking to dramatically expand its power. It has largely been successful in having Washington topple safeguards that were created to protect the average American from the dangers of living in a country where a handful of modern-day Citizen Kanes—in the guise of General Electric, Disney, and Rupert Murdoch—can help determine so much of what we are told each day.[2]

Our country's electronic media feel no real compulsion to serve the public interest. Public service became a dirty word in the industry—used only when lobbyists had to ask for even

more political handouts from policymakers. The failure to ensure meaningful public-service programming is a major reason
why our TV news doesn't stray far beyond the sound-bite,
chatty banter, or diatribe. It's why there is so little investigative
reporting, with the so-called watchdog of the press becoming
the proverbial lapdog. Think about Enron, WorldCom, harmful
prescription drugs, and many other scandals that were not reported on until it was too late. Consider also the consequences
of having a news media that failed to warn us of the growing
disenchantment and anger from abroad about U.S. policies that
could provoke—as it did—an attack. We have perfected a media
system where there is abundant room for channels featuring in-
fomercials. But little time is made to ensure that our First
Amendment is well served by providing us with a wide range of
views and in-depth information that is at the core of the media
industry's public responsibilities.

As the late communications scholar George Gerbner consis-
tently reminded us, those who control what stories we hear can
help determine our politics and culture. Promoting a commercial culture is the most important story that General Electric,
Disney, Viacom, and many others want us to constantly hear.
That's why our lives are so dominated by advertising, buying,
and selling. Our new digital media enable us to tell many more
stories that may actually assist us to better govern ourselves, and
begin to redress the race and class problems that haunt the
United States. But to have such stories told, we have to ensure
that our new digital communications readily permit such messages to be meaningfully heard.

That's why we have to do this right. Today, many believe that
our electronic media system is entering a permanent golden age,
where a never-ending series of Web sites, bloggers, and streaming videos along with a mind-boggling assortment of virtual
voices challenge the mainstream "big media" giants. Such independent voices and perspectives will undoubtedly continue to

be part of our digital lives. But there's no guarantee that such diversity won't be electronically sidelined by the plans of today's media and advertising industries to ensure that they remain at the forefront of our attention. As James Surowiecki explained in the *New Yorker,* our largest phone and cable companies wish to become "Internet gatekeepers."[3] If they have their way, it will be an Internet in their image, sponsored by AT&T, Comcast, Viacom, Time Warner, and Fox. These few will also likely own, unless we stop them, many of the nation's principal "old media" news outlets, including daily newspapers, broadcast stations, and TV channels. Instead of having a communications environment that promotes freedom, creativity, and expression, we could witness an ever-dwindling number of major corporations controlling an unthinkable array of the most powerful media outlets.

As we listen to communications policy debates, we should also remember that what the media industry promises lawmakers are mostly lies. The media have no intention—and certainly no track record—of delivering the benefits they regularly invoke as the payment to the public if they receive a favorable decision to their lobbying request. The media lobby is a good example of an institution suffering from a form of repetitive promise syndrome. The media have continually promised that once "freed" from government oversight, the country would witness dramatic advances in health care, a bonanza for employment, and more choice for "consumers." Such words work magic in Washington, serving as a convenient smoke screen for what is really just a power grab. Unsaid to lawmakers is that one of their key goals is to better perfect a system of interactive advertising and personal data collection. This book summarizes what programmers, ad executives, technologists, and academic experts are collectively doing to help further what I call "brandwashing." By also covering recent media industry efforts to win favorable legislation, including the now-infamous 1996 Telecommunications Act, this book seeks to forewarn readers about the power of the media lobby to do and say anything to win its political goals.

This book also discusses how the public, angered about broken media promises and the threats of even more consolidation of ownership, recently raised up in collective protest. Consequently, the plans of the media lobby to sweep away what little remains of safeguards preventing a few to control so much were—for the moment—defeated. We need to be inspired by such actions as we confront many of the same companies that also want to determine the dimensions of our digital age.

Our creation of an electronic broadband media system will be viewed by future generations as one of our society's most significant accomplishments. Will it be seen as one of the highest achievements for a democracy, a place in cyberspace that helped enrich the lives of many and offered new opportunities for an outpouring of cultural and civic expression? Or will it be seen years hence as a new version of what the late scholar Neil Postman aptly described as a medium even more capable of "amusing ourselves to death"? We hold that decision in our hands.

1

Really "Meet" the Press: The Days, Months, and Years When You Didn't "Read—or See—All About It"

TV's coverage of the September 11, 2001, attacks was praised as one of journalism's "finest hours." Not since the assassination of President John F. Kennedy in 1963 had the medium devoted so many commercial-free hours to reporting the news. Newspapers also dedicated more resources, including the printing of special sections, to better cover the tragedy. But senior executives at TV networks, broadcast stations, and newspapers also had another story on their mind right after the World Trade Center crumbled to the ground. Their focus was on Washington, DC—but not on the Pentagon or the White House. It was on the FCC. For on September 13, 2001, the FCC announced that it would review and presumably eliminate a key policy long opposed by the most powerful media companies in the United States. The broadcast-newspaper cross-ownership rule and other safeguards, including limits on cable TV industry ownership, stood in the way of their ability to buy more media properties. Get rid of these rules, and with our increased revenues, print and electronic journalism will flourish, the companies promised regulators.

From fall of 2001 through 2004, practically every media owner would lobby Congress and the Bush administration–controlled FCC seeking a favorable outcome for their political agenda. But the public was never really informed about what the media companies were asking policymakers to do during that time. They were kept unaware of the hot pursuit of favors at the FCC and in Congress by the owners of their favorite newspaper and TV news program. They were not given the details of how the news and entertainment they now receive might change—or what was being promised in terms of new services for them.[1]

As they lobbied for a favorable decision, media companies pointed to their September 11–related reporting as an example. Broadcasters told policymakers that their 9/11 programming illustrated how they were serving the "public interest." In addition to expanded news coverage, the four commercial networks also cited a jointly produced "star-studded telethon," which had raised millions for victims. But simultaneously, they also bemoaned their loss of advertising revenues from not being able to air commercials following the attack and during the subsequent economic downturn. "Let us buy more media outlets so we can continue to support our news operations," they whispered in the halls of Congress. Eliminating the media ownership rules was how, they said, "the government could help them out."[2]

There was a perverse irony in pointing to their September 11 programming as illustrative of the vigorous state of journalism in the United States. Equally ironic was their proffered solution, suggesting that further consolidation would help strengthen reporting. For what was not said to policymakers was that there had been a growing affliction for many years within the news business. Media consolidation, including the waves of mergers of radio and TV stations, newspapers, cable companies, and broadcast networks, had taken its toll. Driven to please the interests of Wall Street, a media system had emerged that greatly reduced the ability of reporters and producers to meaningfully inform the public.

By the 1990s, news organizations were firmly ensconced within giant corporate empires, imprisoned by a structure that forced them to respect rather than challenge government and commercial power. Far-flung media companies were increasingly relying on the lobbying of governments here and abroad to further their business strategies. Financial resources for newsgathering were limited by parsimonious parent companies that continually sought higher profits each quarter.

As a November 2001 Project for Excellence in Journalism study, "Gambling with the Future," reported, "Local TV journalism" was now "on dangerous ground." Consultants advised news departments about "what to cover and what not to cover," based on what could generate "the most advertising dollars." More than half of the 118 news directors surveyed said that advertisers regularly press them to "kill negative stories or run positive ones." It was "getting harder every year" to protect the news from the influence of advertisers, explained one news manager. News directors noted they were having to "produce a thinner and cheaper product."[3] Even on network-owned stations, "video news releases" created by advertisers ran on local news as if they had been produced by the station.[4] The situation was also dire at the national TV networks. The elimination of FCC public-interest policies had led to a growing reliance on "soft" over "serious" news. Nightly newscasts were increasingly running pieces on celebrities, crime, and sports. TV news bureaus abroad had been shuttered by corporate cost cutting. Newspaper journalism was also reeling from cutbacks in news staffs, despite an increase in profits.[5]

The very force of consolidation itself had contributed to an inability of the news media to adequately inform the public of the growing threats to the United States from abroad. As *Editor and Publisher* magazine would write in reporting on the *9/11 Commission Report* findings, the "watchdog" of the news media had been found "asleep."[6] TV and newspapers had not focused on what was clearly a growing threat. The ratings-driven twenty-four-hour news cycle had also contributed to an information culture in which the speed of reportage now regularly trumped analysis and discussion.

In addition to failing to warn the public about the developments that led to September 11, the news media played a significant role in helping the Bush administration win approval to wage war in Iraq. Not only did the print and electronic press allow the Bush administration's "weapons of mass destruction" premise to go unchallenged they also helped to promote the myth's legitimacy. Even before President Bush asked Congress for the authority to wage war, the media had helped foster a public belief that former Iraq dictator Saddam Hussein had masterminded 9/11. As researchers at the University of Maryland's Center for International and Security

Studies documented, the White House was able to set an agenda for the press that was meekly followed by major media outlets. Skepticism, let alone serious reporting, was largely kept in a state of suspended animation.[7]

During fall 2001, American flag pins were prominently worn by news anchors and patriotically branded animated logos adorned newscasts. The Bush administration had reached out to the media industry to help rally the country, and the broadcast and cable networks were eager to comply. But invisible to the public, this show of support was also accompanied by lobbying from the TV and newspaper industries about media ownership. Had Americans known, they might have asked themselves how the unabashed display of TV loyalty to the Bush administration played into what industry lobbyists were saying to Congress and the FCC.[8]

When they say it isn't about the money, it's about the money.
—Fred Friendly, on the attitude of the networks toward their
news departments

The media have long been a part of politics. What is less known is that big media has regularly used the tools of politics to advance their interests over everyone else's. The country's most powerful media companies have developed a formidable political machine. They each have their own lobbying offices, hire well-connected political consultants, and are members of influential trade associations. Disney/ABC, General Electric/NBC, Viacom/CBS, Time Warner, and News Corp./Fox are just a few of the conglomerates that maintain well-funded political operations in the nation's capital. Many of these companies also sit on the boards of lobbying "trade associations," such as the National Association of Broadcasters (NAB) or the National Cable and Telecommunications Association (NCTA). Representatives of Cox, Gannett, Post- Newsweek, Tribune, Scripps, Media General, Belo, and Advance/Newhouse have recently served on either the NAB or NCTA boards. Most major newspaper companies, including the parent organizations of the *Washington Post* and the *New York Times*, also belong to the Newspaper Association of America (NAA) advocacy group.

The media lobby's deep pockets also permit it to hire well-connected political help. Concerned that the public outcry over the FCC's 2003 media ownership decision would drive a congressional override (see chapter 6), NBC, CBS, and Fox enlisted the aid of the influence-peddling firm of Cassidy and Associates. Cassidy's role was to give them access to top Republican lawmakers, who could protect the networks' newly won FCC increase in station ownership limits. Cassidy had connections to key Republicans, including, as the firm stated on its Web site, "the Speaker, Majority Leader, Conference Chair, and seven other leadership offices."[9] Cable giant Comcast, apparently fearful that there would be political challenges to its corporate agenda, hired Bush White House chief of staff Andrew Card's lobbyist sister-in-law, Lorine Card.[10] The NAB, along with many other media companies, relied on Democratic superfixer Tony Podesta to bolster its political deal making.

In addition, media companies controlling our news have a huge policy agenda in Washington beyond ownership. Since many of them have a stake in other fields—such as General Electric's work on defense and nuclear energy, or Disney's involvement with tourism and manufacturing—their lobbyists also work on many other special-interest issues. Companies such as Time Warner or Comcast also regularly lobby at the state and local levels on such issues as tax breaks and cable rates. Media firms play a major role in contributing to political campaigns, hosting tony events during presidential nominating conventions and providing "airtime" to powerful lawmakers.

The CEOs of many media conglomerates have a clear political allegiance either to a candidate, a political party, or an ideology. No journalist working for Murdoch needs to be told about Murdoch's role as a major supporter of the GOP via Fox News or the *Weekly Standard*. Nor that Viacom/CBS CEO Sumner Redstone endorsed the election of George Bush in 2004 because from a "Viacom standpoint, the election of a Republican administration is a better deal . . . deregulation and so on."[11] Who at Time Warner during the 1990s didn't know that then–CEO Gerry Levin was constantly going to Congress and the courts to overturn every rule limiting cable TV's monopoly power?[12]

Failure to Communicate

> *The freedom of the press can remain a right of those who publish only if it incorporates into itself the right of the citizen and the public interest.*
>
> —*Commission on Freedom of the Press, 1947*

The concentration of control of our nation's media outlets and its impact on journalism have been a concern for more than a half century. In the late 1940s, the Commission on Freedom of the Press, chaired by Robert H. Hutchins, wrote a landmark work. The "Hutchins Commission" report, *A Free and Responsible Press*, recognized that media consolidation was connected to growing problems in U.S. journalism. The "chain" ownership of newspapers and broadcasting (the single-company ownership of many outlets across the country) would have a negative effect on the press's ability to promote diverse and antagonistic viewpoints. They would, instead, likely "show hospitality" to the ideas of their owners.

A Free and Responsible Press reflected on the lessons from World War II and the potential prospect for peace with the founding of the United Nations. Composed of scholars, writers, and philosophers (and funded by *Time* magazine founder Henry Luce), the commission was concerned that the consolidation of media ownership would ultimately harm the ability of the United States to meaningfully evolve in an increasingly global society. The commission was also aware that technologies would greatly expand the reach and influence of the new press lords. Empowered by technology, large news organizations "can spread lies faster and farther than our forefathers dreamed when they enshrined the freedom of the press on the First Amendment to our Constitution," the commission warned.[13]

One can see the spirit of the Hutchins Commission recommendations in the FCC policies developed during the 1960s and 1970s that encouraged a diversity of media ownership and promoted public-interest programming. The FCC's regulatory regime played a key role at that time in promoting more quality news programming. Broadcasters were afraid the FCC might actually crack down on the industry, threatening their extremely profitable programming oligopoly. Concern over the regulatory consequences of the late 1950s' quiz scandals (where contests were fixed by the networks) and alarm over Kennedy administration FCC chair Newt Minow's "Vast Wasteland" speech criticizing the quality of TV both helped spur serious documentary programming on the networks. Network news budgets were fatter as a result because they helped keep the FCC wolf at bay.

But TV news never recovered from the FCC's "slash and burn the public interest" efforts started by the Reagan era FCC. The commission, along with a largely complicit Congress and backed by the broadcast lobby, discarded the notion that there was a public interest for TV to adhere to beyond generating enormous revenues. The FCC turned a blind eye to the corporate takeovers of the three major broadcast networks—ABC, CBS, and NBC—during the 1980s. Seeking to cut costs and recognizing there would be no recrimination by the Reagan FCC, the new network owners butchered their news divisions. There were major layoffs, overseas bureaus were closed, and documentary/investigative programming was eliminated. Policies by the FCC at that time were also responsible for the rise of "tabloid" TV, setting the stage for the coarse nature of much programming, such as on Fox. Even with the introduction of twenty-four-hour cable news, such as CNN, the information programming Americans saw was dictated by the established economic and regulatory conventions for TV. Without any overriding public policy requirements, the purpose of TV news was now primarily to keep viewers engaged so they will watch the next commercial. Ratings-driven decisions created news programming that was light on information, analysis, and criticism. Contrarian views were strictly off-limits.[14]

Don't Ask, Don't Tell Me

Today, the business of news is business, not news.
                    —*Gilbert Cranberg, Randall Bezanson,*
                           and John Soloski, Taking Stock

Newspaper journalism suffered as well. Publicly traded media firms were pressed to deliver ever-rising profits to their Wall Street investors, despite considerable annual growth. A bottom-line mentality began haunting newsrooms. As explained in *Taking Stock*, news has become far less important to newspaper holding companies than the revenues to be made from advertising or some other profitable aspect of their wide-ranging businesses. A system has been put in place at newspapers where executives—including news managers—are financially rewarded by their participation in practices actually harmful to journalism, such as cutting newsroom budgets.[15]

By the early 1990s, even the largest newspapers were reeling from a sort of compression—the inability to have the depth of resources necessary for reporters to do their job. Investigative reporting, although still practiced, was becoming far less frequent. Not-for-profit groups had to be created by journalists to fill an increasingly large vacuum at news outlets. Enterprise reporting, as it is sometimes called, was now being outsourced. Both the Center for Investigative Reporting and the Center for Public Integrity, two such nonprofits, have conducted the kind of intensive inquiries that mainstream media should have been doing.

Journalist Ben Bagdikian's *Media Monopoly* is a clarion cry against the dangers of consolidation. The landmark book, first published in 1983 and updated over two decades, has been largely ignored by policymakers.[16] Meanwhile, the problem of media concentration grew more evident during the 1990s and into the new century. Yet despite an unprecedented series of media-related legislation, legal action, and FCC proceedings, there has been little reporting by news organizations about what their own companies are doing (see chapter 2).

The list of outlets that largely failed to report on the FCC's

2001–2003 ownership proceeding is alone an indictment of our news system. Practically every company was politically involved in some way, either lobbying directly or through its trade group. Eric Boehlert of the online magazine *Salon* was one of most perceptive critics of the FCC coverage debacle. As he wrote in May 2003, neither the broadcast or cable networks nor most of the nation's major dailies covered the first and only public hearing on the commission's proposal, which would have ended many safeguards. There was also, as Boehlert noted, little broadcast or cable news coverage prior to the June 2003 FCC vote on new ownership rules.[17]

Broadcast and cable TV news have steadfastly avoided reporting on media issues, given that their owners are all involved in lobbying. But reporters didn't have to be told to largely stay away from covering these issues, let alone what their own industry and parent company were doing. As Center for Public Integrity founder and investigative journalist Charles Lewis explains,

> What journalist is going to propose to his editors or owners that they expose the special interest influence-peddling of the media? That's an idea that will kill a promising career. Many editors and reporters exercise self-censorship or anticipatory restraint, when it comes to investigating the media. It is kind of like an ostrich sticking its head in the ground, seeing nothing. Meanwhile, the American people are not informed about how the media barons are profiteering from democracy, and why it matters. An entire part of our national discourse is muted, with no debate, because the media doesn't want to shine a spotlight on itself.[18]

Newspaper editors are also to blame for their decision to place most media policy stories in the business section. Adding to the problem has been that media policy was not viewed as an important beat; media business reporters were forced to cover many industries at once, along with issues related to consumer privacy, new gadgets, cable rates, or mobile phone service. Since newspaper coverage sets the agenda for TV news, the failure of the print press to prominently focus on media-related stories has contributed to what is ultimately a news blackout. Not a single major news organization has engaged in investigative reporting of the media lobby.[19]

Countless times, when reporters were asked to cover stories of policy changes or the implications of media mergers, they would claim that readers or viewers were simply not interested. The cases were "inside baseball," covered only by the specialized trade publications. Or they would say, "We've covered such things in the past." Such reporters were visibly surprised when media policy became one of the most spirited and discussed issues in 2003. Millions of Americans formally opposed the Bush FCC's media ownership plans. Few journalists, however, reflected that perhaps the public may have been more interested in the issue all along, but simply didn't know much about what was really going on.[20]

All the News We Won't Print or Televise

Given this great diversity, there is no longer any valid rationale for retaining a government-imposed limit on common ownership of newspapers and broadcast stations at the local level.
        —New York Times Company, formal comments to the FCC,
                                                December 2001

Perhaps there is no better example of a failure to be candid about its media industry lobbying than the New York Times Company. The corporate parent of the *New York Times*, *Boston Globe*, seventeen other daily papers, and eight TV stations filed a lengthy document with the FCC in early December 2001. The filing, filled with statements from Times executives and media industry experts, vociferously argued that the commission should end its long-standing policy preventing common ownership in the same market of a newspaper and broadcast TV station. The Times told the FCC that the "newspaper/broadcast rule no longer serves any legitimate purpose in today's media-saturated environment," claiming that the "repeal of the rule will result in an increase, not a decrease, in diverse and competitive sources of news and information available to the public."[21]

Neither the general public nor the communities served by the Times Company ever learned the full details about what was being promised if the commission eliminated the cross-ownership policy. Nor were they told what the potential negative consequences might be. Thus, viewers and readers of the Times Company news outlets could not weigh-in with their own views or even engage in the debate. It would take months for the *New York Times* to report that its parent was seeking to overturn the FCC rule.[22]

In each of the communities it served, the Times Company informed the FCC, there was now a "plethora of competing local media voices." The company pointed to one of the smallest markets where it owned a TV station: Fort Smith, Arkansas. Perhaps the residents of that community would have liked to have known that according to the filing, those living there "now have access to a striking multiplicity of voices." Among those identified by the Times Company in its filings at the FCC were radio stations owned by "John Brown University," "LeRoy Billy," and "Vision Ministries." There was also the publication every Wednesday of the *Hometown News*. The company assured regulators that the residents of Memphis, Tennessee, where the Times Company also had a TV station, had nothing to fear from a policy change because there were stations run by Clear Channel, Trinity Broadcasting, the Board of Education, Bountiful Blessings, Inc., and the K-Love Radio Network. In a separate document titled "Media Sources in the USA," the Times pointed to the "Drudge Report," "Break Point—A Christian Perspective on the News," and the "Laura Lee Show" as evidence that diversity of expression was alive and well.

There was also high-minded rhetoric full of commitments made to the FCC by the Times Company, which claimed that "public interest benefits" would be delivered "upon elimination of the cross-ownership rules." There would be "more news and information services . . . at a higher quality," the company promised. The public would greatly benefit from the "synergies and efficiencies" as TV and newspaper news staffs were combined. Some of the company's digital TV capacity would be tapped as well in order to create "new services such as all-news DTV channels." (The Times Company, like all other station owners, had benefited from the 1996 Telecom Act digital TV spectrum giveaway to the broadcast lobby, each station now had an extra set of the public airwaves.) But these words were for FCC eyes only.

Nor would *Times* readers learn about how the company's various media holdings may have influenced or shaped its reporters' coverage of communications issues. For example, missing from its pages were the implications of major investments in cable, including a 2002 $100 million joint venture with Discovery Communications. Through the deal, the Times was also now a partner with Discovery's major shareholders, including John Malone's Liberty Media, Cox Communications, and Advance/Newhouse. Surely reporters on the media beat at the company's papers must have recognized that the Times was now part of cable's closed programming world. After all, Discovery's partners had promised to help ensure that no new additional "basic programming service featuring documentary, science and nature programming" would ever appear in the United States.[23]

> *The* Los Angeles Times *is still very strong journalistically, but one wonders how long it can stay strong.*
> —*John Carroll, former* Los Angeles Times *editor*

Perhaps no company lobbied as hard for the newspaper-TV cross-ownership rule's demise as Tribune. The Tribune Company operates an empire of newspapers (including the *Chicago Tribune*, *Los Angeles Times*, and *Baltimore Sun*), TV stations, programming services, cable channels, and the Chicago Cubs. Tribune's many media outlets rarely explained to their readers what the issues were, let alone what the company meant when it told the FCC that the "Newspaper Rule harms the public by denying access to the superior quality news and information that results when publishers own local broadcast outlets." Like the Times Company, Tribune swore to the FCC that a "super-competitive media environment" existed in the United States. It was "folly" for the FCC to have a policy on newspaper-broadcast cross-ownership. There wasn't even a legal premise left for any regulation of TV at all, it claimed.[24]

Companies like Tribune hold tremendous sway with media policymakers. After all, officials argue, we should heed the proposals from those who really run the business. But while the Tribune Company was making claims to the FCC that its interest in deep-sixing the media ownership rules was aimed at enhancing competition and improving journalism, it failed to inform the agency that in reality, the corporation was much more interested in expanding its highly profitable entertainment ventures. Tribune basked in the glory of being, as it noted in its annual 2004 report, the "leading syndicator of first run, hour action drama" for TV, including the *Beastmaster* and *Mutant X* programs. Given Tribune's dominance in newspaper markets and its profitable partnerships with Comcast, Time Warner, and Microsoft, it probably didn't expect to see the vibrant competition it predicted in its arguments to the FCC.

Indeed, even as Tribune spent hundreds of millions buying new TV stations, it was also firing dozens of reporters to bolster its bottom line. Such "business" decisions would undoubtedly never be mentioned as Tribune lobbied policymakers. But it didn't just work to influence federal officials. The company also made sure that civic-minded charitable foundations wouldn't threaten its plan by supporting public-interest efforts. When the Carnegie Corporation of New York brought together a working group of journalists, journalism school deans, and media scholars in June 2002 to discuss what could be done to address the crisis in reporting, a Tribune executive helped ensure no action would be taken. It was at a time when the FCC was deliberating media ownership issues, with public calls for the submission of independent research about the state of journalism. Orville Schell, dean of the University of California at Berkeley's Graduate School of Journalism, recommended that Carnegie and the expert group "might want to appeal collectively to the FCC, or at least provide it with an academically researched argument in favor of more responsible journalistic programming."

Such an intervention would have been welcomed by advocates and officials such as FCC commissioner Michael Copps. But the opportunity was immediately lost as Tribune Publishing president Jack Fuller vigorously argued against the idea. "Please, don't go to the government to solve the problem of public information in our society," he said. "Nothing has been changed, in the nature of governments or human nature, that suggests government is going to be the solution to our problem here."[25] What Fuller didn't mention, however, was that at precisely that moment, he and Tribune were aggressively asking "the government" for help in the form of favorable policies worth billions of dollars.[26]

It Is Clear There Is a Crisis in U.S. Journalism Today

The basis of our governments being the opinion of the people, the very first object should be to keep that right; and were it left to me to decide whether we should have a government without newspapers, or newspapers without a government, I should not hesitate a moment to prefer the latter.

—Thomas Jefferson, 1787

Along with its failure to cover the real story behind the run-up to the Iraq war, the press in the United States bears a major responsibility for the failure of the country to address some of its most pressing problems. From the rising income gap between the rich and the poor, to the tens of millions without health insurance, to our tattered relationships globally, our news media have become incapable of protecting the public interest. Instead of focusing the nation's attention on its troubles and helping to champion solutions, our major news media are squandering their journalistic resources. They have become timid, self-serving, and a hazard to our economic and political well-being.

Where was the reporting that should have exposed early on the scandals of Enron and WorldCom? As economic writer Jeff Madrick has explained, the news media itself played an important role in helping create the mirage of the "new economy," cheerleading us all the way to the dot-com bust. It's not just domestic issues but also "foreign affairs" that require a new focus by the news media. Until the media begin to help Americans better understand their relationship with the politics and economics of the global South, our country will continue to be the target of rage.[27]

Much of mainstream journalism will continue in a crisis until there is an acceptance that we must change the public policies for the media industries. This will be difficult to do, as the media industry advocates for ever-more consolidation and a weakening of what's left of public-interest policies. But there are a number of approaches that should be considered, including major policy reform for mainstream news media outlets and a new regulatory regime for broadband Internet communications. This will be discussed in the final chapter.

2

Consolidation Dance: Featuring Clinton, Gore, Gingrich, and a Cast of Lobbyists

Never before had a law been signed in the Main Reading Room of the Library of Congress. The president predicted that this bipartisan legislation would bring "revolutionary" changes to the country. The bill reflected the nation's "best values" and would strengthen our democracy. Soon, the president declared, the United States would benefit from advances in education, health care, and job creation.[1] The vice president, who had played a major role in advocating for the bill, said that the country was "charting a new path to our national future. . . . It is not a mid-course correction. . . . It is a new flight path to an entirely new world."[2] The speaker of the House of Representatives, known for his command of the issue, praised it as "a jobs bill" and a "knowledge bill." He predicted the law would "bring more health care of better quality at lower cost."[3]

Helping to host this "historic" event, which was attended by prominent political and business leaders, was another well-known figure. In remarks that conveyed that less lofty aspirations might be realized, Ernestine—actress Lily Tomlin's telephone operator character—spoke about how the new law would bring us the "super-duper infomercial freeway." Tomlin was supposed to add some comic relief and Hollywood glitz as the Telecommunications Act of 1996 was signed by the president. But the real joke was on the public, with the charade acted out by President Bill Clinton, Vice President Al Gore, Speaker Newt Gingrich, and most of the other elites attending the ceremony.[4]

Much had been made by the Clinton administration, the GOP,

and the telephone, cable, and broadcasting industries heavily lobbying for the new law that this was a bill designed to quickly provide Americans with the benefits of "advanced" digital communications. But the Telecom Act was never meant to serve the public interest in such areas as jobs and education, let alone in communications. The law did little to ensure that the Internet would improve the lives of Americans. That's because it was written to further enrich the nation's media and telecommunications conglomerates, along with Washington's unholy trinity of power: politicians, lobbyists, and lawyers.

On taking office in 1993, the Clinton administration had made the development of what it called the National Information Infrastructure (NII), popularly known as the information superhighway, one of its top policy goals. The NII would purportedly deliver profound changes to everyone. Vice President Gore, the administration's lead official on communications issues, spoke of the "communications revolution" that would bring the public a new form of "empowerment" as technology helped to transform us from "consumers into providers."[5]

There were high expectations from media reform advocates in the early 1990s that the new administration would support policies designed to provide the country with a more diverse and democratic media system. They believed that the Internet could fundamentally challenge the media monopolies of broadcasting and cable TV, helping to counter the harmful impacts of media consolidation. The Net would also restore vitality to journalism, which had been beset with problems arising from mergers and cost cutting in newsrooms. As the Internet merged with TV, a powerful new medium could flourish, freed of the corporate and public policy constraints that limited choice and diversity in video programming. But advocates also understood that the largest media and telecommunications companies had no intention of losing their clout. These companies would not only want to maintain their domination of today's media but extend it into the emerging interactive world. It would be critical to develop policies that would help preserve the new digital medium's democratic structure while also constraining the ability of "old" media giants to become stifling digital gatekeepers.

Public-interest leaders hoped that Gore would recognize the need for strong safeguards. After all, as a senator, Gore had been one of the leading critics of the cable industry, decrying its monopolistic control over video programming. Gore understood that the dramatic changes in technology were unleashing what was already called two-way broadband communications. While it was evident that electronic commerce would prosper on its own, the potential role that the Internet could play promoting civic participation required a set of public policy measures. Otherwise, the democratic uses of the Internet would become secondary to the drive for corporate profits. Here was an opportunity to reverse years of what Washington and the industry termed "deregulation." It had left the country's major media in the hands of a few, helping to usher in a bottom-line mentality in news and entertainment programming.

> *The most major surgery on the Communications Act since it was enacted in 1934.*
>
> —*Al Gore, 1993*

In one of his first pronouncements about the NII, in 1993, Gore said that the country would need to revise its telecommunications and media laws in order to achieve its goals for the Internet's future. "The Administration will support removal . . . of judicial and legislative restrictions on all types of telecommunications companies: cable, telephone, utilities, television and satellite," Gore stated. "Market forces," he said, would "replace regulations and judicial models that are no longer appropriate." Such changes were necessary because it was "private investment" rather than the government that was going to build the NII. But while Gore said that the administration would seek to relieve the business sector of "suffocating regulation," it would also strive to protect the public from "unfettered monopolies."[6] Gore endorsed the concept of an "open platform" to protect the Internet from control by either cable or phone companies. To his credit, he also called for new policies that would ensure there would not be a generation of so-called information have-nots (later called the "digital divide").[7]

A broad initiative was developed by the administration to help spur the NII: the Information Infrastructure Task Force. There were governmental committees, white papers, advisory boards, public hearings, and pilot projects, all designed to foster a set of policies and strategies that would support the development of an NII.[8] In his 1994 State of the Union address, Clinton announced that the transformation of the country's media system was one of his highest priorities. He called on Congress to quickly approve legislation that would provide "instant access to information," which "will increase productivity, [and] will help to educate our children. It will provide better medical care. It will create jobs."[9]

Soon after, Gore made a trip to Hollywood to speak about plans for the NII. The vice president was paying political homage to many of the administration's supporters in the entertainment and media industry, along with the country's most powerful telecommunications moguls. Despite their polite reception to Gore's speech, it was evident that the phone, cable, and broadcast industries would each use their considerable lobbying power to advance their own economic interests, cloaking them in the guise of helping the country fulfill the promise of an NII. They had no intention of permitting an open platform to develop that would challenge their position in their respective markets.

Everything would play to their advantage. The phone industry would soon hire one of Gore's top aides. Other media companies and trade associations also hired lobbyists who had special contacts in the administration and the key congressional committees. An infrastructure of think tanks and industry-supported nonprofit groups showered support for an agenda favorable to the media companies. Representatives from Silicon Valley expanded their Washington, DC, political operations, sending in top CEOs to meet with the administration and Congress. They made it clear, through their own white papers, that the best path for the NII was to allow "market forces and competition" to determine the Internet's future.[10]

Such recommendations from the CEOs of Apple, Intel, AT&T,

Hewlett-Packard, and others had an effect. The administration looked to Hollywood, Silicon Valley, and Wall Street both for policy direction and as sources of campaign contributions. While there would be much rhetoric about the potential of the NII, the administration ultimately would not take any risks that would shake up the corporate media status quo.

Compounding the administration's closed-door approach was the change of power in the 1994 election. Most critically, the GOP won control of Congress, ushering in a leadership shift in the key committees overseeing media and telecommunications. Republicans were eager to appeal to big business, reflecting their philosophy, but also in response to new campaign contribution fund-raising schemes the GOP had developed for industry. They helped craft a bill that was seen as one of the biggest giveaways to private interests in the twentieth century. The legislation passed with overwhelming bipartisan support.

So on that February day in 1996, Clinton and Gore blessed the act's approach to media ownership, saying that "by providing safeguards in the deregulation of monopolies and preventing undue concentration in the mass media, this legislation will promote and protect competition." Gore noted that it was "probably the biggest win for bipartisanship on a substantial piece of legislation we've seen in this Congress."[11]

Yet just a few months before, Gore had bitterly criticized the legislation. "America's technological future is under attack by shortsighted ideologues, who pretend to understand history, but in fact have no understanding whatsoever," he had said the previous September. Gore warned that the bill, strongly backed by Gingrich's GOP, would foster ever-greater consolidation and monopolization. "The telecommunications bills pending before the Congress . . . and especially the House bill, represent a contract with 100 companies. The highest bidders, not the highest principles, have set the bar."[12]

Gore's critique was correct, of course, before he and the Clinton administration performed a 180-degree turn to both praise and take credit for the law. Instead of promised competition, the Telecommunications Act of 1996 would hasten further communications and media industry consolidation by sparking a frenzy of deals and mergers. There would soon be fewer owners controlling the nation's daily newspapers, broadcasting stations, cable systems, and telephone companies. Jobs would be lost and there would be no dramatic improvements in education and health care.[13]

Going, Going, Gone

This is the kind of deal that was intended when the telecom bill was passed.

—*Mel Karmazin, Infinity CEO*

We now know that the Telecom Act was the "starting gun" for a communications industry shopping spree. Leading media outlets were traded as if they were pork bellies on the commodities market. Even before the president signed the bill, mergers were made in anticipation of the law—including Capital Cities/ABC with Disney. Soon after the bill was signed, newspaper and broadcast giant Tribune scooped up ten TV stations for $1.3 billion. Tribune would spend another $6 billion to take over Times Mirror, the publisher of such newspapers as the *Los Angeles Times*, *Newsday*, and the *Baltimore Sun*. Westinghouse Electric/CBS and Infinity Broadcasting merged, creating a new $4.7 billion radio powerhouse. Viacom then acquired Westinghouse/CBS for $50 billion. Murdoch became one of the largest owners of TV stations, adding twenty more outlets to his Fox network. Time Warner bought Turner Broadcasting in a $6.7 billion deal. The nation's largest cable company, Telecommunications, Inc. (TCI), was acquired by AT&T for $48 billion. Telecommunications companies were also in play, epitomized by the 1998 $37 billion purchase of MCI by WorldCom.

The frenzied pace of mergers and acquisitions would soon lead to the largest media combination in U.S. history, when AOL and Time Warner announced a $160 billion merger in 2000 (see chapter 9).[14]

Major communications firms vanished overnight. Gone were "Baby Bells" Pacific Telesis, Nynex, GTE, and Ameritech. Gone were cable giants Continental Cable, TCI, and MediaOne. Some of the biggest TV and radio station groups disappeared as they were folded into even larger empires, such as New World, Chris-Craft, and Jacor.[15]

The act did not deliver more jobs. By 2003, there were a half million *fewer* employees working for telecommunications companies. The law was supposed to generate $2 trillion in economic growth. But within a few years, the market value of telecom corporations was about $2 trillion *less* than when the bill was signed. Consumers had been promised that the act would "save them . . . $333 billion in lower long-distance rates, $32 billion in lower local phone rates, and $78 billion in lower cable bills." Yet monthly fees for cable and local phone rates soared by 50 and 20 percent, respectively.[16]

The Telecom Act was supposed to be a boon to the radio business, encouraging programming diversity. But the exact opposite occurred, as radio became ever-more homogeneous with stations gobbled up by conglomerates. Two companies soon dominated the industry: Clear Channel and Viacom (Infinity). Ten thousand people lost their jobs, including severe cuts in radio newsrooms.[17]

Nor was there any of the promised competition between phone and cable companies that was supposed to offer Americans new options for voice and video communications. The pledge by TV broadcasters that there would be new forms of public-interest programming serving the public was forgotten.[18]

> *There is no ringy-dingy any more.*
>
> —*Lily Tomlin, 1994*

The Telecom Act is a tragic case study in how our officials continually fail to create media policies that benefit the public. Time after time, media and telecommunications companies use the same rhetoric to convince policymakers to pass laws or rules that benefit their economic interests. Overlooked by officials is how such policies diminish the democratic potential of our media system.

The media industry's political success is not solely based on how it effectively creates and frames its messages, of course. There is the outpouring of millions in campaign cash given to lawmakers and the political parties. Of great help too is the revolving door between the media industry and policymakers that provides lucrative employment for so many ex-officials.

Much of what was said by the media companies during the debate on the 1996 Telecom Act was repeated as they sought favorable decisions by the FCC in 2003 on media ownership. They can be heard again now as cable, telephone, broadcast, and Internet giants work the halls of Congress, state legislatures, and even city halls. The same lobbying themes are trotted out again and again.

What was the magic word as the Telecom Act was debated that helped instill a sense of political suspended animation, opening the congressional floodgates to an outpouring of special-interest provisions? *Competition.* Like an elixir guaranteed to cure all ills, the companies that hated competition would suddenly transform themselves into cutthroat capitalists, driving down prices while laying down miles of fiber-optic cable to everyone's home.

In 1996, the refrain was that if lawmakers would help unleash competition, the nation would witness a communications transformation. Eliminate policies that restrain us, the broadcasting, cable, and telephone companies said, and we will aggressively compete with each other. Consumers will receive telephone service from cable providers. Video programming will flow over phone lines. Given favorable rules, local broadcast TV stations will become the public's link to the information superhighway. Everyone will be connected to a digital universe for free. All this competition, each industry claimed, will be a financial boon to consumers ("your constituents") as monthly cable and telephone bills plummet. Congress must not impede the inevitable progress and financial prosperity that will surely come from new technologies such as the Internet.

The bill's opponents, who wanted to maintain and even expand rules limiting media power, were dismissed as being out of touch. Industry lobbyists claimed that public-interest advocates didn't understand that we were now living in a new economy. Federal rules intended to promote competition, diversity of expression, and public service threatened to dim the opportunities made possible by the dot-com boom. Besides, any concerns critics had about media monopolies would be answered by the new technologies.

Typical of those who alleged that competition would bring us into a new era was writer and technology investment adviser George Gilder. He was just one from a legion of experts, representing so-called think tanks financially backed by industry, who provided support for the media lobby's agenda. Gilder had made a name for himself by writing such books as *Microcosm* and *Life after Television: The Coming Transformation of Media and American Life* (published with advertisements from Federal Express).

Testifying on the bill, Gilder warned the Senate Commerce Committee that if it failed to enact what he called the "freedom model of de-regulation," the U.S. economy would suffer a $2 trillion blow, harming the "stock market . . . incomes and job growth." Let companies and industries merge without any restrictions, and soon new technologies would "overthrow all the hierarchies and monopolies, pyramids, and power grids of the established communications infrastructure."[19]

That such hyperbole would have any impact on lawmakers reflects the sad state of what passes for serious debate in Washington, DC, especially on communication issues. But the media and telecommunications industries have benefited from an almost thirty-year campaign to discredit the critical role public policy plays in fostering an equitable and diverse communications environment. Regulation had been given a reputation as onerous, unfair, or even undemocratic. Deregulation, the sweeping away of policy safeguards—except those actually desired by industry—was the idol many lawmakers now worshipped.

Bolstering the impact of Gilder's pronouncements was the perception that he was representing many of the views of Newt Gingrich, then at the apex of his power. After all, Gilder was connected with the Progress and Freedom Foundation (PFF), the high-tech think tank founded to help advance Gingrich's ideas. Gilder had helped write a number of PFF's key publications, including its self-proclaimed "Magna Carta for the Knowledge Age." The PFF had issued a media "manifesto" in May 1995 partially credited to Gingrich himself. It was time to "cleanse the detritus of the past" by ending what the PFF termed New Deal–type policies. The FCC should be eliminated, since its rules had "inflicted staggering costs upon American consumers and the economy." Newspapers, TV stations, cable systems, and telephone companies must be permitted to merge at will. Media ownership rules should be scuttled. "Mass privatization" of the public's airwaves would turn them over to the highest bidder. What little was left for the government to do on communications could be accomplished by a small office at the White House.[20]

So-called think tanks such as the PFF perform an important political role for industry, helping create new points of pressure on Congress or the FCC. By urging that the FCC be eliminated, the PFF also relieved the media companies from having to attack the agency's policy role themselves. The tactic was designed to place supporters of media policies further on the defense, since now they would have to defend the agency as well.

A whole slew of such groups played a key part in supporting the corporate agenda for the telecom bill (see chapter 4), including Citizens for a Sound Economy (now Freedom Works), the Heritage Foundation, and the American Enterprise Institute.

The PFF and its allies found a glowing reception from the late twentieth century's version of robber barons, such as Robert Wright of General Electric/NBC, Gerry Levin of Time Warner, and Murdoch of News Corp./Fox. The media lobby would use Gingrich's GOP, deregulatory proponents like the PFF, and the Clinton administration in a campaign designed to sweep away limits to its power and gain one of the biggest windfalls in U.S. history.

How Congress might help . . .

—GOP leaders, January 1995

Congress had been considering a rewrite of the 1934 Communications Act since the 1970s. Bills had been written, but failed to pass, as competing interests and campaign cash paralyzed lawmakers. But when the Republicans took over Congress in January

1995, the media industries recognized that this was their golden moment. The GOP wanted to champion the interests of big business. Immediately after taking power, the new House leadership organized two days of closed-door sessions with the CEOs of some of the biggest media companies. The goal, said Republican leaders, was to "learn how Congress might help their industry." Among the notable "teachers" for GOP lawmakers were Murdoch of News Corp./Fox, Wright of General Electric/NBC, Thomas Murphy of Capital Cities/ABC, Howard Stringer of CBS, and John Curley of Gannett. At a Heritage Foundation–sponsored dinner for the executives, Gingrich attacked the news coverage of the Republican congressional takeover, including outlets owned by his "guests." Sources told the *Washington Post* that Gingrich's "complaints of brutal treatment from the press seem to have been sympathetically received."[21]

Gingrich's message was that media companies better make sure their news divisions played ball with the "Republican Revolution" or else face the consequences in Congress. The meeting with the executives, as recounted by media critic Ken Auletta, was part of a larger scheme to help enhance GOP power. Soon after the event, the CEOs "got calls from the fund-raisers and the party chairman" asking for political contributions. They were also urged, as part of the GOP's "K Street Project" (run by Tom DeLay) "to get rid of their Democratic lobbyists and hire Republicans."[22]

Despite the threats, the media industry knew a good thing when it saw it. Here was the powerful majority in Congress bending over to help, and asking little in return. After all, campaign contributions and other favors for politicians were a way of life, regardless of the party in control. As for reining in criticism of the Republican agenda, the executives knew that reporters working for the broadcasting, cable, newsweekly, and daily newspaper industries didn't really need to be publicly reminded that the passage of the Telecommunications Act would affect their careers.

During the bill's passage, the press would not focus on how their own outlets or industry would benefit, and on what their corporate parent's Washington, DC, lobbying offices were doing. TV and radio would just deliver sound-bites about how the proposed law would be a boon to competition and consumer pocketbooks. Newspapers wouldn't challenge the bill's fundamental premise that competition and diversity were just around the corner. The failure of the press to cover the bill and its own corporate role was one of the major indicators for reform advocates that further consolidation would harm the news media's ability to serve as a watchdog. As noted by scholar Dean Alger, the three broadcast networks' prime-time newscasts barely covered the bill from when it was introduced in 1995 to its final passage—offering a total of about twenty minutes over nine months. Much of the coverage was taken up with side issues, such as concerns over so-called Internet indecency and TV violence. Some of the reports were just a few seconds in length. Newspaper editorial coverage of the bill was strongly linked to whether their company also owned broadcast stations. Those that did were silent on the bill's controversial provision awarding stations public airwaves worth billions.[23]

As public-interest groups worked the press, one was aware that many reporters were thinking about how any potential ownership changes brought on by the legislation might affect their own careers. Reporters at *Time* magazine, for example, had to be aware that the cable industry—including parent company Time Warner—was supporting the legislation. Journalists at major dailies likely knew too well that their next boss could easily be from one of the big media companies lobbying for the bill. But reporters would not want to say that they were worried or feared for their future employment. There were excuses. Some claimed that this was a story too technical, wonky, or "inside the Beltway." Of course, this was exactly the reason they should be covering the Telecom bill critically. For this was a story, after all, that would help to change who controlled U.S. news outlets, affecting the public's "right to know." Even enthusiastic reporters at respected news outlets who expressed an interest in more in-depth coverage learned from their editors that there were limits to what could be done.[24]

It wasn't only the GOP wanting to help get the bill swiftly enacted. There was also pressure coming from Democrats. Both parties wanted to take credit for having played the key role in passing a new communications law, which was supposedly going to be a boon for the public. Gore, Gingrich, Senate majority leader Bob Dole, and others pressed the various commercial interests to "stop stalling" and come to an agreement among themselves on the legislation. If they failed to do so, then Congress would act on its own—which might not fully support what each company or industry desired. As new House Telecommunications Subcommittee chair Jack Fields (R-TX) told Mike Mills of the *Washington Post*, "I've tried to make clear we are not going to wait. If they can't come to some kind of resolution quickly, then we're going to move forward."[25]

Such "let's-make-a-deal" exhortations quickly had an effect. As the *Post*'s Mills observed, "Every sector appears poised to get what it wants in the upcoming overhaul of the 1934 Communications Act." A "sort of mutual nonaggression pact" had been formed by normally feuding industries. Cable wasn't objecting to "broadcasters' efforts to loosen ownership rules or get freer use of their broadcast frequencies." Broadcasters now ignored the cable industry's proposal to dismantle rules limiting rate increases (something they had recently helped enact). The only industries still arguing over the terms of the legislation were the Baby Bells and long-distance companies such as AT&T.[26]

Bouncing "Checks and Balances"

The First Amendment rests . . . on the assumption that the widest possible dissemination of information from diverse and antagonistic sources is essential to the welfare of the public, that a free press is a condition of a free society.
      —*Justice Hugo Black,* Associated Press v. U.S., *1945*

Despite the oratory about a new day dawning for competition in the Internet era, what the broadcasting, cable TV, and newspaper industries really wanted was to use a new Telecom Act to eliminate the remaining policy constraints on their power. Over the decades, and created by laws, FCC regulations, and court decisions, a form of checks and balances had developed. Responsible regulators at the FCC and civic-oriented political leaders had understood that the electronic media system enabled a few to hold sway over mass public opinion. This concentration of power needed to be tempered through a variety of policies, including one designed to foster a "diversification" of ownership. Having many different owners of communications outlets such as radio and television stations would encourage a variety of programming perspectives. Another check was the rule requiring radio and broadcast TV stations to undergo regular license renewal reviews, demonstrating that they were serving their communities by airing public-service programming.

The broadcasting industry had long chafed at the handful of public-interest rules in place. The four commercial over-the-air TV networks—Fox, CBS, NBC, and ABC—wanted to scrap the cap, or ceiling, on station ownership, both locally and nationally. There was such a cap on the number of TV or radio stations a single corporation could nationally own outright (although they could assemble a vast network comprised of their own and affiliated stations). Other broadcasters also desired to simultaneously operate multiple TV stations in the same town, creating what they call duopolies, triopolies, or more. Newspaper companies, including Tribune and Gannett, wanted to buy TV stations so they could operate lucrative media combinations. That would require the elimination of the broadcast-newspaper cross-ownership policy.[27]

These FCC rules and laws historically had mixed results. Even with limits on ownership, a few companies readily dominated broadcasting, cable, and newspapers. Nor was there much real diversity of content—with TV broadcasting, for example, having embraced the same cookie-cutter formula for much of local and national programming. Cost-cutting measures, a previous round of megamergers during the 1980s, and lax federal oversight had helped decimate the quality of broadcast news. Persons of color and women had no significant ownership role at all in radio, broadcast TV, and cable.[28]

But despite their limitations, media ownership rules represented something important to preserve. They reflected legal and philosophical approaches to ensuring that the First Amendment served the public, not just media corporations. The media industry has continually argued that the First Amendment is primarily designed to benefit them. Any limits on its power, such as ownership safeguards, the industry claims, is a violation of its constitutional rights. But it's the public who must be guaranteed a communications system that ensures as much robust and diverse news and debate as possible, especially via the most powerful media. The sweeping elimination or weakening of these rules would have even fewer large companies running the nation's newsrooms, unaccountable at all to the public. Such a victory for industry would be harmful to our democracy, said the bill's opponents.

But with both lawmakers and the media lobby claiming that the country would soon be experiencing an unprecedented outpouring of content diversity, there really wasn't room for any serious introspection concerning the ills of our communications system. The illusion created by the Internet boom served as an effective facade for what was just an old-fashioned power grab.[29]

Eight TV Stations for the Price of One

Those with a stake in the broadcast TV business also desired something more than just an approval to further consolidate. They planned to use the Telecom Act to help advance their campaign to become more of a major power in the cable business. The majority of viewers by now relied on cable and satellite companies to receive TV. Cable and satellite offered viewers multiple channels; TV broadcasters could only deliver one. Cable companies were able to reap the financial rewards from two sources: monthly subscribers and advertisers; broadcasters supported themselves only through advertising.

Broadcasting's leaders knew that its future as a business was in jeopardy. TV was changing. Soon, as video and Internet technology merged, programs and advertising would be delivered interactively. Viewers then could select what programs they wished to see. Advertising that was finely targeted to viewers based on information that had been collected about their viewing habits and interests was going to be the preferred method for commercials. Broadcast executives understood that cable's two-way technology (through its wires, set-top boxes, and so on) would make it the dominant medium for TV and even Internet service. They feared that their business would soon be relegated to the back roads of a video wilderness, while cable prospered.

The broadcast lobby had devised a plan where it would use its political clout to get a chunk of cable's profitable future. At the top of its congressional wish list with the Telecom Act was to win a giant slice of new public airwaves for free—worth tens of billions of dollars. In the twenty-first century, electronic real estate such as airwaves (spectrum) is the equivalent of owning railroads and vast fields of oil wells in the nineteenth and twentieth centuries. Broadcasters believed they could use these new airwaves as part of a strategy to gain more control over cable.

Broadcasters had built a successful political operation by combining the individual lobbying clout of the TV networks with the wide-ranging and influential membership comprising the NAB. Occupying a large, modern building near the Capital's K Street lobbying corridor (and a short walk from the then-headquarters of the FCC), the NAB included many of the country's most powerful media companies. Among its members were Fox, CBS, Tribune, Hearst, ABC, and Cox. NAB members also ran major daily newspapers, including the *Washington Post*, *Atlanta Journal-Constitution*, and *Dallas Morning News*.

The NAB was legendary for its ability to get Congress and the FCC to hand it victories. In 1992, as part of a broadcast lobby–led campaign against the cable TV industry (fueled by public uproar over ever-raising subscriber rates), it won a federal policy that was worth billions to both networks and stations. Cable was required by the new law to basically pay for running much of commercial broadcasting programming. But instead of cash, broadcasters were able to require cable companies and later direct broadcast satellite companies to turn over invaluable channel capacity to them (known as retransmission consent). As a result, within a few years, broadcasting-related companies actually controlled the majority of cable TV programming, reaping monthly revenues from subscribers. Few viewers understood that the broadcasters had been able to use their clout to help dominate the programming services coming from their principal rival, cable. (Among the channels established with retransmission consent were Disney's ESPN 2, Scripps Howard's Home and Garden Network, and News Corp.'s Fox Movie Channel).[30]

Broadcasters also had another scheme to get the federal government to help bail the industry out. During the 1980s, the NAB had mounted a public relations effort claiming that the United States was falling technologically behind Japan with its development of high-definition TV (HDTV). HDTV would bring viewers a more three-dimensional-like picture, including vivid images and crystal-clear sound. But broadcasters were actually less interested in HDTV than in making sure no one else would ever be awarded the airwaves they now controlled or coveted. Public safety officials, among others, were then pressing for policies that might force broadcasters to give up their underutilized TV frequencies.

Through the influence of powerful lobbyists, especially former FCC chair and industry attorney Richard Wiley, the FCC blessed broadcasting's plans to develop digital HDTV services. But broadcasters needed Congress, via the Telecom Act, to order the FCC to give them an extra piece of the airwaves for digital broadcasting.

We need to begin broadcasting digital TV right now, the broadcasters told Congress. This will help keep the United States at the forefront of technological change and innovation. But to do so, we need you to ensure us that there's another government giveaway of spectrum—similar to what stations had originally received with their current public airwave licenses. Never mind that there never was a good business model to warrant providing broadcasters a new channel for digital over-the-air transmission. So not said to policymakers was that the broadcasters had developed another strategy designed to grab a sizable chunk of capacity from their principal competitors, the cable and satellite industry. They would use a form of the old bait-and-switch scheme.

Murdoch's Fox keenly understood that once the broadcasters received a digital channel, they didn't really need to use it for HDTV. Digital technology would permit TV stations to slice a single HDTV channel into four, six, eight, or more high-quality TV channels. With it, local TV stations would overnight be transformed into multichannel providers. They would tell Congress that they were going to give the public HDTV—one souped-up channel—but what they really wanted was to be able to deliver multiple channels and other digital content. Soon, the industry had coalesced around a plan that was designed to get the Telecom Act to require the FCC to award each station a new digital channel with what broadcasters termed "spectrum flexibility." Such flexibility would enable TV stations to do whatever they wished with their new public airwaves. The broadcast lobby believed that it would eventually be able to get Congress or the FCC to require cable operators to hand over even more capacity. Broadcasters then would be able to demand that cable give them preferential treatment when it came to delivering two-way TV or even when consumers accessed their Web sites via cable broadband.[31]

To start their campaign to win more airwaves, broadcasters began to complain that they were being left out of the administration's plans for the NII (or "infopike," as *Variety* put it). Such pressure worked, and soon the Clinton administration supported their call for spectrum flexibility. NAB chief lobbyist Eddie Fritts told the industry's annual gathering that given "the flexibility for innovative use of our spectrum, today's broadcast system is tomorrow's superhighway."[32]

The future viability of broadcasting and our public service mandate will be compromised.

—Ron Loewen, Cosmos Broadcasting Corporation,
March 17, 1994

But for Congress to approve in a Telecom Act what critics called an outrageous digital giveaway, worth at the time as much as $70 billion, the broadcasters knew they would have to rely on their "we're-serving-the-public-interest" refrain. Broadcasters brought up this phrase whenever they wanted something from Congress or the FCC. In exchange for supposedly providing public-interest programming, radio and TV station owners had been given a free license to operate on a scarce and an enormously valuable piece of public property—the airwaves. But public-interest programming rules were practically nonexistent. For decades, broadcasters had fiercely opposed any suggestion that would have led to some meaningful public-interest programming. They had bitterly fought a policy requiring a few hours a week of educational children's shows as well as a modest proposal for a few minutes of free airtime for political debates. The NAB and broadcast groups spent millions fighting off such requirements, notes the Center for Public Integrity.[33] A compliant FCC and Congress had made the notion of serving "the public interest, convenience and necessity" a joke. Stations did as little as possible in terms of what could be charitably called public-service programming. Gone were serious documentaries and ample airtime for community views, let alone creative locally produced programming. A station got its license renewed by claiming that its airing of local news, including covering storms and high school sports, demonstrated its commitment to the core public-interest principle of the 1934 Communications Act.

Promises, Promises

TV broadcasters, like the media lobby in general, will promise policymakers anything they believe will help them win their agenda. They have no real intention of following through. Broadcasters' statements that "promise them everything" will be forgotten in an unread *Congressional Record*.

As the Telecommunications Act was debated in Congress, three themes were heard from broadcasters. The first was that despite the record to the contrary, the industry devoted its existence to selfless public service. Broadcasters now praised to the skies what they called "the genius of the 1934 Communications Act," and its "creation of the public interest standard," claiming stations had taken their "special responsibility . . . to serve the public interest" by giving the country diverse programming and "local responsiveness."[34] They knew that hardly any member of Congress would dare to raise a voice in disagreement. There was a widespread perception among politicians that crossing broadcasters would mean revenge from local TV news departments, especially at election time. Lawmakers feared that they would no longer be favorably covered or reported on at all. Besides, giving the testimony were station executives from the town or state capital where often both the chair and ranking committee member were from. A form of political insurance, the NAB clearly understood that no legislator would incur the wrath of the owner or manager of the most powerful outlet from their district. They would be facing someone who had contributed to their campaigns or at the least played golf with.

Broadcast industry witnesses reminded Congress, as it debated the Telecom Act, how local stations annually aired charity telethons, covered high school sports, distributed toys at hospitals during Christmas, and donated airtime for public-service announcements (even if they ran at 3 A.M.). They also made a round of new public-interest commitments. Once they had their digital TV service running, broadcasters would send out "electronic newspapers," "medical information," emergency communications such as school closings on a "real-time" basis, and details about local sports.[35] They also made promises based on what was politically popular with key policymakers. Suddenly, the NAB became a leading champion of those low-income Americans who couldn't afford online access. They said that they too were concerned about a growing digital divide on the Internet, assuring lawmakers that by awarding them both new digital spectrum along with the flexibility to use it, Congress would "help prevent the development of information 'haves' and have-nots. . . . [O]ur digital transmissions will expand the scope of services that we can offer to those stops along the information highway that we already reach almost universally—hospitals, schools, universities, libraries and, of course, American households."[36]

A second refrain from the broadcasters' political hymnal was "re-

lief." Like every other special-interest lobby, broadcasters always argue that rules or regulations prevent them from fairly competing
with rivals such as cable. Their businesses now require assistance from
the government. We need relief, they plead, so we can survive. Instead of tears or sympathy, these lobbyists were really working on
some form of government handout—either an outright gift of public property or favorable legislative welfare designed to help their
revenue stream. Broadcasters working on the Telecom Act told
lawmakers that the existing limits on station ownership were "regulatory barriers" that prevented them from serving the public. "Let
us own more stations in our market, give us free digital airwaves
along with the 'flexibility' to use it as we choose." Otherwise, testified broadcaster Bertram Ellis, we will not be able to "afford . . .
to do . . . news, public service, and other local programming."[37]

Another favorite tactic was to warn of the dire consequences
that awaited members of Congress unless Washington approved the
requested list of broadcaster demands. Millions of Americans
would likely no longer see their favorite soaps, sitcoms, and game
shows. Broadcasting would cease to exist. Constituents would undoubtedly blame their member of Congress for making TV sets go
blank. Testifying in 1995, Ellis also declared that "America's free,
over-the-air, locally-based television system will not be able to sustain itself and survive."[38] Never mind that TV broadcasting had
made a healthy $34 billion in 1995, up 9 percent from the previous
year. Congress rarely, if ever, takes a serious look at the media industry it is passing legislation on.

It was a foregone conclusion that such pleadings and threats
would work their magic. Broadcasters would receive their publicly
funded digital age bailout worth tens of billions of dollars. But
there were critics in Congress, especially Senate majority leader
Robert Dole (R-KS) and Rep. Edward J. Markey (D-MA), who
suggested that broadcasters should have to pay something for the
new digital spectrum. If not cash to the Treasury, what about some
public-service programming? The broadcasters' answer: of course
not. No new requirements were necessary. There would be such an

outpouring of free new services, the public would be well compensated, replied the industry.

But such talk of payment made the broadcast lobby nervous. It used its deep pockets to fund a public relations campaign aimed at winning free airwaves without paying a dime. A blitz of ads warned that "free-over-the-air" TV would disappear unless Congress protected the industry. Viewers were told that soon one's "favorite shows . . . gone. Local news, weather and sports . . . gone. The Olympics for free . . . gone. That's what some in Congress have in mind." There was even a toll-free number (1-888-No-TV-Tax) to help send the message to Congress from constituents. What little their public-interest opponents such as Media Access Project could muster in a low-budget "stop-the-giveaway" campaign was ineffective in halting the TV industry's political juggernaut.[39]

It wasn't only the broadcasters who relied on tried-and-true formulas to help win their objectives. The cable industry also offered up the same promises it had made Congress almost fifteen years earlier, when it had won a major political victory to free itself from most government oversight (see chapter 8). Policymakers never seem to acknowledge having even an odd feeling of political déjà vu as they approve favorable treatment for the second time. As it had done before, cable said that if given what it wanted, the industry would provide competition to local phone companies. Instead of having a monopoly by one industry over telephone service and another monopoly controlling cable TV, there would be at least two major competitors fighting each other by offering both video and voice service. Decker Anstrom, cable's chief lobbyist, told a Senate hearing in 1995 that all Congress had to do to make it happen was overturn recently enacted federal rules that had helped limit skyrocketing monthly subscriber rates for cable TV service. With the "tens of billions of dollars" in new revenues, once companies could begin again hiking their fees, cable would be "the other wire," Anstrom testified.[40]

Cash and Carry

You buy war bonds on both sides.

—*Media executive*

Millions of dollars poured into Congress from the cable, broadcasting, and telecommunications industries, especially to Republican lawmakers willing to help support the inclusion of special-interest provisions in the legislation.[41]

Long ignored by the media and telecommunications interests, newly named Senate Commerce Committee chair Larry Pressler (R-SD) suddenly became a fund-raising powerhouse. He immediately began "leaning heavily" on the companies now under his purview, including "a $1,000 a plate fund-raiser attended by 200 industry lobbyists" only weeks after the 1994 GOP election victory. Pressler made a rushed visit to Hollywood studios, picking up cash at Fox, Sony Pictures, and the Walt Disney Company.[42] Ted Turner, Murdoch, and Disney's Michael Eisner helped Pressler raise entertainment industry donations.[43]

Senator Trent Lott (R-MS) was a committed ally of the broadcasters, partly based on his long friendship with NAB chief Eddie Fritts; they had been classmates at Ole Miss. Practically every conglomerate had a lifelong friend in Rep. Billy Tauzin, a powerful member of the Telecommunications Subcommittee. (Tauzin changed his party affiliation to Republican several months after the GOP assumed control of Congress.)[44]

Money also filled the coffers of Rep. Jack Fields (R-TX), the chair of the subcommittee responsible for communications. Even while in the minority, Fields pulled in more special-interest media and telecommunications contributions than anyone else in the House. His door was open to any corporate lobbyist. Other powerful members of Congress took money, but were especially loyal to interests based in their district. For example, House Commerce Committee chair Thomas Bliley was an advocate for the long-distance telephone companies, since AT&T had a facility in his district.

A band of dedicated public-interest and consumer advocates such as the Consumer Federation of America, the Consumers Union, the Center for Media Education, and the Media Access Project led the effort to resist this accommodation to special interests.[45] Through the advocacy work of these groups and with the help of Rep. Ed Markey (D-MA), Gore and Clinton eventually played important roles in tempering some of the worse provisions of the bill. The administration threatened a veto unless some changes were made, including a lower cap on the national ownership of TV stations (from 50 percent of the national audience down to a compromise of 35 percent). Gone from the Republican-backed plan was a provision that would have allowed newspapers and TV stations in the same community to merge. The industry and its allies were at work to the very end, however, making sure that the bill's few critics did not have the political leverage to demand changes. Senators such as John McCain (R-AZ) and Robert Packwood (R-OR) were among those who claimed the bill was too regulatory since it preserved some safeguards, but in a much weaker form. While such a statement was not supported by the facts, it served as an effective counterweight against those calling the bill a total sellout to the media lobby.[46]

Even at the last minute, Murdoch's Fox Corporation, an important GOP ally, was engaged in an effort to weaken TV ownership limits. Frustrated by its inability to eliminate the national station ceiling, Murdoch's lobbyists placed a "poison pill" in the final bill. The industry would now have a congressional mandate to further wreak havoc on the FCC protections. The rest of the TV industry also did its part to ensure that the final bill would reward them. As the House and Senate Conference Committee met in mid-December to iron out any differences, NBC president Bob Wright held a Washington, DC, party featuring the stars from the network's *Frasier* series. Network lobbyists were able to use the event to advance their agenda.[47]

The bill's only real last-minute opposition came, ironically, from conservative GOP Senate majority leader Dole, who was opposed to allowing TV broadcasters to have billions of dollars worth of free new airwaves for digital TV. Senate Commerce Committee chief Pressler promised Dole that if he would drop his opposition and let the bill pass, there would be a congressional "Camelot Moment." Dole did.[48]

Negotiations between the White House and congressional leaders led to the final bill, just days before Christmas 1995. Gore told the *Washington Post* that Clinton was pleased and would now sign it into law, dropping his earlier promise to veto it. "This is an early Christmas for consumers. It's a terrific bill . . . every concern the president expressed about the initial legislation has been dealt with on a bi-partisan basis."[49]

The telecommunications bill debate illustrated once again that the administration, despite its last-minute intervention, embraced an ideology where the media industries and the influence of their political machine overwhelmed concerns for the public interest. Clinton FCC chair Reed Hundt, for example, had vacillated as pressure from industry and the GOP was applied to the concept of policies supporting the public interest. As Republicans took up the idea in early spring 1995 that the FCC should be abolished, or at least reduced in power and size, Hundt's office responded that he shared much of the same philosophy. We are "fostering a new era in which competition will gradually phase out regulation," FCC "officials" (meaning Hundt's aides) told the *Washington Post*. Hundt himself said he agreed that "you've got to throw out many of the old rules."[50] As Neil Hickey of the *Columbia Journalism Review* wrote, although "Congress tweaked the bill to get [Clinton's] OK . . . it's still the most potent instrument in legislative history for promoting mega mergers and consolidations, and for fostering gigantism in media companies by relaxing ownership rules and hauling down barriers to inter-industry matrimony."[51]

That Congress was convinced it had made the necessary bipartisan compromises was evident in the final bill's near-unanimous vote. In the Senate, the bill passed 91 to 5 (McCain was one of the no votes, once again claiming that the act was too regulatory). The final tally in the House was 414 to 16.[52]

Industry representatives hailed the measure, alleging that the bill's provisions were the equivalent of an industrial "Berlin Wall being broken down." GOP leaders said that the 1996 Telecommunications Act was their "most substantive legislative accomplishment" in the 104th Congress. The senior Republicans who had shepherded the bill through—Sen. Pressler and Rep. Bliley—declared that the new act was "the greatest jobs bill of the decade."[53]

Stripping Away the Safeguards

The 1996 Telecommunications Act was a victory for the media industry. The new law now claimed it was in the public interest to permit greater control over the majority of the nation's media outlets by a few companies. The act required the FCC to award additional free airwaves to existing TV station owners, along with the flexibility they requested. Broadcasters would be able to keep their old channels for many years, controlling several streams of vital public spectrum for free.

TV and radio stations won an increase in the number of years they could hold on to their licenses before a renewal review. The previous policy required TV stations to go through the renewal process every five years, and radio had been at a seven-year term; now both had eight-year periods. This meant one would have to wait eight years before objecting to a TV station renewal. The industry understood that even the most hardened media advocate would likely be focused on other concerns so many years and TV seasons later.

An even more serious loss for the public was the elimination of the "comparative" renewal process. No longer would the commission be able to even consider competing applications for a station license to "determine which applicant would best serve the public interest, convenience, and necessity." In other words, incumbent stations would now receive an automatic renewal of their eight-year terms just by sending in a postcard to the FCC.[54]

The act increased the number of stations the TV networks and other major broadcast chains could control from 25 to 35 percent of the national audience. This would enable the networks and other large broadcasters to buy more properties throughout the United States. It also required the FCC to begin a rule making that would lead to multiple ownership of TV stations in a community by a single company. Congress also set the stage for mergers in the TV business by repealing a number of rules related to mergers between the broadcast and cable industries. Cable also won the right to raise rates, ending the brief efforts of the FCC to keep a lid on monthly fees. In radio, any cap on the total number of radio stations "which may be owned or controlled nationally" was scrapped. The end of ownership limits permitted a company like Clear Channel, which owned forty-three radio stations in 1995, to assemble nearly twelve hundred stations by 2005.[55]

But the industry was apoplectic that it had not won its entire agenda, including ending the cap on TV station ownership, and eliminating the ban on controlling a newspaper and a broadcast outlet in the same town. That's why Murdoch and his allies had inserted their poison pill provision into the act.

The Little Time Bomb . . . Quietly Began Ticking

Murdoch's Fox and other media industry lobbyists, noted Alicia Mundy in *CableWorld* magazine, "devised a plan to keep the cap issue in play after the Telecom bill, in whatever form, passed." Looking back several years later, Fox lobbyist Peggy Binzel, who helped engineer the poison pill provision, told Mundy that "you have to think long term. You have to convince a corporation that, when dealing with Congress, the front door may be locked, but there's always a window somewhere." According to Mundy, this plan was supported by McCain.[56]

Murdoch's amendment became Section 202(h) of the 1996 Telecom Act, which ordered the FCC to review all its ownership rules every two years. Congress (really the network lobbyists that wrote the provision) specified that the commission had to determine "whether any of its ownership rules . . . are necessary in the public interest as the result of competition. Based on its findings in such a review, the Commission is directed to repeal or modify any regulation it determines is no longer in the public interest."[57] The industry understood that such language was a potential sledgehammer. The FCC would not be able to effectively conduct a serious review of the entire TV industry in such a short time period. The industry would be able to use its clout to force the commission to act on its behalf. If it failed to do so, media lobbyists were ready to spend whatever legal fees necessary to have the federal courts force the FCC to overturn the remaining rules.

Section 202(h) was used to wreak havoc on what was left of the media policies Congress hadn't vacated in the Telecom Act. It was Section 202(h) that enabled Fox and the other networks to sue the FCC for failing to eliminate the rest of the media ownership safeguards. It would also serve as the key legal rationale for FCC chair Michael Powell's quest to sweep away FCC rules during 2001–3. Neither Powell, the courts, Congress, nor most of the news media ever acknowledged that Murdoch's operatives had engineered the poison pill's inclusion in the law. But ironically, as will be discussed in chapter 6, Murdoch's strategy eventually set the stage for the most serious public outcry opposing media consolidation since the 1934 Telecommunications Act was enacted.

So-called competition, as we know, never did emerge, as ever-fewer cable, broadcast networks, and local phone companies quickly dominated their markets. New, creative and risk-taking ventures for TV programming never materialized. TV companies were able to control more stations nationally and also in the same market. Radio became a widely acknowledged disaster, with a growing lack of diverse music and news programming. People of color and women continued to fare poorly in terms of ownership of any media outlets or services. Whatever was done by the bill and the FCC to promote competition in the telephone markets was quickly challenged by the Bell companies.

Lobbying by the school and library communities led to the only real public-interest provision related to the superhighway. The E-rate extended a policy known as universal service designed to make communications services affordable, especially for rural and low-income consumers. Now schools, libraries, and rural health facilities would be able to receive some federal support to help with the costs of wiring classrooms and connecting computers to the Internet. Despite all the talk about wiring schools, it took the legislative initiative of the groups to ensure that the provision made it into the bill. The other superhighway provision in the act, aside from attempts at Internet censorship with the tacked-on Communications Decency Amendment, would also be used as another poison pill by corporate lobbyists. The law required the FCC to do what it could to ensure that "advanced services" such as high-speed Internet access were made available in the country as soon as possible. Cable and phone giants would seize the provision to win approval for even more mergers and, as will be discussed in chapter 10, control over the Internet itself.

The phone, cable, and broadcasting companies used the Telecommunications Act to further their business goals. No comprehensive vision for "charting a new path to our national future" had been created. There wasn't any real plan to wire the country or unleash the new media to advance education and health care. Congress simply hadn't been interested in fostering new approaches to communications that would help spur greater civic and cultural content from digital TV and broadband technologies. It relied on an unproven assumption that more competition was needed and that deregulation was the path to take. While the Internet did soon provide for a greater range of expression, the kind of public policy regime that could have helped ignite greater creativity and experimentation with digital media wasn't ever considered by lawmakers.

Many of the key politicians who gave us the 1996 Telecommunications Act found work in the media and telecom industry. Gore eventually went into the cable TV business, helping run a channel that featured viewer-created commercials. Gingrich would be working as a technology consultant for various Internet-related ventures, including one specializing in interactive sales. Pressler sits on corporate boards, including high-tech firms. Fields was employed as a lobbyist for telecommunications companies. Tauzin decided not to take the job running the Motion Picture Association of America when he left Congress. The Hollywood companies running the association balked at his request of being given hundreds of thousands of dollars more a year than the job's $1 million annual salary. Press reports said he was dissatisfied that the studios wouldn't pay for the two new homes he wanted—one in New York and the other in Los Angeles.[58]

The revolving door between high-paying media industry jobs and official Washington, especially the FCC, continues to undermine the potential for our communications system to serve the public interest. That's one reason why we should really view the FCC, as discussed in the next chapter, as the Federal Conglomeration Commission.

3

The Federal Conglomeration Commission

The FCC has generally been an invisible part of the U.S. government, known mostly to industry leaders, lobbyists, and officials. Yet this "independent" agency has far-reaching authority over the nation's communications system. Practically all the elements of our information age society—broadcasting, cable TV, satellite services, telephones, cell phones and other wireless devices, and the networks that make up much of the Internet—are under the FCC's jurisdiction. Over the next several years, the FCC will help determine how the Internet and other digital media can better serve our democracy. It's likely that this agency will do what it has always done: permit a few privileged corporations to benefit from a resource that belongs to all of us.

The commission will decide, for example, whether we have access to the high-speed Internet service known as broadband in our neighborhoods; how much we have to pay each month for our phone, TV, and online bills; if we have a real choice among competing Internet providers, or just one or two media giants; and whether we have the ability to select an unfettered array of programming, including news, entertainment, and community information. The FCC will be responsible if our cable or telephone company becomes a powerful digital gatekeeper, controlling much of the content coming into our homes; if our local newspaper or favorite radio and TV stations are owned by the same company; and whether those Americans who face economic hardships have ready access to the digital media, so they can participate in the affairs of the nation. All this and much more will be addressed in some way by the FCC.

But because the commission is currently incapable of protecting the public in the digital era, it is likely that none of its actions will truly benefit us. That's why the FCC and the communications policy process must be thoroughly reformed. Otherwise, decisions about our communications fate will be left in the hands of lobbyists and officials looking for their next well-paying media industry job.

A Lobbyist's Home Away from Home

As they walk up to the FCC's front door, visitors will likely notice a policelike van stationed by the entrance. Concrete blocks now provide a barrier to keep the 600,000-square-foot, $200 million building more secure. But while the nation's capital has put more security in place since September 11, 2001, the FCC's barricades are also a legacy of protests that erupted in 2003. For the first time in decades, members of the public appeared at the FCC in sizable numbers, objecting to plans by the GOP majority to jettison media ownership policy safeguards. Unused to as well as uncomfortable with public participation, the commission decided it needed to better protect itself from potentially angry, demonstrative citizens.

But the barricades have not made a dent in the steady stream of lawyers and lobbyists that come to influence the agency. The FCC has long been the second home to a legion of such political operatives, whose occupation is convincing the staff and commissioners to approve policies that benefit a particular company or industry. It is not uncommon to see competing teams of lobbyists sitting near each other in the waiting room that serves the five commissioners. In the relatively small world of Washington communications politics, many of these lawyers and industry representatives know each other well. They are likely to be former senior commission staff, not infrequently including ex-commissioners and ex-chairs. It is a cozy club where influence peddling is viewed as merely doing business as usual.

Until 1998, the commission was based near the heart of Washington's K Street corridor—known for its blocks of pricey real estate filled with the lobbyists, political strategists, legal operatives, and former elected officials who grease the decision-making wheels of the federal government. Media and communications (which also include many technology-related issues) are an important part of this "industry." Almost $1 billion has been spent by the major media-related firms in the last few years lobbying the federal government, including the FCC, for favorable rulings.[1]

At its former location, media industry lobbyists had unfettered access to the FCC building, especially the eighth floor where the commissioners had their offices. "Up on the eighth floor" became industry shorthand for where decisions were being made and where pressure had to be placed. The tradition of influencing commissioners on the eighth floor followed the agency when it was forced to relocate to its current, larger facility, known as "the Portals." The FCC reworked its floor plan so that once again, the commissioners could be found on the eighth floor.[2]

At the heart of the commission's mission is to define how, if at all, the electronic media industries should serve the "public interest, convenience, and necessity." Part of the FCC's founding legislation in 1934, this public-interest mandate from Congress has given the agency a vital role in helping determine how well our electronic media serve our democracy. But since its inception, the FCC has not generally served the public well. The commission has instead focused on the interests of the various corporate sectors it oversees. It is only on rare occasions that the agency will actually craft a policy that benefits viewers, listeners, and now with the Internet, users. The commission has long been captured by the very parties it is supposed to oversee and regulate. Traditionally, the commission has spent its time helping the various companies make more profits rather than ensuring that our society prospers. The public is at best treated as consumers, merely customers for commercial services. The FCC does little to advance citizen rights in the electronic media; in fact, it often works to undermine what little rights we have left in determining how communications networks in the United States should provide for the public interest, convenience, and necessity.

How far the FCC will go to fulfill industry demands for favorable decision making generally depends on the proclivities of its leader. The chair of the five-member commission is more than just a titular executive. He (and there has not yet been a woman chair since the commission's creation) dominates the agency's decision-making process, largely determining the agenda. He is the public voice of the agency, and largely overshadows everyone else. While each of the five commissioners is limited to just three legal advisers, the chair can draw on the agency's nineteen hundred employees who staff its bureaus and divisions. So, if the chair desires, there will be an FCC plan to eliminate safeguards ensuring diverse media ownership. If the chair cares to, the agency will keep a sharp eye on how the major communications companies under its jurisdiction conduct their business. Or, as it did with such giants as Adelphia, WorldCom, Global Crossing, and Enron's fiber-optic subsidiary, turn a blind eye. Is the chair concerned whether consumer charges for cable TV services skyrocket? Should the nation be alarmed about a lack of in-depth TV news, or that there are few African American and Hispanic owners of TV outlets? Whether and how such questions are addressed is determined by what kind of person holds the chair. (See chapter 5 for a discussion of recent FCC chair Michael Powell.)

Generally, candidates for the FCC have connections to industry or to powerful political patrons who do. Once nominated by the president and confirmed by the Senate, commissioners serve a five-year term and can be renominated for additional terms. Commissioners, sadly, see their time at the FCC as their meal ticket for subsequent lucrative employment within the industry. They usually go directly to work for the media or telecommunications businesses after they leave office. The revolving door between the FCC and the communications industry means that chairs and the commissioners know they will soon be raking in high salaries as lawyers and lobbyists. They likely will end up trying to persuade their former agency to some degree. Only in rare cases do they consider working in the nonprofit sector, such as with academic or public-interest organizations.[3]

Every former chair for the last three decades has gone to work in one way or another with the media and telecommunications industry. With such lucrative employment ahead of them while they serve as "public" officials, how can they be trusted to make decisions that would harm the prospects of those companies or industries they likely will serve once in the private sector? The fact is that they can't be relied on to act with the public interest in mind as long as they know that a golden parachute into the Fortune 500 is just around the corner. As one aide to an FCC commissioner privately remarked, "People leave here on Friday and are lobbying me the following Monday!"

Beyond the lawyers and lobbyists, the commission is also besieged by an infrastructure of industry-funded trade associations, think tanks, paid-for consumer groups, and consultants. Media companies always have an open checkbook to hire academic experts who for a lucrative fee will gladly support whatever position their corporate sponsors wish to advocate. Companies use in-house lobbyists as well as outside firms to target the commission. Both Democratic and Republican lobbyists are on call to help a company effectively glad-hand the appropriate commissioner. Often, the companies or trade associations will arrange to have powerful congresspersons contact commissioners or their staff. For example, a letter from the chair of the key Hill committee that oversees FCC operations, including its budget, serves as a potent reminder to commissioners that powerful interests are closely watching them. The media and telecommunications companies also arrange for phone calls, faxes, and e-mails supporting their position to be sent to the commission. Many of these are either from their employees or through groups that receive financial contributions or other help such as some free public-service announcement time from the companies.

Although the FCC is formally considered an independent government body, in truth there are frequent off-the-record communications between federal officials and the commission. For example, a call from the lead communications policy aide at the

White House to the chair's chief of staff will make it clear what is expected from the agency. The back-channel discussions between the White House and the FCC were striking during the Clinton administration. The two worked together to develop the same approach to policy issues. For example, at one White House meeting with top media policy advisers on how to ensure digital TV served the public interest, advocates were asked, "What is the low-hanging fruit on the issue?" meaning what was the least they could do without political ramifications from industry.

Ultimately, the whole policy process at the FCC is stacked against the public, but perfect for the well-organized and wealthy communications lobby. For instance, when it proposes a new or revised policy, the commission will ask for written submissions known as "Comments." But while the FCC is officially considered the expert federal agency on electronic media, it relies on outside submissions from industry for its information. Consequently, media and telecommunications companies, with their limitless resources, are able to flood the commission with slanted information and analysis. A company might submit hundreds of pages of Comments and then provide a round of what are called "Reply Comments" (responding to assertions made by others, including public-interest and consumer groups). Industry filings often contain several appendixes, including charts, supportive academic papers, and other data. The commission usually accepts this corporate analysis as valid. After all, FCC staff say to themselves, why would (fill in your favorite company) not tell us the truth?

In reality, however, a game goes on. The FCC has been unwilling to engage in an independent research effort that might actually challenge the dominant positions proposed by industry. This has left us with a regulatory agency that cannot act to protect the public. If the FCC is incapable of establishing its own objective and in-depth record on issues, how can it accomplish its duty to protect the public interest? It simply cannot. Staff at the commission have developed a "don't ask, don't tell" attitude toward media industry developments. They really don't want to know about information that is contrary to the positions held by the media industry.

FCC decisions should always strive to protect the average American. Diversity of expression in programming along with affordable rates for phone, cable, satellite, and Internet communications should be at the core of the commission's concerns. But they're not. For the FCC, only the economic interests of industry deserve protection. Thus, the FCC has little awareness and interest in examining media industry developments with the public in mind.

The constant pressure of political influence from the industry, the White House, and Congress; the FCC personnel policies; and an industry-can-do-no-wrong mentality are further compounded by the role of money.[4] According to the Center for Public Integrity, the broadcast industry alone forked out more than $222 million from 1998 to June 2004 to influence the federal government. That doesn't include the $26.5 million in campaign contributions that broadcasters poured into the political coffers of candidates for federal offices. Telecommunications companies such as the Baby Bells spent $498 million. Cable racked up $120 million for lobbying expenses during the same period.[5] All this cash means that few political leaders are willing to get up and challenge industry. They are a well-paid part of it.

The practically nonexistent division between industry and government is one reason why the FCC considers corporate welfare the paramount public welfare. While lip service is given to competition and consumer concerns, what really happens is a polite arrangement designed to further the interests of the most powerful industry participants. The principal framework embraced by the commission when it considers important issues such as big media mergers is often how they will affect the financial bottom line of a company or the industry as a whole, not how these transactions will really affect the lives of Americans.

One reason that explains why the FCC prefers to serve a few moneyed special interests over the public is this: our FCC chairs and commissioners end up cashing big checks from many of same companies they once oversaw. They have helped to set a tone where commission staff sees selling out as just part of one's career path.

From FCC Chair to the Corporate Boardroom

Newton Minow, chair of the commission from 1961 to 1963 during the Kennedy administration, is justly remembered for his "Vast Wasteland" speech when he excoriated the then three TV networks for their lack of quality programming. On leaving the commission chairship, Minow became a partner at Sidley and Austin, one of the country's most successful law firms working for the media industry. He also served on the boards of CBS, Tribune, and ad giant Foote, Cone & Belding.[6] Chair E. William Henry (1963–66) went to work as a communications lawyer for a number of firms. Richard Nixon appointee Dean Burch (1969–74) also went from the commission to a law firm, but he eventually left private practice to run Intelsat, the nonprofit organization that manages global communications satellites.[7]

The archetype of a former chair cashing in is Richard Wiley (1974–77). Wiley is an omnipresent power broker at the FCC and with the media policymaking apparatus of Washington. Almost thirty years after he left office, Wiley's power is such that he is sometimes referred to as the FCC's unofficial "sixth commissioner." His Wiley Rein & Fielding firm boasts that it has the largest communications law practice in the country. The firm has represented a *Who's Who* of media-related giants, including the NAA, NAB, Time Warner, Gannett, Clear Channel, CBS, Verizon, Microsoft, and General Electric. It has historically had strong connections with the GOP.[8]

As a former chair, Wiley has instant access to top FCC officials, who know their future careers may depend on being hired or recommended by Wiley. When he speaks, policymakers understand he is talking on behalf of the interests of the country's media magnates. As Stephen Labaton of the *New York Times* notes, Wiley has been the "top lawyer and chief Washington strategist" for the largest media companies. His firm has "supplied more lawyers to the important telecommunications posts in the Bush administration than any other firm."[9] A Bush administration's chief for communications policy (located at the Department of Commerce), Nancy J.

Victory, formerly worked at Wiley (while her husband remained head of Wiley's telecommunications group). She returned to Wiley after her government stint. Wiley "alums" also fill important posts at the Bush White House and in various cabinet departments. Other former Wiley attorneys are lobbyists and political advisers to some of the country's most powerful leaders, including Senate majority leader Bill Frist (R-TN). Some become judges, destined to hear cases that will undoubtedly affect Wiley's clients.

FCC chair Kevin Martin is a former Wiley employee. Martin named a former Wiley partner as head of the commission's influential Media Bureau. Ex-FCC commissioners can always find a comfortable spot at Wiley. For example, former FCC commissioners Mimi Dawson (1981–87) and James Quello (1994–97) are associated with the firm. Among the thirty-five partners working on media and communications at Wiley Rein & Fielding are many former FCC officials, including senior legal advisers to the commissioners as well as key people who used to run the agency's various bureaus and divisions. Wiley Rein & Fielding media lawyers play a prominent part in helping to shape the media and communications policy debate through a variety of professional activities, such as holding down editorships of law journals or filling leadership roles at the American Bar Association and the Federal Communications Bar Association (FCBA).

As the leading partner working on communications, no one works as well as Richard Wiley in shaping the policy decision-making process behind the scenes. It was Wiley, for example, who recommended his "good friend" Michael K. Powell to be the FCC chair as part of his role as head of the then incoming telecommunications policy transition team for the Bush administration.[10] Wiley has held formal positions directly influencing the FCC and national policy even while he was working to advance the private interests of his clients. For instance, he headed up the FCC's official Advisory Committee on Advanced Television Services, which made key recommendations to the commission on digital TV. Ultimately, the federal policy on digital TV was a huge boon to broadcasters, including Wiley's clients. Not surprisingly, in 2002

Wiley received the highest honor that the NAB can award: its Distinguished Service Award.

Wiley will do practically anything to advance the interests of his clients, including helping to run a public relations campaign. For example, in a series of 2003 op-eds for newspapers run by Dean Singleton of the MediaNews Group (owner of the *Denver Post*, the *Oakland Tribune*, and many others), Wiley argued that the time was ripe to eliminate the rule prohibiting the same company from owning both a newspaper and a TV station in the same town. But Wiley didn't identify that his client was the NAA, the key trade group lobbying to kill that safeguard. Nor did he tell readers that publisher Singleton was the immediate past president and main congressional advocate for the NAA. And Wiley didn't mention that his firm had held more meetings with FCC staff in the five months proceeding the June 2003 ownership decision than any other law or lobby firm.[11]

Appointed by Jimmy Carter, Charles Ferris served as chair from 1977 to 1981. Like Wiley, Ferris now runs one of the preeminent Washington, DC, law firms that lobby the FCC—Mintz, Levin, Cohn, Ferris, Glovsky and Popeo. Ferris has traded on his insider status as former chief U.S. media policymaker to assemble a client list filled with major cable, broadcast, telecommunications, Internet, and satellite companies. And also like Wiley, the Ferris firm offers a hospitable welcome to FCC staff and other media policy officials wishing to cash in.[12]

Mintz, Levin has long been one of the leading firms defending the interests of the cable industry, including Comcast, Cablevision, Time Warner, and the NCTA. One of its lawyers working on cable matters is Cameron Kerry, the brother of former presidential candidate John Kerry.[13] The Mintz, Levin firm has been one of Senator Kerry's most generous campaign contributors.[14]

Mark S. Fowler was a media and communications lawyer "representing radio, television, domestic and private radio stations" before being tapped by President Ronald Reagan to run the FCC (1981–87). Fowler radically swept away public policies that required broadcasters to perform public service. He also worked to weaken media ownership limits. Fowler believed that since TV was "just another appliance—it's a toaster with pictures," there was no need for any public policy oversight of the industry. On leaving the commission, he returned to communications law with a major Washington, DC, firm. Fowler also served as an investor and director in broadcasting and telecommunications businesses.[15]

Dennis R. Patrick replaced Fowler, serving as the GOP chair from 1987 to 1989. After leaving the commission, he went to work for Time Warner, and ran his own media and telecommunications investment business.[16] Next came Alfred C. Sikes, a Republican who served as the FCC chair from 1989 to 1993. Sikes also came from the media industry, including broadcasting. A self-proclaimed expert on new media, Sikes went to the Hearst Corporation after his FCC term to run its interactive media division. He was also on the board of directors of broadcast satellite giant Hughes Electronics.[17]

The election of Clinton saw the commission's longest-serving commissioner, James Quello, take office as acting chair from February to November 1993. Long seen as the broadcast lobby's "man" at the FCC, Quello had worked his way up in the commercial radio business, becoming a general manager and network vice president. Appointed by President Nixon in 1974 to fill a Democratic slot (even though he leaned Republican), Quello served as a commissioner for twenty-three years. Afterward, Quello began raising money from the media industry to help endow an academic institute that would support the corporate telecommunications political agenda: the James H. and Mary B. Quello Center for Telecommunication Management and Law at Michigan State University. The media lobby was willing to pay Quello back for all the favorable policies he had delivered over the decades. Among the "Inner Circle," "Benefactors," and "Patrons" of the Quello Center were Fox, the NAB, AT&T, Clear Channel, Comcast, NBC, Tribune, Viacom, and the Motion Picture Association of America. In 2001, Quello began working at the Wiley law firm.[18]

Reed Hundt, who had been a friend and high school classmate of Vice President Gore, became FCC chair in late 1993 and served until 1997. Also a media and telecommunications lawyer, Hundt made a swift return to the business sector on retiring as chair. He soon became a millionaire with his postchair activities. Hundt was frequently sought by the press as an expert. As a former FCC chair, he was regarded as someone with unique expertise who understood both the market and public-interest issues involved in telecommunications. But in this role, Hundt often sided with industry, including supporting big mergers. Yet his own web of corporate connections was seldom revealed in the stories quoting him. For example, he hailed the takeover of Bell South by giant AT&T, enthusiastically telling the *Washington Post* that the public should approve of such megamergers. "It's a sport. It's a competition. . . . It's like NFL linemen. You want 'em big, you want 'em fast, but most important you want 'em big." Yet just a few years before, when he served as FCC chair, Hundt had described a similar merger between AT&T and SBC as "unthinkable." Hundt's private role working for key players in the telecommunications industry should have signaled to the news media that he was not a neutral observer.[19]

Following Hundt as chair was FCC general counsel William E. Kennard (1997–2001). Prior to serving at the FCC, Kennard was also a communications lawyer in Washington. After his term he went into the private sector, directing the Carlyle Group's Global Telecommunications and Media Group. Kennard also serves on a number of boards, including the New York Times Company.[20]

Powell, the chair between 2001 and 2005, became an investment adviser for media and telecommunications interests when he left the FCC. (His career is discussed in chapters 5 and 6.)

Although former chairs Hundt, Kennard, and Powell don't lobby the commission in the same way as Wiley, Ferris, and others, their role is often to help represent their firms and interests before policymakers. A former chair working for a media or telecommunications company is seen as an invaluable asset, providing credibility and easy access to top decision makers, if needed.

Cash and Carry

It isn't just FCC chairs who leave and make six figures from the industry they used to oversee. Commissioners jump on the gravy train, too. Practically every living former commissioner is also working for a law firm, or with some media and telecommunications company. Among the rare exceptions are Nicholas Johnson (1966–73) and Gloria Tristani (1997–2001), who have devoted their post-commission careers to education and nonprofit public service.

Senior FCC staff don't even blink an eye about assuming high-paid media industry jobs where they will end up lobbying their former employer. Marsha MacBride was Powell's chief of staff. That was before she was hired away by the NAB lobbying group to run its "legal and regulatory affairs department." The NAB also swooped up top FCC aide Jane Mago, who had served as Powell's general counsel. Murdoch's DIRECTV took on Susan Eid, a Powell key legal adviser. This is not just a problem with Republicans, of course. Democrats are equally complicit. Kennard's chief of staff John Nakahata went to work lobbying for the telephone industry. One of Kennard's top media bureau aides, Susan Fox, left to lobby for Disney/ABC. Ruth Milkman, senior adviser to Hundt, is part of a legal team of former high FCC officials at a firm working for cable and telecommunications companies.

The migration of high-ranking FCC officials to industry is just part of the accepted process in government where the regulator soon sells out to the highest bidder. This permanent, elite force of ex-FCC officials helps ensure that media empires in the United States remain under the control of a few, competition is diminished, commercialism continues to reign, and creativity is forced to remain at the margins of the mainstream media system. These individuals and employers defend such a practice, of course, as the norm in the capital and much of the country. Doing well means selling your access, contacts, and insider knowledge for six-figure salaries and all the perks. They fail to see how they contribute to a culture of corruption that undermines the ability of the U.S. communications system to fulfill its obligation to strengthen democracy.

The employment merry-go-round and the political ideologies of the FCC chairs influence how commission employees conduct their work. Whatever their chair's particular worldview is—say, on the need of the marketplace to determine policy—will be embraced. Staff are palpably fearful of crossing a line where they will end up disagreeing with the agency's head. Consequently, there is little intellectual freedom at the FCC. The agency simply cannot be counted on to take a critical look at what is really going on in the media business. This is not due to the staff being overworked or inefficient. The overall orientation is that the media company or industry can do no wrong—so the staff lack the zeal to conduct the kind of extensive investigative inquiry that would likely lead to troubling concerns about plans to restrict competition and deny the public access to diverse content. If they were truly insulated from industry, the staff would realize that they would have to have the FCC intervene in some way. Such was the case, for example, during the agency's review of important mergers (AOL with Time Warner and Fox with DIRECTV), when key staff revealed that they didn't have time to keep up with the media industry trade publications or explore other documents that exposed plans to quash competition and dominate emerging new markets, such as interactive TV.[21]

Private Clubhouse

The commission's lawyers and other policy-related personnel also routinely mingle with industry lobbyists. They even have their own organization, the FCBA. The three-thousand-member group is supposed to be concerned with professional education and charitable work, but FCBA committees regularly meet to address the critical issues facing the FCC, usually with some agency official as a guest speaker. These events provide the industry with important information about commission proceedings and facilitate better inside connections to decision makers.

Thus, the FCBA is really there to facilitate a special relationship between the lawyers who lobby the FCC for industry and the agency itself. There is, for example, a Fall Reception with the FCC Bureau Chiefs. A communications law firm can be a Gold or Silver sponsor. Or members can attend the annual FCBA Foundation Golf Tournament at a country club—courtesy of such underwriters as AT&T, BellSouth, and Verizon. Having a cocktail hour with a commissioner at a posh California resort is within easy reach, courtesy of such sponsors as SBC Communications, T-Mobile, and Yahoo! The highlight is the Annual Chairman's Dinner—a roast held each December. It's one big schmooze fest where the FCC chair and commissioners hobnob with lawyers and lobbyists in a holiday atmosphere.[22]

The "well connected," as the Center for Public Integrity calls them, are largely invisible to the public. But they are at the center of the political culture that helps make basic decisions that affect every American and many more outside the United States. The quality of our media system, the ability of journalists to report critically and in-depth, and our country's policies in helping shape global communications—all of these are highly influenced by the elite media lobby. Based in high-priced real estate, with large TV screens for teleconferences connecting them to their offices around the world, and with the deepest pockets to provide campaign contributions, fancy parties, and dinners, these influence peddlers play a key role in determining much of what goes on with the media, both in Congress and the FCC.

Clinton deputy chief of staff Roy Neel left the White House, where he helped oversee media policy for his friend Gore, so he could earn $1.2 million a year running the telephone lobby. Neel's tenure at the United States Telephone Association coincided with his White House pals making crucial decisions about the future of the Internet and telecommunications. At the G. W. Bush White House, Helgi C. Walker, who helped oversee FCC policy for the president, took a new career path when she went to work for Wiley Rein & Fielding—to help Wiley's big media clients get more favorable attention at the FCC.[23]

Of course, one doesn't have to be a former White House or Hill employee to wield power when it comes to media policy in the United States. It also doesn't hurt if your former lobbying firm partner, who happens to be your brother, is the White House chief of staff. That was the case for Tony Podesta, who went from running the liberal People for the American Way to eventually representing the NAB, Viacom/CBS, the Motion Picture Association of America, the Washington Post Company, the Recording Industry Association of America, and Universal Studios. (Tony's brother, John, co-ran the firm before he went to work for the Clinton administration. He now runs the Center for National Progress.) Combining show business panache with a let's-grease-the-wheels-of-government ethos, this Democratic Party high roller exemplifies how lobbyists are able to exert authority, regardless of the party in control of government. In summing up his philosophy for *Wired* magazine, Podesta was candid about how lobbying works: "We have no permanent allies. We have no permanent enemies. We just have interests." Podesta joined forces with Republican stalwart Daniel Mattoon to help ensure his firm would prosper during the era of GOP domination in Washington. The firm's numerous lobbyists include the son of House Speaker Dennis Hastert.[24]

All of the major media companies have their own lobbyists. They usually have both Republicans and Democrats on staff—although the GOP's K Street Project, designed to force companies to hire more Republicans to run these groups, has added more conservatives to these positions. As the Center for Public Integrity carefully documented, big-spending companies like Disney/ABC, Viacom/CBS, and News Corp. totaled $56 million in lobbying expenditures as the FCC considered its media ownership rules. "Smaller" media companies such as Gannett, Clear Channel, and the Washington Post Company spent a million or more each for lobbying. Cable, satellite, and telephone companies tallied huge sums as well. Time Warner alone had a $46 million tab for promoting its policy agenda. DIRECTV spent nearly $13 million. But Verizon outstripped them all, with a sum of nearly $102.5 million. All of this had to shape FCC decisions.[25]

There is also a network of trade associations, such as the Motion Picture Association of America, the National Cable & Telecommunications Association, and the United States Telephone Association, that constantly supplies political pressure.

National Association of Power Brokers

The NAB is like "a dead mackerel in the moonlight—it both shines and stinks."

—James Fly, FCC chair, 1939–44

Founded in 1923, the NAB is one of the most effective of these groups. Combining traditional lobbying clout with access to the airwaves for politicians, the NAB's role, as it says on its Web site, is always to be "Driving Broadcasters' Agenda Forward." The group's lobbyists fan out to the FCC, the Hill, and the White House to advance the industry interests. With the billions generated by the broadcast TV business, there's no problem raising the many millions needed to ensure the political fix. From January 1998 to June 2004, the NAB spent more than $43 million lobbying officials.[26] As an incentive for broadcasters to join, the organization's Web site lists a handful of its political accomplishments, including the bills it defeated and the FCC policies it advanced.

The Television and Radio Political Action Committee (TARPAC) is NAB's political action committee. More than $500,000 was given to candidates for the 2004 election, with Republicans getting the majority of that funding. (The cable trade association spent more than $1 million in the same period.)[27]

These groups also have celebrity events where FCC commissioners and others can hobnob with the elite. Every year, there are conventions or trade shows in places like Las Vegas or New Orleans. Until the Center for Public Integrity blew the whistle on industry, FCC staffers received free trips where they were wined, dined, and intertwined with the industry's agenda.[28]

Then there's the presidential election. Media and telecommunications companies make a special effort every four years to help ensure that whoever is in the White House will be grateful. Kerry was given huge sums of money from media industry heavyweights, including executives at Viacom, Sony, and even Fox. Meanwhile, executives at Comcast, Time Warner, and Clear Channel, for example, were Bush "pioneers" (what Bush's reelection committee called those who raised $100,000 or more). Media companies wall-papered the nominating conventions with parties and special events. Lobbyists spent their time at the conventions volunteering to help the candidate, all the while knowing there could be a big payback if their person won.[29]

Then there are the former lawmakers. Many make their living after Congress working as lobbyists. Among the many ex-members of Congress from both parties who went to work influencing communications policy are former House majority leader Richard Armey (R-TX), House Telecommunications Subcommittee member Steve Largent (R-OK), and Rep. Patricia Schroeder (D-CO). In addition to such persuasion, former Hill members also serve on the boards of some of the biggest media companies. Former Senate majority leader George Mitchell (D-ME) has been the chair of the Walt Disney Company; Sam Nunn, former Democratic Senator from Georgia, sits on the board of General Electric, the parent company of NBC, Universal, and so on; and former Sen. William S. Cohen (R-MA) served on the Viacom board.[30]

The boards of many of these media giants also include former top White House officials, college presidents, technology venture investors, and civil rights leaders. Their job, in part, is to give the company political cover and help ensure that trouble from their own constituencies doesn't explode. It is doubtful whether these individuals have asked themselves about the consequences to the public at large from the political positions their companies take.

For example, Comcast has on its board the former president of the University of Pennsylvania and the current president of the Rockefeller Foundation, Judith Rodin.[31] Time Warner had former G.H.W. Bush administration trade representative Carla Hills; News Corp. (Fox) has former Bush Department of Justice official Viet Dinh.[32] Former Clinton administration economic chief Laura D'Andrea Tyson served on the board of Murdoch's Fox Entertainment Group.[33]

All the political clout that the media industries assemble, including capturing prestigious officials and experts, is brought to bear on the FCC. Their interests are seen as the most legitimate and worthy of the agency's support. Meanwhile, the interests of "average" Americans are sidelined or ignored.

Over the last several years, the FCC has made access to records much more transparent. Its computer system makes looking up some information easy. That's a good change from the past. Concerned members of the public can also file comments to important proceedings online as well. Commissioners can be e-mailed, and some take the time to read such correspondence. Occasionally, there will be true public-spirited commissioners who will put the concerns of Americans ahead of the corporate lobby. But such FCC appointees are a rarity.

The FCC must be required to engage in a major reform of its practices. To do so will take a serious effort aimed at making sure the agency's mission is to serve the American people, not wealthy special interests. I will discuss what can be done with the FCC in the final chapter of this book.

4

The Art of the Front

It takes, as they say, a "village to raise a child." So when it comes to lobbying policymakers, political operatives prefer to have a "helping hand" for their agendas. The nation's capital is home to impressive-sounding organizations and well-degreed individuals who are part of the media industry political apparatus. They play an important, and mostly invisible, role in advancing the goals of the communications lobby in Congress and at the FCC.

There are the think tanks that publish supportive position papers; the independent scholars and academic research organizations that weigh in with footnoted arguments claiming that the science upholds the industry position; and consumer groups that advocate for policies that exactly match the requests of media and telecommunications companies. They issue a steady stream of reports, books, press releases, regulatory filings, and legal briefs; conduct background sessions on key issues for the media and lawmakers; and invite powerful decision makers to luxurious events such as retreats in Aspen, Colorado. If, say reporters and congressional staff, group or person X (a nonprofit organization, think tank, or scholar) supports media mergers, claims public-interest rules are an anachronism, and believes that there should be a more limited role for the FCC, such policies must be right.

But in most cases, these organizations and individuals are either on the payroll of the media companies or hope to get a big check from them soon. They represent a chain of groups fronting for the media and telecommunications lobby. While a great number of them work inside the confines of Washington, DC, many such groups are also part of a network of related organizations located in state capitals and other cities. These organizations are deployed to weaken the effectiveness of independent nonprofit groups that advocate for the public at large. Policymakers and many journalists often remain clueless that these think tanks or groups may actually be housed at the office of a lobbyist for the media industries. Or that telecommunications companies often provide generous support of the groups' annual budgets. Reporters who cover the media generally do not engage in the more in-depth, investigative journalism these issues require. Consequently, public relations pronouncements from groups and companies often get written up instead of being critically analyzed.

While many of these organizations are committed to their own worldview, too often their financial relationships with the very media company or industry that benefits from their advocacy is overlooked. If one follows the money, one can see that groups and their independent experts frequently have received funding from the same corporate source. Without the continued generosity of media companies, for example, many of these so-called think tanks, consumer groups, and other nonprofits wouldn't be able to operate effectively. That's why it's important to ask, Where does the money come from and how does it relate to the position being endorsed?

Progress and Freedom Foundation: Fighting for the "Rights" of Big Media

The Progress and Freedom Foundation (PFF) became a major political presence soon after the Republican Party took over Congress in 1994. It was the technology think tank of then House speaker Gingrich. Gingrich used PFF events to pontificate on the glories of technology and the GOP, and how they would soon transform the United States. All we would need to achieve such a technological nirvana, said the PFF, was to get rid of all the federal rules and regulations, including the FCC.[1]

More than a decade later, the PFF remains one of the key groups supporting the political goals of media and telecommunications industries. It backs, for example, cable TV companies' efforts to have monopoly control of the valuable "last mile" of broadband Internet connections. The PFF supports the elimination of federal safeguards on media ownership. It is opposed to community control of local communications broadband networks. The PFF says in its report to the IRS that it doesn't engage in lobbying. Although technically correct, the group's real role is to influence and shape the passage of public policy favorable to its supporters.

On a regular basis, the PFF creates task forces, publishes "fact" books on the digital economy, releases lengthy white papers, and holds events. Lawmakers past and present are usually in attendance. Former FCC chair Powell found the PFF a particularly supportive environment, and regularly used it as a launching pad for many of his policy statements. The PFF's financial supporters helped it raise more than $3 million in revenues, according to its IRS report for 2003–4.

With the media industry talking about the need to revise the 1996 Telecommunications Act to make it more corporate friendly, the PFF sprung into action. In February 2005, it launched a major initiative designed to further weaken public-interest policies. Likening its call for a revision of the nation's media laws to the Declaration of Independence, the PFF listed its "grievances" against "the current regulatory regime for the many ways it 'mistreats' digital communications technology." Seizing on a time-honored approach designed to undermine respect for public-interest rules, it "charged" U.S. media policymaking with various "offenses." An advisory board of well-known experts had been tapped to work with the project, including politically sympathetic officials from the last five presidential administrations. Background papers on key media topics were sent to the Hill and reporters.[2]

But missing from the PFF's "Digital Age Communications Act" missive, as with all its prodigious output of documents, was an acknowledgment of who actually supports the organization financially. To be fair, such a list of supporters is available on the PFF Web site. But the PFF knows it is unlikely that reporters and policymakers will take the time to go online to learn who might have a vested interest in the policies that the group supports. In dozens of articles about the PFF, there has rarely been any mention at all of its Fortune 500–type funders who are paying for this piper's tune.

So when the PFF says it is opposed to rules that would limit the number of media outlets a single company can own, it surely must be pleasing to the companies precisely supporting that position and the PFF: Disney, News Corp. (Fox), and Viacom (CBS). When the PFF objects to the call for safeguards to prevent cable companies from having control over the broadband Internet, it surely isn't a surprise to its like-minded supporters Comcast, Time Warner, and the National Cable & Telecommunications Association. As the PFF issues a call to sweep away federal rules requiring our largest phone companies to provide competitors reasonable access to their monopoly lines, it likely warms the heart of BellSouth, SBC, Verizon, and the U.S. Telecommunications Association—supporters all.[3]

The PFF's real role is to help industry frame the debate about key communications and information technology issues. It provides a cloak of intellectual capital designed to advance the industry's political capital. Much of the PFF's work suggests that it is tapping into serious and respected academic and scholarly approaches to policy. But many of the academics have taken handsome sums of money to write papers on behalf of the PFF's own supporters or work as consultants for the industry. This is also not told to reporters and policymakers. So, for example, in announcing its new Digital Age Communications Act rewrite, the PFF listed a number of academics participating in "working groups" that would supposedly study an important media issue, and then report back to Congress and the administration about their findings. On the Regulatory Framework committee was Howard Shelanski of the University of California at Berkeley. A professor of law and head of Berkeley's Center for Law and Technology, Shelanski's impressive accomplishments are listed by the PFF. But the group failed to mention that the professor had also worked for the NCTA, helping the cable lobbyists argue against any federal safeguards for the cable industry. The NCTA is, of course, a supporter of the PFF.[4]

Nor did the PFF mention that Professor Simon J. Wilkie, serving on its Universal Service/Social Policy working group, spent some of his time as a paid consultant helping companies develop "less restrictive regulation and market-oriented solutions." When not teaching at the California Institute for Technology, Wilkie was an "affiliate" at the ERS Group, a telecommunications consultancy firm fighting what it calls "regulatory constraints." Wilkie's ERS bio cited "consultancies" that helped Murdoch's News Corp. buy DIRECTV and assisted Comcast with its acquisition of AT&T Broadband. As noted, both Comcast and News Corp. provide financial support to the PFF.[5]

PFF supporters give generously, allowing the group to maintain a high profile. The PFF spent about $2.2 million advancing its agenda during the period from April 2002 to March 2003. About half of its revenues were used to support its "communications policy" deregulatory strategy, according to IRS filings.[6] Its key officers and "senior fellows" were well paid, some taking home $200,000 a year. For its annual Aspen Summit Conference, it paid $136,000 so Washington and industry insiders could enjoy the comforts of the St. Regis Aspen hotel. One year later, as talk of Telecommunications Act reform was building, the PFF's budget was nearly $1 million larger, with more than half earmarked for its communications policy projects. The increase in budget support for the PFF illustrates one tactic of the major media companies. As they aggressively move ahead to win their policy objectives, they unleash their allies to campaign on their behalf. While real public-interest groups have to constantly scramble to raise modest resources from independent funding sources such as charitable foundations, groups like the PFF can always depend on the kindness of their friends.

The PFF board exemplifies the relationships that place the group well within the confines of the corporate sphere. The PFF board chair is George Keyworth, a former science adviser during the Reagan presidency and now chair of the Keyworth Company. His eponymous firm assists companies in developing "strategies for growth based on emerging and changing technologies." Keyworth serves on the board of PFF supporter Hewlett-Packard.[7] Director Larry Harlow worked for the Reagan and G.H.W. Bush administrations before taking the helm of Timmons and Company, a subsidiary of lobbyist and public relations giant Hill & Knowlton, which has represented PFF supporters Intel and Motorola. James C. Miller III, PFF "director emeritus" and a former head of the Federal Trade Commission under President Reagan, is also chair of CapAnalysis, a division of Washington legal and lobbying firm Howrey Simon Arnold & White. Howrey has represented PFF financial supporters Disney, BMG, Sun Microsystems, and Apple Computer.[8] Also based at CapAnalysis is PFF co-founder Jeffrey Eisenach.[9]

Organizations such as the PFF play another important role, serving as a comfortable home for those federal officials who exit government to take lucrative posts with industry or their allies. They help give instant credibility to a PFF as well as access to their former colleagues. Take, for instance, former FCC chair Powell's "special counsel" on broadband policy, Kyle Dixon. Described as the "seven-year FCC veteran and Powell confidante," Dixon was hired by the PFF to run what it calls the Federal Institute for Regulatory Law and Economics (FIRLE).[10] FIRLE is a good example of how corporate media money permits a PFF to create what seems like an endless series of spin-offs.

FIRLE describes its mission as a "pioneering effort devoted to influencing federal policymakers." It claims to provide the "analytical tools" so lawmakers can "master fundamental legal and economic concepts to avoid policy responses that are unnecessary or that yield unintended consequences."[11]

One selling point FIRLE makes is that it has the backing of "leading academics, practitioners and scholars." Officials are no doubt pleased to come to what the PFF describes as a "mandatory" event and spend three days at the luxurious "Aspen Meadows Resort of the Aspen Institute." Despite the surroundings, the PFF promises that its scholarly "partners" from the University of Colorado Silicon Flatirons Telecommunications Program and the George Mason University Interdisciplinary Center for Economic Science provide attendees with "reading assignments, lectures, small group discussions and a series of 'hands-on' economic experiments." But these partners are tied to the PFF in a variety of ways. For example, the Silicon Flatirons Telecommunications Program counts on Comcast, Disney, Time Warner, T-Mobile, and Qwest for support.[12] The PFF president serves on Flatiron's board. The PFF's other academic partner, the Interdisciplinary Center for Economic Science, has long been the academic home of pro-corporate technology interests. The center is just one way the PFF is connected to a network of corporate-friendly think tanks across the country that routinely work together.[13]

Like a series of interlocking corporate board directorates, the ideological and financial affinities of these organizations foster all kinds of mutual relationships. So it isn't surprising that members of the PFF's advisory group working to further weaken federal media and telecommunications safeguards come from the Heritage Foundation, the Cato Institute, the Competitive Enterprise Institute, and the Manhattan Institute. All of these organizations share the same worldview and mission. Their job is to help industry frame the debate and influence the news media and policymakers.[14]

Cato: Leave Big Media Alone

One of the other most active think tanks is the libertarian Cato Institute, which never slows down in its efforts to support the media lobby. Cato's $12 million annual budget (based on its IRS filing for 2003) enables it to be one of the most visible nonprofits in the field. In its IRS statement, Cato lists the almost $9.9 million it spent on generating various publications as well as the $2.75 million for the "476 forums and seminars" it sponsored. Cato has ten full-time staffers working in its "communications" division, including a "director of broadcasting." TV appearances, daily messages sent by digital mobile devices, and even a "Cato University" offering home study courses are all part of its formidable machine.

Cato has a major focus on communications policy, as part of its broad agenda including health care, education and children's policies, and environment. The group's "director of communications studies" helped ally the PFF with its work on a proposed new

Telecommunications Act. Cato's "Tech, Telecom, and Internet" area lists a dozen subtopics, including broadband policy, wireless communications, and Internet governance. It's not a surprise that Cato, with its antigovernment and generally pro-business orientation, vociferously defends private interests.

Of course, it is rewarded for its media positions by corporate funders. In 2005, Cato's corporate media and telecommunications sponsors included Comcast Corporation, Freedom Communications, Microsoft, SBC, Time Warner, and Verizon. The group has constantly taken political positions that exactly dovetail with their supporters' lobbying agenda. At least one powerful media mogul usually sits on Cato's board, and that person backs the very policies the organization takes that will help enrich industry interests.[15] Murdoch and cable titan John C. Malone have served on the board. (Tobacco giants Altria and R.J. Reynolds are also backers; these companies have an obvious interest in advertising regulation, also a key concern of media companies.)[16]

The think tank's network of scholars and speakers working on media issues often have direct financial affiliations with those industries. Yet these corporate connections are not clearly identified. For example, Cato lists well-known communications attorney Robert Corn-Revere as one of its "Free Speech, First Amendment, and Technology" speakers. Cato's biographical listing of Mr. Corn-Revere is devoted to his legal scholarship. Not mentioned is the fact that among his "representative clients" at his Davis Wright Tremaine legal and lobbying firm are the Association of National Advertisers, the Motion Picture Association of America, the NAB, Fox Entertainment, and Viacom.[17] Cato author Lawrence Gasman, prominently featured on Cato's home page in February 2005 for his policy analysis "Who Killed Telecom," calls on policymakers to abandon all regulation and "simply let market forces do their work." Not mentioned is that Gasman's Communications Industry Researchers has numerous telecommunications clients including AT&T, BellSouth, and Verizon.[18]

You Can Fool All of the Politicians All of the Time

One of the media industry's favorite methods is to sponsor what appears to be a bona fide public interest or research group, but is really run by a pro-corporate lobbying operation. Such is the case of Issue Dynamics, Inc. (IDI), run by "founder and president" Samuel A. Simon.

Simon's biography on his corporate Web site is impressive, including some legitimate past public-interest credentials.[19] He was once a consumer advocate, working for Ralph Nader. He's the chair of the boards of such do-gooder-sounding organizations as the National Consumers League and the Telecommunications Research and Action Center. His list of media appearances is formidable, including *Nightline*, *Face the Nation*, *Today*, and *Oprah*. Perhaps the tip-off in his official bio is another accolade. Simon is credited with having "pioneered the practice of bridging gaps between industry and non-traditional consumer groups . . . to achieve win-win solutions for clients." That's Washington, DC–speak for helping industry undermine public-interest efforts. Simon's "win–win" methods have landed him such clients as AOL, Comcast, BellSouth, Qwest, SBC, and Verizon.[20]

One of IDI's roles is to help its media and telecommunications clients keep track of potentially troublemaking organizations. It operates an "Internet Monitoring" service that keeps a digital eye on the online activities of public-interest groups on a daily basis, reporting back to its clients what various Web sites and/or e-mail lists are saying that could be of concern.[21]

Simon's company does more than just opposition research. One of the company's specialties is what it terms "relationship management." IDI, for example, creates "strategic alliances" that help bring nonprofit organizations to the aid of corporate agendas.[22] IDI lines up groups that appear to be serving a higher social purpose—say, concerns over civil rights and disabilities—and influences their actions to help its clients. It hires former public-interest types who then trade on their relations with the groups they once worked with. One of IDI's "accomplishments" was the creation of a group that has positioned itself as a public-interest organization, but has really served as a telephone industry political support mechanism: the Alliance for Public Technology (APT).

APT was created to advance telecommunications industry goals while Congress debated what eventually became the 1996 Telecommunications Act. The group held events with members of Congress, lobbied the news media, participated in FCC proceedings, and testified before Congress. APT was funded by the media and telecommunications industry, however. Based out of the same offices as IDI, APT gave the illusion of being an organization whose primary concern was the public agenda. It attracted many supporters from the civil rights, disability, legal, and academic community, all eager to help advance pro-consumer interests. While APT may have framed its stance in terms of the need for "universal service" (a program to ensure low-income and rural consumers pay affordable phone rates) or concern over the digital divide, the ultimate goal was to ensure it delivered political help to those "sponsors and affiliates" who paid the bills. APT's real role was to provide "public interest" cover for the claims of its Bell company supporters. During the debate over the 1996 Telecom Act, the Bell companies wanted favorable rules that would allow them to extend their monopolistic control over the telephone market into the broadband era. APT's policies dovetailed with their position. Policymakers had no clue that the group was actually directed and funded through a political operative working for the phone companies.[23] Since its inception, APT has served as an extension of the media and telecom industries' lobbying apparatus.

IDI's role was and remains to help neutralize the impact of independent media reform groups such as the Consumers Union and the Consumer Federation of America. Not only did IDI receive assistance from APT in attracting and retaining corporate clients, it was also paid by APT. For the tax year 2002, for example, IDI received a $147,104 "management fee" from APT. In 2003, IDI took a slight cut—taking $134,604 as its fee from APT that year.[24] Simon must also have been pleased when APT awarded him with its highest public-service award in 1999.

IDI has helped bring other nonprofit groups to the aid of its corporate clients. It secured the endorsement for Bell company positions from organizations such as the Black Leadership Forum, the League of United Latin American Citizens, and the American Association of People with Disabilities. All of these groups have received funding from corporations working with IDI.[25] Sometimes, IDI itself funnels funds to the group that is aiding its clients. In 2003, the Gray Panthers, which supposedly represents the interests of older Americans, ran full-page newspaper ads attacking long-distance giant MCI WorldCom at a cost of $200,000. According to press reports, IDI "raised" the money for the Gray Panthers group. IDI was at the time representing local phone companies such as Verizon that were fighting the long-distance company.[26] John Stauber, who heads the Center for Media and Democracy, described IDI as "one of the leading players helping corporations find public interest groups that will accept industry money and front for industry causes."[27]

IDI also sponsored a so-called research group that aimed at undermining the ability of communities to establish consumer-friendly high-speed Internet networks. The New Millennium Research Council, an IDI spin-off, was used to head off one of the biggest threats to IDI's phone and cable company clients. If cities across the United States offered their residents a low-cost alternative to high-speed Internet service, it would pose serious competition to a Verizon or Comcast. In 2005, the council released a well-publicized report criticizing local governments that backed such public networks, claiming that cities couldn't be trusted to build a state-of-the-art system. There was no mention in the forty-page document of IDI or its corporate clients.[28]

Heartland Attack

Scattered across the country are offshoots and subdivisions of the pro-corporate communications lobby, conveniently cloaking their activities as independent experts and academics. Take the Chicago-based Heartland Institute, which has taken aim at community broadband networks, issuing a series of critical reports and press releases. This is another example of how such groups are used to advance their backers' political interests. Heartland has played a key role working to counter the growing public movement to promote low-cost and universally available Internet connections, such as wireless or wi-fi networks. In September 2004, Heartland's development team was making the rounds of the Washington, DC, telecommunications lobby, trying to raise money from BellSouth and the United States Telecommunications Association, two of the leading opponents of community broadband. A month later, the group released a "policy study" blasting the local governments that promoted community broadband Internet services.[29]

Heartland teamed with IDI's New Millennium Research Council to issue another "study" critical of broadband community networks.[30] Joining the two groups on the broadband report was the like-minded Competitive Enterprise Institute Technology Council, the Beacon Hill Institute, and the Institute for Policy Innovation. They are all connected through the well-funded State Policy Network of organizations funded by industry and right-wing foundations. Over 150 members and affiliates are listed on the State Policy Network Web site, including major organizations such as the Heritage Foundation, the Hoover Institution, and the Manhattan Institute.[31]

This network of organizations has significantly bolstered the goals of the media industry. In the inside-the-Beltway world of Washington, such "outside" experts (that is, groups based elsewhere) are often welcomed. If they have a well-known leader, a "guru" with name recognition, so much the better. One such organization is the Seattle-based Discovery Institute. Co-founded by new media financial commentator and investor George Gilder, the institute (part of the State Policy Network) has been a booster for a media world in which big business can safely tread. Like the PFF, Discovery reinforced the media and telecommunications industries' positions on public policy, arguing for the sweeping away of rules during the 1996 Telecom Act debate. In 2006, Gilder and

Discovery were back, lobbying the FCC to eliminate public policy safeguards for communications. Few policymakers questioned Discovery concerning where its money was coming from in 1996 or more recently.[32] (Lately, Discovery has also been a major proponent of the so-called Intelligent Design movement.)

Freedom for Our Backers—Not for You

As the debate on the rewriting of the 1996 Telecom Act heated up, one group suddenly appeared around the country calling for policies that would sweep away rules ensuring that communities could directly benefit from cable and broadband networks. FreedomWorks, formerly Citizens for a Sound Economy, claims on its Web site that it's helping to achieve "Lower taxes, less government, more freedom." But what it really does is to make certain that its funders—which include Verizon and AT&T—can achieve their political goals. Verizon and other Bells were working to kill off the rights that cities and counties currently have to insist that companies providing cable TV service must first negotiate an agreement with local government. Such franchising, as it is called, enables cities to craft deals that help address unique needs, from wiring schools to providing financial support for community communications services. The Bell companies dislike the idea of permitting citizens and city officials to have any say in how the companies plan to use what they consider "their" wires. So, they turned to FreedomWorks, which was happy to launch a "Choose Your Cable" campaign.

Former GOP House majority leader Dick Armey runs FreedomWorks. While he now is a big supporter of proposals that would further concentrate control of the media in fewer hands, prior to his Bell company–supported role he was a proponent of what he called "media independence." That was Armey's term for diverse media ownership, something he once publicly called for just a few years ago. The former majority leader had blasted the negative impact of media concentration in his home state of Texas as one of the reasons his son lost an election for a seat in the House of

Representatives.[33] But now, with big phone company support, Armey's FreedomWorks is happy to lead the way for less media independence.[34]

The major trade associations are usually front and center in the fight on media policy. But they also like to have their own "in-house" pet nonprofits that can be used as launching pads for high-profile initiatives or to add another name to those supporting their efforts. The Media Institute in Washington, DC, helps serve that role for the NAB, NCTA, and others. Founded in 1979, it is a wholly owned part of the industry's defense team.[35]

The Media Institute tries to wrap its pro–big media activities around the First Amendment, but it really protects special interests. It's clearly the rights of the institute's financial supporters, however, that it is designed to protect. Among the sponsors of the organization are associations that represent virtually every newspaper, magazine, ad agency, and broadcaster in the United States. These sponsors fund the Media Institute's Cornerstone Project, which works to protect the First Amendment rights of "print, broadcast, cable, satellite, and cyberspace" companies. A major public relations effort for the industry, Cornerstone arranges meetings with editorial boards, places news articles and op-eds, and distributes electronic and print public-service announcements.[36] Serving on the board of the institute in 2005 were executives from the largest media firms, including the Washington Post Company, Gannett, Belo, Viacom, Clear Channel, News Corp., Tribune, Time Warner, and Cox.[37]

The Media Institute can always be counted on to support whatever position its backers are taking. It has opposed any limits on media ownership, requirements for free or lower-cost airtime for political candidates, and rules that would require stations to serve the public interest in the digital TV era.[38]

Halfway House

The Center for Democracy and Technology (CDT) has won a reputation as one of the leading groups working on digital communications issues, including copyright and privacy. It was established in 1995 by Jerry Berman after he was forced to leave the director's job at the Electronic Frontier Foundation. Some of the foundation's officials were angered by Berman's deal making on federal policy, including his support for the FBI's Digital Wiretap legislation. Berman decided to create his own group with money, he said, coming from "foundations and different cross sections of the communications industry."[39]

The CDT occupies a strange middle ground when it comes to front groups. It presents itself as the leading nonprofit organization working to protect freedom in the digital age. But the CDT, in effect, serves as part of the communications industry political support system, helping to change the policy conversation. By focusing on privacy issues raised by government practices or the data-collecting efforts of rogue private companies, the group diverts attention from its corporate backers who are at the heart of the privacy problem. For example, instead of supporting privacy policies that would restrict the amount of personal data collected from us online, the CDT has focused the debate on a few so-called bad actors from the advertising industry that use "spyware." If the group called for serious safeguards that would restrict the online collection of personal data, it would be a problem for many of its key backers such as Time Warner (AOL) and Microsoft.

The scope of the CDT's financial backing from the media and online industry is impressive. In 2004, the CDT was supported by data collection company Axciom; e-commerce giants eBay, Google, Yahoo, and DoubleClick; telecom providers AT&T, MCI, and Verizon; software behemoth Microsoft and the Business Software Alliance (representing Apple, Cisco, IBM, and many others); and Time Warner, the NCTA, Hewlett-Packard, Intel, and American Express. Supporters of the CDT have been generous, helping it receive $5.5 million in donations between 1998 and 2001. President and executive director Berman has brought home almost $250,000 a year in salary and benefits.[40]

The creation of spin-off groups that help corporate supporters achieve their policy goals is also one of the CDT's major accomplishments. Take the Internet Education Foundation (IEF), housed in the same offices as the CDT. The IEF was founded in 1997 to help protect the digital media industry through so-called self-regulation as a way to ward off calls by consumer advocates for new policies on privacy and data collection.[41] Its board includes representatives from the CDT, Microsoft, the Recording Industry of America, Verizon, and Time Warner as well as nonprofit groups. But some of these individuals work for organizations that receive funding from the media and telecommunications industries as well. There is a representative from the Institute for Policy Innovation, which supports the political positions of Time Warner and others, and also works with such right-wing-funded groups as the Heartland Institute.[42]

The IEF's Advisory Committee is made up of most of the major media and telecom companies and trade groups that have a stake in federal policymaking, including Microsoft, the Motion Picture Association of America, the NCTA, News Corp., Time Warner, Verizon, the Association for Interactive Marketing, the Direct Marketing Association, the Association of National Advertisers, Comcast, the Cellular Telecommunications and Internet Association, General Electric, the NAA, the United States Telecommunications Association, and the U.S. Chamber of Commerce. Media lawyers and lobbyists are also on this committee.[43]

The IEF became the nonprofit that helped the industry create a variety of initiatives to ward off policies it opposed. One such example is "GetNetWise," which promoted "online safety" at a time when there were calls for federal laws on collecting data from children and youth. The IEF received $558,000 in donations in 2003. It spent most of it on projects related to "public and policymaker awareness on Internet policy and technology." The CDT's Berman, who is also both the chair and a staff member of the IEF, received extra annual compensation—nearly $20,000. From 1999 to 2002, IEF's backers forked over almost $1.9 million.[44]

Why the financial generosity to the IEF? It's because the IEF's most important project is ensuring that industry has greater influence with the lawmakers who pass all the technology and media legislation. The IEF "facilitates" the Advisory Committee to the Congressional Internet Caucus. This advisory group helps shape the agenda for the Congressional Internet Caucus, a group of around 170 members of Congress from both parties. The corporate-dominated Advisory Committee enables the biggest companies to strongly influence the national policy agenda.[45] The IEF's Advisory Committee helps develop the various forums and conferences attended by lawmakers that focus on technology-related issues. Among the issues of concern to the companies addressed by the caucus are privacy, digital rights management, and Internet "global governance." Prominently featured as speakers have been executives from Microsoft, eBay, and VeriSign—all CDT funders.

Twenty-First Century Philanthropy

The big media companies not only pay hefty membership fees to support groups like the IEF. They have also established grant-making foundations that dole out millions. While the companies will cloak their donations as charity, a great deal of the giving is based on buying allies and neutralizing potential opponents. By funding activities that fit into a corporate agenda, these big media foundations ensure that many policy issues will only be addressed in a way favorable to their interests. Nonprofit groups grateful for the income won't be interested in supporting efforts designed to rein in their benefactors.

AOL created its foundation in 1997, and it became the AOL Time Warner Foundation in 2001. One of its first major projects concerned "21st Century Literacy," which helped push the role of technology in education (something that would, of course, benefit AOL). It developed a digital divide network in partnership with other foundations. The generous donations from AOL, it appears, helped ensure there would be few low-income advocates fighting to check the online and cable giant.[46]

One of the biggest potential challenges to companies like AOL Time Warner and the cable and telephone monopoly could have come from civil rights groups. "Minority" ownership of media outlets, including programming services, is practically nonexistent. Further consolidation of ownership would only continue to undermine the potential of our media system to foster greater diversity. If civil rights groups launched a serious challenge, it could cause major problems in Congress. So one of the first grants made by AOL's foundation was to the Leadership Conference on Civil Rights, the umbrella for most of the nation's groups concerned with civil rights. The foundation would pay for "a new Web site, www.civilrights.org, to put the power of the Internet behind the nation's civil rights agenda." The Web site was just one of a number of projects that the AOL Time Warner Foundation funded for the Leadership Conference on Civil Rights, including its "Digital Opportunity Partnership" project aimed at "creating digital opportunity for the civil rights community." Time Warner was able to use its relationship with the Leadership Conference and other civil rights groups in 2004 to advance the cable industry's political agenda.[47] As documented in a 2004 report by the investigative group the Center for Public Integrity, a Time Warner lobbyist worked with the Leadership Conference to organize opposition to calls from consumer groups for cable industry reform. In 2003, AOL Time Warner, Microsoft, and Dell sponsored a "Technology Town Hall Meeting" as part of the National Council of La Raza's annual meeting. Comcast has helped underwrite the Congressional Back Caucus Foundation's annual meeting.[48]

Another AOL strategy was to create tools for grant seekers, designed to make them grateful to the company's largesse. It established "Helping.org," an online service for charitable donations. The AOL foundation co-sponsored "Network for Good," another Internet resource for nonprofits (Cisco and Yahoo! were the other supporters). Since all of the online donations would go directly to the nonprofit charity (instead of a percentage taken out for processing expenses), philanthropic groups were even more in AOL Time Warner's debt.[49]

The Verizon Foundation gave $71 million in 2004, funding scores of organizations, including major educational, civil rights, and religious groups. Comcast, AT&T, and Cisco are just some of the media-related companies that groups count on for operating support. Of course, the Bill and Melinda Gates Foundation, with nearly $29 billion in assets, is a major funder for the education and library field, in addition to its global health initiative. It's doubtful that many nonprofit groups will want to pursue a federal antitrust breakup of Microsoft for fear of alienating the foundation run by the Gates family.

Corporate foundations play a leadership role in determining policy for the philanthropic and nonprofit sector, including such key organizations as the Council on Foundations and the Independent Sector. They have been able to help ensure that the nonprofit community plays a less effective role in media and telecommunications policy debates. In 1995–96, as the Telecommunications Act was being debated, corporate media-related foundation executives argued that the Independent Sector should not advocate for rules that would benefit the public interest, including not-for-profit organizations. They sat on the committee determining public policy and discouraged the group from committing resources to help fight for diversity in communications. The organization was too fearful to speak out. Among the media and telecom foundations that play a role in the Independent Sector today are the BellSouth Foundation, the Chicago Tribune Foundation, Cisco Systems, and the General Electric Foundation.[50]

Naming Opportunities

As the lights went down in the corporate boardroom at Fox Studios in Los Angeles, "Naming Opportunities" suddenly appeared on the large viewing screen. This wasn't a preview for a new movie or TV series. It was a pitch from deans, professors, and other officials in the Department of Communication of the University of California at Santa Barbara (UCSB) to their show business advisory board. UCSB officials explained that they had plans to construct a building to house their Center for Film, Television, and New Media. All they needed was $15 million. Generous donors would be recognized, via the naming opportunities, with their moniker on reception halls, screening rooms, and a "Palm Garden Plaza." (Eventually, for example, there would be a "Michael Douglas Lobby and Reception Hall.")[51]

Clearly, the constant search for funding from cash-starved universities has also affected the role that the academic community plays in media policy. But fund-raising wasn't the only item on the agenda for UCSB. Concerned faculty wanted to address the issue of media consolidation. They hoped that academic resources could be developed on important public-interest questions. But powerful members of the advisory committee, including the then head of production for Murdoch's Fox TV studios (Gail Berman, who eventually went to work for Viacom), criticized such a move. Berman seemed to think there was no need for public policies, such as limits on media concentration. Nothing should get in the way of what companies such as Fox wanted to do. This was soon echoed by some of her other media industry UCSB adviser colleagues. The message to UCSB was clear. If it wanted the industry to help "name names" that would give the school lots of dough for a new building, supporting public-interest policy on media ownership was taboo.

Universities, especially journalism, communications, and technology programs, should be playing a public-interest role in the policy debates about the future of the U.S. media. But these universities are in a scramble to secure additional donations for capital campaigns, endowed chairs, and operating support. Communications and journalism departments are fearful of alienating the business contacts their students will need for internships and jobs. Practically everywhere there is a media studies program, media companies are pursued as donors. Consequently, academia has become largely incapable of addressing important questions concerning the media. Academics are one of the few groups in our society awarded both the time and independence to stake out policy issues. They should be weighing into the debate with independent analysis, research, and even advocacy. There are exceptions, of course, such as Patricia Aufderheide, Ben Bagdikian, Lawrence Lessig, and Robert W. McChesney.

But scholars at many of the schools with communications programs end up working for and defending the media and telecom industry lobbies. Since the culture of higher education continuously seeks more and more funding from corporations and donors, the major media companies have been embraced with open arms. It wasn't a surprise that colleges and universities didn't even try to sound the alarm over the FCC's 2003 media ownership proposal. They understood that to have done so, would have meant a loss of funding.

Perhaps the archetypal university taking media industry money to help further corporate goals has been MIT's Media Lab. Media and other corporations are pitched to be "sponsors" on research efforts that will pay big commercial dividends. MIT says that the $600,000, three-year minimum contract is a small price to pay to "gain access to the work of a 300-person research laboratory." That fee gives the sponsor "full intellectual property rights" for work done by the lab. Much of the lab's work focuses on furthering the commercialization of life through the use of digital technologies. In 2005, its sponsors included Microsoft, Comcast, Google, Time Warner, and Sony, among others.[52]

One would have hoped that criticism of the big media agenda would have come from Los Angeles–based academics. After all, many members of the show business community have been hurt by consolidation. Outlets for distribution have dried up; there has been a loss of opportunities to craft more serious work for TV, especially for writers, and independent TV producers have basically become extinct. That's why so many Hollywood-based groups actively fought the FCC's 2003 media ownership proceedings.

But schools like the University of California at Los Angeles's (UCLA) School of Theater, Film, and Television ignored the debate, and thus failed to develop a position that would represent the interests of the public. They and the University of Southern California's (USC) Annenberg School of Communications rely on the media industries based in Los Angeles for financial support and connections. Annenberg's Board of Councilors includes executives from General Electric/NBC, Fox, and Charter Communications, and Leslie Moonves, the CBS chief. Its Center for the Digital Future receives support from Hewlett-Packard, Microsoft, SBC, Sony, Time Warner, and Verizon.[53] (Luckily, due to the support of TV pioneer Norman Lear and the work of Marty Kaplan, Annenberg's Norman Lear Center has made important contributions to the public interest. USC did sponsor one forum during the FCC debates, but it was primarily organized by advocates.)

The Columbia Institute for Tele-Information at Columbia University is one of the leading academic media research centers. Among its official "Affiliates" are some of the biggest names in the industry: Cablevision, Time Warner, SBC, and Verizon. Its advisory board is chaired by Richard Wiley. Other board members include representatives from the Affiliates group.

Individual academics are not typical fronts. But they often take money from media companies to advance their lobbying interests. These scholars rarely reveal how large a fee they have received. Nor do they tell policymakers about the list of related clients they have in the media and telecom industry.

Bruce Owen is an economist who has taught at Stanford University for many years. During the 2003 FCC ownership fight, Owens and his colleagues lent their support to Fox, NBC, and Viacom, which were trying to weaken media rules. An "academic" paper supplied by Owen's "Economists, Inc.," backed up network claims and was submitted to the FCC. On the paper's front page was a citation designed to convey Owen's academic qualifications: he was the "Gordon Cain senior fellow in the Stanford University Institute for Economic Policy Research." But there was no mention of the donors to the institute, which included many of the Wall Street firms backing the big media companies' lobbying efforts such as Goldman Sachs, JPMorgan Chase, and Deutsche Bank's Alex Brown. Nor, of course, was there any mention of how much he and his Economists firm received from the three TV networks. His curriculum vitae lists just a few of his "consulting" clients, including Cablevision, Comcast, Cox, Gannett, Liberty Media, and the NAB.[54]

Academics such as Ben Compaine regularly argue that media

consolidation is a "myth." Compaine, who once worked at MIT, has published a series of articles that claim, as a 2005 one does, that "the empirical reality does not support the notion in the United States . . . [that] consumers of content via the media have fewer choices of sources." But nowhere in "The Media Monopoly Myth" does he identify the funders of the article's sponsor: the New Millennium Research Council. The council, as noted earlier, is based out of IDI and is supported by Time Warner, Comcast, SBC, and others. Nor does he identify himself in his "Myth" as a "Principal" in a "consumer e-commerce Web site" as well as a "Current Principal" at a consulting firm working with Time Warner, SBC, and AT&T.[55]

Comcast reached out to University of California at Berkeley professor Michael Katz in 2003 to help the cable industry fight consumer safeguards to address skyrocketing rates.[56] Katz, who is simultaneously the Sarin Chair in Strategy and Leadership, the Edward J. and Mollie Arnold Professor of Business Administration, and an associate dean for academic affairs at the Haas School of Business, was chief economist at the FCC under Hundt. But while Katz's FCC paper did identify Comcast as its sponsor, it should also have acknowledged the many other corporate funders of his Haas Business School. They likely may have been opposed to any call from a prominent faculty member that even suggested there should be a policy restraint on business.[57] Nor was there any mention of Katz's role as the director of the Center for Telecommunications and Digital Convergence, whose mission is to "help businesses . . . understand the sweeping developments taking place . . . and to use that understanding to attain competitive advantage and implement sound public policies."[58] Among the projects undertaken by Katz's group is a "series of executive workshops." Such a pro-business focus should have been identified to the FCC and the press. But in the game of hiring scholars, financial ties to vested interests are rarely identified.

Bears and Bull

One of the media industry's lobbying tricks is to parade before FCC officials so-called financial experts from Wall Street who support their positions. The FCC, like other government agencies, is loath to get in the way of the stock market. So if it hears from a well-known "analyst," such testimony can have a powerful impact.

Victor B. Miller IV of Bear Stearns & Co. has played such a role. Miller has been a big booster of media deal making—and has opposed public-interest safeguards on media ownership. In spring 2003, in his position as managing director of Equity Research, Radio, and TV Broadcasting, Miller made the lobbying rounds with Wiley. On the agenda was the media ownership rule making before the agency. Miller and Wiley, according to documents, spoke about the "financial implications of the proceeding for the media industry." He met with commissioners, their chief aides (including Powell's legal adviser), and the head of the commission's media ownership working group. As the *Wall Street Journal* reported the day the FCC voted to weaken many of its ownership rules, Miller had "become a trusted industry sounding board" to "Commissioners and staff."

During the 2002–3 FCC review of the rules, Miller filed hundreds of pages of documents that supported ending or weakening media ownership safeguards. He wanted to see TV networks and large station groups own more stations, both locally and nationally; he also backed permitting the cross-ownership of newspapers and stations. But while Miller says he never made it a secret that his firm was working for many of the media giants supporting FCC rule changes, in several of his commission filings—done by the Wiley law firm—there is no mention of such financial relationships. Miller should have noted that Bear Stearns had financial relationships with Fox, Disney, Viacom, Comcast, Cumulus Radio, Radio One, and Sinclair Broadcasting, among others. Of course, Miller's lawyer's firm was representing Clear Channel and the NAA as well.[59]

For centuries, powerful interests have used their resources to advance political and economic agendas. Politicians, business leaders, academics, and other influential members of the public have taken the money and run into the arms of their donors. In the political culture of Washington, DC, such arrangements occur regularly. But too often the public is unaware that there are financial connections between the media companies and their supporters. With a frequently uncritical press, these big companies and trade associations are able to bask in the glow of well-positioned and paid for cheerleaders. Given the limited resources of the public-interest groups working on media and telecommunications issues, it's made it more difficult to secure reasonable public policies that would benefit more than just a handful of special interests.

Many of the groups and academics that support the industry agenda don't do it for the money alone. They are ideologically aligned with the concept that corporations should be free to do as they please, regardless of the public consequences. These supporters prefer a system in which companies fight each other in the commercial arena, winner take all. One can't convince them with arguments that the United States must have rules and policies designed to make our media culture as diverse as possible.

But even though groups take policy positions that are in sync with their values, it's still the money from the corporate interests that makes their work possible. Many nonprofit groups would be incapable of sponsoring all those studies, scholars, and media events. There would be no fancy trips to resorts. Perhaps that's one reason many groups don't clearly disclose who is paying for all the work.

The relationship between the media companies and these front groups will continue. It makes political sense for the lobbyists to pull the strings of their supporters. What's paid out in terms of annual donations or grants is a pittance compared to the return: policies that favor their interests or the trashing of ones that would favor the public. Yet the public needs to be forewarned. When the news media reports about a favorable study on how the broadcast, cable, or high-tech industries are serving the public well, follow the money.

5

The Powell Doctrine

The tenure of Michael Kevin Powell as chairman of the Federal Communications Commission (2001–5) serves an as important case study of how the FCC chair wields power. It underscores why presidential appointments to the commission, made in collaboration with Congress and often industry, should be carefully reviewed and the entire process reformed. The level of scrutiny used to review judicial nominations is needed to ensure public accountability in FCC appointments.

The country will ultimately pay dearly for Powell's tenure. During Powell's term, the bankruptcy of communications companies such as WorldCom cost investors billions—setting back the economy and leading to the loss of thousands of jobs. And by abandoning the public policies that helped ensure the Internet's evolution as an open network, Powell placed its future into the hands of the cable and telephone monopolies.

Ironically, those who care about the media and the public interest should be also grateful to Powell. So sure of the correctness of his worldview about media and telecommunications, Powell alienated constituencies from the Left to the Right (including groups such as Moveon.org, Common Cause, and the National Rifle Association). By refusing to address the concerns about consolidation, Powell helped galvanize an emerging media reform movement. More than anyone else in the FCC's recent history, Powell made visible the crucial role played by the commission.

The Son Also Rises

Powell's career had been on a fast track, undoubtedly aided by the fact that he is the son of General Colin Powell. His rapid ascent in the late 1990s was remarkable. As *Salon* magazine noted, "In just a few short years Powell has hopped from a coveted court clerkship to a prestigious law firm to a chief of staff at the Department of Justice, all with the aid of A-list Beltway mentors from both parties."[1]

The public should have been forewarned of Powell's views, a communications philosophy based on the belief that the forces of so-called competition would provide the digital age equivalent of serving the public interest. His vision of a competitive landscape meant that the FCC would essentially step aside and permit private interests to determine how the public should benefit. Policymakers should let the "genius" of an unfettered marketplace determine winners and losers. The government had little or no responsibility to protect consumers, small businesses, independent producers, or journalists. Consumers (as Powell defined the public) would receive new technological services and access to more diverse content.

Powell first served as an FCC commissioner, appointed through the kind of backdoor Beltway deal making that routinely goes on in Washington. The FCC's five members are statutorily divided by party affiliation. Presidents appoint three from their own party, while the remaining two must be from the opposition. In 1997, President Clinton nominated four new FCC commissioners, including Powell. At the time, John McCain was chair of the Senate Commerce Committee, the panel that oversees the FCC and must confirm nominees to it. Clinton had been forced to develop a package of nominees that the Senate would support, including his own choice for chair, William Kennard. With McCain and then Senate majority leader Lott's backing, Powell's nomination was ensured.[2]

The appointment of Kennard, who had been the FCC's general counsel under prior Clinton chair Hundt, dominated the press coverage of the confirmation hearing. Little was asked of Powell during his turn. One congressional aide involved in the process admitted that "we really don't know that much about him." But since Powell had worked as chief of staff for Clinton Justice Department antitrust chief Joel Klein, he was seen as having knowledge of the frequently contentious issues involving telecommunications and media. Besides, he had a blue-ribbon GOP pedigree and powerful political godfathers.[3]

Powell began his commission term without any significant public scrutiny. Shortly after being sworn in, he referred to himself as a "moderate" and not a "blind ideologue." It quickly became clear, however, that Powell was highly critical of the approach to policy taken by the commission. In a telling speech as a newly appointed regulator, Powell explained to a legal forum that "the night after I was sworn in, I waited for a visit from the angel of the public interest. I waited all night, but she did not come. And, in fact, five months into this job, I still have had no divine awakening and no one has issued me my public-interest crystal ball." In a subsequent speech, Powell likened the commission to an out-of-date, black-and-white hero of radio and early TV: the Lone Ranger. The Lone Ranger (referring to the FCC Democrats) was holding on to its past, ignoring the realities of the modern media landscape of cable and the Internet, Powell said.[4] He argued that there was no real reason to be concerned about the relationship between diversity of content and media ownership. "The FCC Ranger cannot bring itself to take full cognizance of this change and face whether it is time to retire the mask and let other forces do the job," proclaimed Powell. The "natural forces of the market" should replace the government's role in ensuring "competitive prices, competitive opportunities for programming, and robust options for viewers." Powell frequently cited the Austrian-born twentieth-century economist Joseph Schumpeter, who developed the concept of "creative destruction." This theory argued that the undermining of one company or technology by a new challenger helped spur economic growth. The trumpeting by Powell of Schumpeter dovetailed with much of the ethos evoked by the then high-tech boom of the 1990s and the success of companies such as Enron. Technological innovation was seen as a never-ending path to soaring stock market share prices. There was hardly a role for government at all.

In December 2000, Powell laid out this theory in one of his hallmark speeches, "The Great Digital Broadband Migration," while still just a commissioner. As he often did, Powell framed his analysis in sweeping terms, linking today's changes in media to such historical precedents as the founding of "Western Civilization." He told the politically sympathetic PFF gathering that "rather than talk of reform, a relatively pedestrian incremental notion, we need to consider the Schumpeterian effect on policy and regulation. That is, what are the implications of creative destruction economics on economics-regulatory policy."[5]

The "Brightest Light"

According to the *Village Voice*'s Brendan Koerner, Powell's elevation to the chair was ensured by the support of Republican Tauzin, the wheeler-dealer chair of the House Commerce Committee. Tauzin had listened to the "Broadband Migration" speech and immediately hailed Powell as the "brightest light on the commission, the brightest mind." Just a few weeks later, Powell was named FCC chair by President Bush (who had also named Powell's father the secretary of state). Tauzin had helped pick someone who, like him, would advance the giveaways to the big media supporters of the GOP.[6]

By the time Powell was to be confirmed for his second term, at a May 17, 2001, Senate hearing, much was already known about his approach. (He had assumed office as the chair two days after the Bush inauguration.) Yet little was done to explore what his beliefs really were. Various pet issues of the senators were raised, from broadcast spectrum to rural broadband. Further media consolidation and its associated dangers were mentioned by Sen. Ron Wyden (D-OR). But as *Variety* noted, it was "an out-and-out love fest."[7]

Given that Congress and the White House were controlled by his party, it would have been politically impossible to stop Powell's reappointment. Yet a group of determined senators who took media policy as seriously as they (sometimes) do Arctic drilling for oil or a federal court appointment could have forced a more public discussion of Powell's views. But with most members of Congress under the influence of the media and telecommunications industries, few had the inclination to oppose Powell. The collegial "buddy" atmosphere that often permeates official Washington, where members of Congress are disinclined to oppose a colleague's position lest they suffer retribution, also plays a role in limiting such challenges.

Which member of the Senate Commerce Committee would rise to oppose Powell at his confirmation hearing after his introduction by chair McCain? Powell had an "exceptional and distinguished record . . . extraordinary talent and leadership abilities," said McCain. The senator thanked Powell for "his willingness to serve our country," and also noted his "distinguished military career." He was "confident" that Powell would engage the issues "in the fair and balanced manner for which you have been justly praised."[8]

Powerful lobbyists such as Robert Okun of General Electric/ NBC hailed Powell as well, saying he "makes people feel pretty comfortable; he's not a polarizing kind of guy." Okun, already planning for the network's effort to eviscerate the media ownership rules, was confident that Powell would succeed. "He's politically savvy and experienced," he told the *Los Angeles Times*. "He understands the importance of maintaining allies of Capital Hill."[9] But the *Los Angeles Times* did report, however, that "none of more than two dozen industry executives and lobbyists" it contacted would speak "critically on the record," acknowledging that Powell would help determine policies worth "billions of dollars."[10]

Even a Democratic predecessor had high expectations for Powell. "No FCC chairman, from day one, has been more politically powerful, more well-connected and more knowledgeable since perhaps Newton Minow during JFK's administration," said first Clinton administration FCC head Hundt.[11] There was even speculation that "he could well become the first African-American president."[12]

Make Mine a Mercedes

At his first news conference as chair, Powell revealed his own perspectives about the direction of the agency under his leadership. "I do not believe that deregulation is like a dessert that you serve after people have fed on their vegetables and is a reward for the creation of competition," he told reporters. "I believe that deregulation is instead a critical ingredient to facilitating competition, not something to be handed out after there is a substantial number of players in the market."[13]

At that press conference, Powell made a comment that illustrated how disconnected he was from the plight of low-income Americans who couldn't afford access to computer technology. He mocked concerns over the digital divide that had left millions outside the online world.[14] "I think there is a Mercedes divide," he explained to reporters. "I'd like to have one; I can't afford one." Powell said that concerns over a gap in computer and online access didn't require federal action, arguing that it shouldn't "be used to justify the notion of essentially the socialization of the deployment of the infrastructure." The remark stirred up protests by some civil rights and media organizations. Although Powell was the second African American ever to be FCC chair, it was clear that he didn't envision himself as someone who would champion traditional civil rights concerns with communications policy.[15]

Despite the early controversy, Powell was seen as a political comer on a meteoric rise. Several months after the "Mercedes" gaff, congressional lawmakers were still in awe. According to *Salon*, "Committee members spent much of the day tipping their hats to one of Washington's fastest-moving movers and shakers."[16]

Powell's philosophy that the market knew best, and that creative destruction would automatically deliver a diverse and competitive communications system, played right into the hands of the media companies. By fall 2002, the nation's largest cable system owner, AT&T Broadband, was taken over by Comcast. That gave overall control of what's called the multichannel TV market to Comcast, along with a huge chunk of the broadband business, since cable was also the leading provider of residential high-speed Internet services. The FCC approval of the melding of the first- and third-ranking companies would have been "unimaginable," noted observers, if it had been done before Powell assumed control. But it was clear that the commission under Powell would not generally get in the way of any media merger, acquisition, or deal.[17]

Under Powell, the cable industry was able to achieve one of its long-desired political victories. It understood that as the Internet evolved, it would face intense competition in video programming, such as from streaming video. This would challenge the way the cable industry ran its business. Cable's monopolistic clout in the multichannel TV business was based on its management of the wire; new programming couldn't be distributed without its permission. The industry recognized that its wires delivering TV services were also perfect for high-speed Internet services. Unlike the phone companies, cable owned content—which it wanted to favor over its broadband pipes. The cable industry also saw a profitable new business in granting other content providers better treatment, such as faster download speeds to home computers. But in order to do so, cable lobbyists realized they would need to undermine the Internet's openness and nondiscrimination. They knew that Powell would be the official who would help them do exactly that.

The Internet had evolved as a dynamic and democratic medium because of the FCC regulation of the telephone network. Phone companies were required to serve, in FCC parlance, as common carriers. This meant they had to operate on a nondiscriminatory basis; they couldn't, for example, refuse to transmit your call to whoever you dialed. The Internet's growth and success reflected these regulatory "roots." There were no Internet gatekeepers. Anyone could create content and have it seen by millions. Successful start-up companies such as Google, Amazon, and eBay have prospered partly as a consequence of the FCC's regulatory regime for the telephone.

Unlike the Internet's open architecture, the cable industry ran a closed shop. So the cable lobby argued that it needed to be free of any nondiscriminatory safeguards—which would, it said, hamper the industry's ability to bring the country more broadband connections. Such rhetoric appealed to Powell's "let-the-marketplace-work" philosophy. A March 2002 decision for broadband cable reflected Powell's worldview that the media system was so dynamic and competitive that concerns about the power of big media companies weren't justified, especially in the Internet era.[18] Now cable would not have to worry about any prohibition against online content discrimination. It was free to privately run its dominant broadband Internet service.

Powell was satisfied that as technology reshaped the media landscape, it would give birth to a content cornucopia made possible by microchips and innovation. While touring the Consumer Electronics Show early in 2003, for example, Powell proclaimed that harddrive recorders connected to TVs were practically a miracle. Thus TiVo, the best known of the personal video recorders, was "God's machine," in Powell's estimation. "I can't wait to walk in the house each day to see what it's recorded for me."[19]

Big Media's Best Friend

But the hallmark issue that marked Powell's tenure was media ownership. The big newspaper and broadcast companies wanted to see the elimination of federal rules setting limits on media consolidation. Like Powell, they argued that today's media landscape made limits on the size and reach of broadcasting and newspaper companies an outmoded concept. Powell decided to use his power as chair to sweep away the remaining rules on media ownership.

He began this effort on September 13, 2001. Powell seized on a little-known provision of the 1996 Telecommunications Act, Section 202(h), as his political map. As noted in chapter 2, this provision was the poison pill placed in the act by Murdoch and other corporate interests. It was designed to force the FCC, or the courts, to do away with whatever ownership safeguards hadn't been jettisoned by the 1996 act. Section 202(h) required the commission to determine whether any of the existing limits were "necessary in the public interest as the result of competition, and to repeal or modify any regulation it determines to be no longer in the public interest." The media industry assumed that Powell and his fellow GOP commissioners would decide that most of the ownership rules were unnecessary.

During 2001, Powell first addressed the cross-ownership of broadcast stations and newspapers as well as limits on cable system ownership. He expanded this effort one year later, launching a comprehensive review of all the broadcast-related media ownership rules. This included radio, local and national limits for the ownership of TV stations, and the cross-ownership of major media outlets, including daily newspapers and broadcast properties.

Newspaper and broadcast companies had long desired to eliminate the key safeguard requiring different owners of a broadcast station and a newspaper in the same town. The purpose of the 1975 rule prevented the same company from controlling a community's two most powerful sources of information. Newspaper and broadcast companies saw big profits in cross-ownership as well as a way to cut spending for journalism. Not only were TV stations cash cows but they also would permit personnel layoffs as companies combined staff from the two outlets.

But the cross-ownership rule, advocates contended, was crucial in ensuring that a locality had competing sources of news reporting. Public-interest groups were also concerned that once TV stations could acquire local papers, the tabloid TV and ratings-driven business models that characterized local broadcasting would impair the mission of print journalism. Newspapers were the last bastion of more reliable in-depth reporting and analysis. Once folded into TV empires, they would come to resemble their dumbed-down counterparts. Maintaining their independence and as much of their editorial vitality as possible was critical for the country.

Powell liked to consider himself an intellectual. To help advance his agenda, in October 2001 Powell established a "Media Ownership Working Group." The new group, said Powell, was to address "one of my top priorities . . . rebuilding the factual foundation of the Commission's media ownership regulations." He used terms such as "empirical," "analytical," "solid factual," and "rigorous" in describing what he envisioned for the group. He was, of course, suggesting that the current slate of FCC media ownership rules were unjustifiable from such an informed analysis. The seven-member working group was composed of Powell's chief aides—hardly the types who would challenge the chair.[20]

For all his analysis, invocation of philosophers and historians, and confidence, the chair had a surprising lack of knowledge about the media industry. Powell and his supporters were blinded by the claims that new digital media was ushering in unprecedented competition and content diversity. He looked at the Internet and emerging forms of technology, and only envisioned a rosy future. But he ignored the impact of the consolidation that had already taken place, resulting in fewer companies controlling major outlets. He didn't want to know about the harm suffered by print and TV journalism due to all the mergers and deal making. Powell wasn't concerned about the decreasing opportunities in TV for independent producers and writers, who were key to Hollywood's creative potential. He also overlooked the domination of the new media by the old companies, with, as *Salon* noted, "every one of the top 20 news Web sites . . . under the thumb of a media giant,"[21] He never reflected that the TV networks and stations wanted limits on ownership ended so they could buy extra TV stations and gain even more valuable free digital spectrum. They had, after all, engineered the airwaves giveaway in the 1996 act precisely to increase the clout as well as value of every TV outlet.

And perhaps most crucially, Powell also refused to consider how his support of policies enabling the largest cable and telephone companies to control the future of broadband might change the Internet's ability to provide a stream of diverse content. Yet Powell was predicating his entire approach to media ownership on the role the Internet would play to ensure robust diversity.[22]

Much was said by Powell and the proponents of eliminating ownership rules about how these rules unfairly impinged on corporate media "free speech" rights. But never acknowledged was how the policies had been designed to provide the public greater access to diverse sources of information. In fact, the First Amendment had been used as a political battering ram by the big media companies to overturn any policy they opposed. Permitting a single company to own most of the outlets of expression in a single community had nothing to do with the spirit or meaning of the First Amendment. Public policies promoting a diverse and competitive media structure were not tantamount to government prepublication censorship. But what Powell's FCC was proposing would, in fact, limit the range of information Americans received and help further weaken an independent press.[23]

By eliminating and diluting safeguards on local ownership, Powell would permit a single company in every major city to own several TV stations, eight radio stations, the daily newspaper, the cable system, and the leading broadband Internet service provider. There would be fewer companies controlling national media outlets as well. Powell's proposed agenda would lead to a mega-megamerger of phone, broadcast, cable, and print interests. This was hardly a scenario to promote the intense competition that was part of Powell's marketplace philosophy, let alone a robust environment to further the First Amendment.

Few challenge the status quo thinking that reflects much of how Beltway insiders discuss media policy issues. There is a kind of official amnesia that goes on, permitting some things to be discussed while other important aspects are sent into an intellectual exile. As the media lobby pushed for overturning the rules, and as Powell's FCC urged quick and decisive action, a number of key points were overlooked. There could have been a discussion about how big media companies had engaged in a political campaign of over two decades to weaken many of the FCC's media rules. Or how they advocated for policies such as the free spectrum giveaway that added to their bottom line. Nothing was said about how the media lobby had developed a "tripartite" strategy. If it couldn't get what it wanted from the FCC, it next went to Congress; failing a successful effort there, off to the courts. Once the media lobby had a favorable decision, it would be time to start the cycle again.

In that sense, Powell was ideologically aligned with Mark Fowler, Reagan's first FCC chair (1981–87), who also enthusiastically embraced eliminating media rules during his tenure. Fowler defended a deregulatory position by claiming that TV was just an appliance, "a toaster with pictures." But as Robert W. McChesney has noted, deregulation isn't the proper description of what the media companies were asking for. They wanted special-interest policies designed to provide additional government protection for the monopolies they had developed over time. Rules that were designed to serve the public were "regulation." Media companies, depicting their lobbying efforts as deregulation, were hardly regulated at all. But both Fowler and Powell used the deregulation framework as a convenient cover for what was really a giveaway to private interests by a government that is supposed to serve more than just the wealthiest interests in the country.[24]

Powell believed he could fundamentally alter U.S. media ownership policy. To this end, he had created task forces, commissioned research papers, and won the backing of powerful corporate and political interests. But what Powell didn't recognize was that he would soon face an unprecedented challenge from forces long dormant when it came to public policy and the media. Those forces would be awakened from their decades-old slumber by none other than Powell himself.

6

Showdown at the FCC

Never in its history had the FCC and the major media companies faced such intense opposition. It became a media lobbyist's worst nightmare. For decades, media moguls expected commissioners to enact favorable rules for them without so much as a whimper from the public. The broadcast networks and stations, for example, believed that federal policy was there to serve *their* interests. While there had always been some form of spirited opposition, most notably from what was called the media reform movement, critics were always at a disadvantage. There was never enough money, time, and people interested in media policy issues.

Public activism on communications issues in the United States was at its high point during the 1960s and 1970s. The era of social and political upheaval had brought renewed interest in how poorly the medium of broadcasting was serving the country. Civil rights groups conducted campaigns to break open the white male domination of management and news personnel at radio and TV outlets. They also often publicly criticized the programming that fostered ethnic stereotypes or failed to reflect diversity. Among the tools used by these campaigns were challenges to the renewal of FCC licenses as well as a variety of strategies designed to shame the media industry into changing its ways. An entire infrastructure supporting media reform developed, funded primarily by philanthropic foundations. It included public-interest law firms, policy think tanks, and activist groups. Whatever progress was made in radio and TV securing greater opportunities for women and persons of color was a result of such activism.

But the industry was working to undo the regulatory apparatus that had made such progress possible. The philosophy, known as media deregulation, had initially taken hold during the Carter presidency. With Reagan's election, though, the FCC embraced deregulation as a religion. Long-standing safeguards were swept away. The loss of regulatory leverage at the FCC was just one of the reasons the media reform movement went into a serious decline over the next twenty years. By the end of the twentieth century, only a few groups remained to represent the interests of the public in media policy.[1]

It was evident to the handful of media reform advocates that the country would require public-interest policies for broadband Internet communications, including safeguards preventing the large cable and phone companies from unfairly dominating the new medium. It was also clear that the battle over broadcast and cable ownership concerned both the new media of the Internet as well as the old media of TV. Both the broadcast and cable industries had secured policies from either Congress or the FCC that directly affected the future of the Internet. TV broadcasters had grabbed control of broadband property (digital spectrum) that could be used to favor the distribution of their content online. Cable companies had also won from Powell's FCC new freedom to operate their broadband Internet systems as private fiefdoms. If the media companies won the ability to further expand their power, by controlling more stations and airwaves, for example, they would be in an even stronger position to influence digital media. Consequently, a number of groups recognized that they would have to try to limit what the companies could do, both for today and with implications for tomorrow.[2]

Fight the Power(ful)

During the initial 2001–2 FCC review of key rules, a small band of organizations fought with every tool at their disposal. The groups included the Consumers Union, the Consumer Federation of America, the Media Access Project, and the Center for Digital

Democracy. While poorly funded and lacking the "person power" of the media industry lawyers and lobbyists, these groups did what they could to both counter and slow down Powell's juggernaut.[3] These organizations helped to generate substantial evidence that challenged the commission's flimsy theories on media ownership.

One of an advocate's key tasks is to effectively frame an issue for the press and public, going beyond the headlines and sound-bites to let people know what's really going on and what's at issue. During 2001–2, these groups made it clear to reporters and others that what Powell wanted would fundamentally place the entire U.S. media system under the control of even fewer large companies. Going beyond the conventional discussion of whether mergers or policy changes economically benefit industry, media reformers explained that much more was at stake. Whatever the FCC did would affect the country's ability to engage in civic debate, impact the institution of journalism, and help determine whether the public would receive diverse cultural content.

Fortunately, the public interest had an unusual ally at the FCC—a member of the commission itself. Helping lead the criticism of the Powell regime was Democratic commissioner Michael J. Copps, a former professor of U.S. history with a PhD. Copps had been a longtime chief of staff for the powerful senator Ernest Hollings (D-SC). Sworn in during May 2001, Copps soon became concerned about Powell's lack of support for the role of the public interest. His perspective about what was at stake dovetailed with the public-interest groups, helping provide this criticism with the blessings of an insider. In a speech shortly after Powell began his 2001 media ownership proceeding, Copps politely rejected the chair's argument that the public-interest concept was vague and unworkable, saying that "in a market-based democratic society, Americans are entitled to a variety of sources of ideas. . . . For each American to benefit from the marketplace of ideas, there must be a diversity of sources of programming available in each community."[4]

While the newspaper lobby had hoped for a swift decision in the 2001 review of the newspaper-broadcast cross-ownership rule, it was disappointed. Fox, Viacom/CBS, and NBC had gone to court to overturn commission policy limiting how many stations they each could own—the so-called national ownership rules. The federal Appeals Court for the DC Circuit ruled in February 2002 that the best way to interpret the 1996 act and the Section 202(h) provision was for the FCC to move swiftly in its review of the ownership rules. This decision suited Powell, who decided to open up a September 2002 proceeding of all the media ownership policies affecting broadcasting, including newspaper cross-ownership.[5]

Everything Must Go!

Powell seized on the court's ruling to create a new initiative that would, he believed, end most media ownership rules. In typical Powellesque form, the September 2002 FCC action wasn't just any proceeding but "the beginning of the most comprehensive look at media ownership regulation ever undertaken by the FCC." The commission would examine rules, "many of which were originally adopted decades ago," it said in a press release.[6] Powell intended to oversee an "everything-must-go sale" at the FCC.

Six ownership policies were included in this review, including newspaper-broadcast cross-ownership, local radio ownership, national TV ownership, local TV multiple ownership, radio and TV cross-ownership, and the "dual" network rule that prohibited one TV network from acquiring another. The FCC also announced that it would conduct a set of research studies to help support its final recommendations.[7]

The commission had placed this most important proceeding in the hands of Powell's chief media aide, Ken Ferree, a libertarian-oriented bureaucrat. Ferree had been named by Powell to run the commission's new Media Bureau, overseeing the broadcasting, cable, and satellite industries. According to *USA Today*, Ferree was known as "the enforcer" on his high school basketball team, "sent in to intimidate opposing players who were getting too physical." Ferree would play such a tough-guy role for Powell, too, helping ensure that the agency delivered the results his boss desired. In announcing the FCC's intention to undertake the review, Ferree likened what the commission intended to do as akin to Copernicus challenging the orthodoxy regarding the celestial relationship between the Sun and the Earth.[8]

In its sixty-eight-page "Notice of Proposed Rulemaking," the ideology of Powell's FCC was evident. The report painted a glowing picture of the U.S. media marketplace, where content was flowing from many sources. Why, it said, there were thirteen hundred full-power and twenty-one hundred low-power TV stations. Two hundred and thirty "national cable programming networks" were available on cable and direct broadcast satellite. There were thousands of radio stations, almost fifteen hundred daily newspapers, and the Internet. Practically every U.S. home had a VCR, it crowed. With such competition, why have any ownership rules at all? it asked. And besides, echoing a favorite theme of Powell's, wouldn't eliminating these policies encourage "innovation in the media marketplace"?[9]

Missing, of course, was any discussion of the state of U.S. print and electronic journalism along with its possible link to ownership patterns and FCC rules. Absent from this media fantasyland was any sense that despite the thousands of outlets, most Americans received abbreviated and formulaic news. Nor was there any mention of the fact that few companies actually controlled the production pipeline for TV entertainment.[10]

The commission asked dozens of questions that required more time, resources, and expertise about industry deal making than advocates could organize in such a short time. "Commenters," as the public (including industry) are called, were given the traditionally brief sixty-day time frame to respond. The commission normally relies on industry-biased information, including reports and analyses done by media company–funded "scholars." But since Powell wanted to claim the intellectual high ground, he ordered up a dozen studies as part of this proceeding that were used to substantiate his approach to media ownership policy. Conducted primarily by FCC staffers or academics with a relationship to the media industry, these reports (with one exception) were intended to provide cover for the relaxation or elimination of media ownership limits.[11]

Instead of bringing in scholars and experts who might have objectively developed a research agenda, Powell merely ordered his underlings to do the job.

These studies produced predictable results. For example, in one study, FCC staffers found that there had been an increase in "the number of media outlets available to consumers." Other FCC Media Bureau research results showed that conglomerate broadcast media stations received more journalism awards than independently owned outlets. The FCC's research arm found "an increasingly competitive environment" for the TV business. A study of radio playlist diversity found that consolidation of the industry had not played a role in limiting what songs were being broadcast. Indeed, this FCC staff report claimed that "listeners in local radio markets may have experienced increasing song diversity."[12]

The commission also relied on two scholars with media industry connections. Professor David Pritchard of the Department of Journalism and Mass Communications at the University of Wisconsin, Milwaukee, was asked by the FCC to compare the editorial record of newspaper-TV jointly owned operations with papers and stations that didn't have such cross-ownership. His findings once again echoed Powell's perspectives. But neither the commission nor Pritchard noted that he had previously been commissioned by a Canadian media conglomerate seeking to weaken cross-ownership policies in that country. Or that he had recently completed media research paid for by Clear Channel Communications, the Infinity Broadcasting Corp., and the Hispanic Broadcasting Corp.[13]

As part of Powell's effort to quell the call to ensure more independent programming on commercial TV, the FCC hired Queens College professor Mara Einstein to do one of the studies. Her fifty-five-page report found that former FCC rules requiring access by independent producers to network TV programming schedules really hadn't worked anyway. Her findings flew in the face of the independent production community's firsthand knowledge of how, once federal rules had been rescinded, they no longer had serious commercial opportunities within the broadcasting industry. But Einstein's report shouldn't have been a surprise. She was, after all, a "twenty-year marketing and advertising professional," with stints at NBC, MTV (owned by Viacom), and ad agencies working for Miller Lite, Uncle Ben's, and Dole.[14]

Powell said that "these studies represent an unprecedented data gathering effort to better understand market and consumer issues so that we may develop sound public policy."[15] But it was clear that these reports were methodologically flawed and biased in favor of the Powell agenda. Quick press work done by advocates helped to blunt some of these studies' immediate public reception. Public-interest groups called on Powell and the FCC to conduct a more independent research process—which they rejected. Yet the FCC had fundamentally gained what it wanted. After all, the commission's press release says that studies had been completed that revealed the diversity of the U.S. media marketplace.[16]

But these FCC activities were beginning to trigger growing public alarm, generating interest from groups not traditionally engaged in media policy fights. Unbeknownst to Powell and the media industry lobby, musicians and the supporters of more diverse and independent music were organizing over the state of radio. The 1996 Telecommunications Act had swept away limits on radio ownership, permitting the growth of Clear Channel Communications into a behemoth. By 2000, Clear Channel controlled nearly twelve hundred radio stations in the United States, including multiple stations in the same market; it had forty stations prior to the act. With its live entertainment subsidiary, which controlled key performing venues as well as many of the radio station playlists essential to success for musicians, the company had helped remake radio into a homogeneous and tightly organized business. Clear Channel and others had also adopted the practice of "voice tracking," which gave the illusion of local service even if their studio personnel were working thousands of miles away. What appeared to be the local disc jockey was someone merely adding the local station call letters and other bits of community information, even though they were likely recording from a studio based elsewhere. Music fans and artists were angry.[17]

One such group was the Future of Music Coalition. Launched

in 2000 by musicians and music lovers, the group understood how "the radical deregulation of the radio industry has not benefited the public or musicians. Instead, it has led to less competition, fewer viewpoints, and less diversity in programming." More than any other organization, the Future of Music demonstrated that the FCC wasn't looking seriously at the radio market and that any calls for further weakening of ownership policies were greatly misguided. In the first of what would be important research reports on the issue, the Future of Music effectively showed that what once had been a locally oriented business was now "dominated by ten parent companies." Two of those companies, Clear Channel and Viacom, had amassed so many stations that they commanded the lion's share of the revenues and listeners. In addition, there was a serious decline in programming diversity, with "few opportunities for musicians to get on the radio." The Future of Music also documented that only four companies, including Viacom and Disney, really controlled radio news.[18]

It wasn't only music that was helping spur the creation of groups concerned about the media. The failure of the mainstream press and TV to meaningfully serve their communities had led activists across the country to form new organizations. Each would play a crucial role in battling Powell. From policy research to street theater–style protests, these organizations would be on the front lines of the fight against Powell's plans.[19]

Powell and the media industry liked to dismiss such critics as disgruntled advocates. But what they didn't realize was that there had been growing dissatisfaction with media ownership policy from professionals within the media industry itself. Many of these individuals and their membership organizations had the financial resources and political clout to fight Powell's agenda. A great number of people working in TV, movies, or journalism understood how consolidation, made possible by federal rules, was negatively affecting their career and profession. A loose-knit working group, which included the key organizations representing TV writers, producers, and journalists, was formed to help oppose FCC ownership changes.[20]

As they had done a year before, Mark N. Cooper, research director of the Consumer Federation of America, working closely with Gene Kimmelman of the Consumers Union relentlessly provided scholarly research and analysis that countered Powell's and the industry's claims. Cooper took on the well-funded research infrastructure the industry relied on to support its goals, including academics from universities such as Stanford, Berkeley, and New York University. Like the other advocates, Cooper was passionate about how growing consolidation in both the old and new media would undermine democratic discourse and free speech.[21]

These substantive reports helped convey the real-world implications of the Powell plan. For example, in December 2002, thirty groups, led by Cooper's Consumer Federation, released a 210-page study that showed the consequences to the nation if ownership rules were weakened. Among the findings was further evidence that U.S. media would be controlled by a few; around three hundred owners would soon run the nation's TV stations and daily newspapers. The research also made clear that such changes would usher in a further weakening of the ability of media institutions to provide a check on private and public power.[22]

The message was clear. Powell and the FCC were engaged in a dishonest intellectual effort—and critics had the research facts to back up their concerns. All along, advocates had called on Powell to participate in what should have been a robust debate about the future of U.S. communications policy. Proposals that would affect what every American would see, hear, and read needed to be made public. Since the major print news media primarily covered the story on the business pages, and TV didn't really report on it at all, few knew about the FCC proceeding, let alone its implications. Newspaper and TV companies, of course, were lobbying the FCC on the issue. But Powell didn't see the need for such a public debate, despite calls from his colleague Copps and various coalition groups to do so.[23]

Foot-stompers

But Powell, ever sensitive to public criticism, was beginning to feel the pressure, as the groups leveled charges against his unwillingness to debate the issue outside the safety of his office. Press coverage suggested that Powell was afraid of having a serious and honest discussion with the public. That's when he agreed to a lone public hearing—scheduled for the dead of winter in Richmond, Virginia. Why Richmond? There were no national news media outlets there, guaranteeing that the event would not receive much coverage. It was home to the *Richmond Times-Dispatch* and its parent company, Media General. With major newspaper and broadcast TV station holdings, Media General was one of the leading companies lobbying for rule changes. Since it controlled the leading print outlet there, the *Times-Dispatch* could be counted on to provide Powell favorable treatment. Powell was also rumored to be interested in becoming the GOP candidate for a U.S. Senate seat in the state. The hearing could bring him some favorable public relations. He would fulfill the call for public hearings and do nothing to seriously jeopardize his agenda. Powell's official statement tried to rationalize why he had selected Richmond and was willing to have only one formal media ownership hearing: "Severe budget constraints and a commitment not to further delay completion of this critical proceeding are also paramount considerations in conducting such a hearing and the choice of venue."[24]

Copps had developed political support from conservative organizations because of his criticism of so-called indecent content on TV. He spoke repeatedly to socially conservative groups about the links he saw between media consolidation and such indecent content. Copps suggested that the tabloidlike quality of TV was fueled by FCC decisions on public policy, including ownership. Advocates such as the Parent's Television Council had long wanted to check the growth and power of the TV networks that they believed were conveyers of cultural "pollution." They recognized that the commission's media ownership proceeding gave them leverage to pursue their agenda. The issue of media consolidation was now garnering interest from across the political spectrum.

The FCC was also unresponsive to the concerns of many in show business. Hollywood producers and writers requested that Powell come to Los Angeles to discuss how consolidation was harming the "creative community" and programming competition. Some of TV's most innovative programming, such as Norman Lear's *All in the Family* and David Wolper's *Roots*, had been developed by independent producers. But media mergers and the elimination of FCC rules benefiting independents had helped make them an endangered species in the industry. The networks, which now were part of global media empires, could dictate both the creative and financial terms to writers and producers. Groups representing the creative community believed that TV programming, as a result, had become more formulaic and less risk taking.[25]

But Powell rejected their request to come to Los Angeles to publicly discuss the ownership issue. The show business groups, joined by other professional unions such as the Newspaper Guild, hoped they could convince the FCC chair to change his mind. They arranged a meeting with Powell's chief aide, Ferree. The groups politely asked again that Powell hold hearings in Los Angeles and other cities. Ferree rejected their request, saying that the chair had no intention of meeting with "foot-stompers," presuming that the Hollywood audience would be there merely to "stomp" their approval of their leaders. It was a wake-up call. After all, the group represented leading TV writers, successful producers, and print and TV news journalists. Surely they would be received with some respect. But Powell's refusal to meet with them underscored that he wasn't interested in learning about what was really happening in the TV entertainment and news business. He was there to implement an ideological position. The foot-stompers meeting, as it was called by the show business groups, helped strengthen their resolve to fight Powell's plans. "The sense of helplessness and anger that he [Ferree] generated by that meeting was enormous," Writers Guild of America, East executive director Mona Mangan told the *Columbia Journalism Review*.[26]

This was just one of the many mistakes Powell and his supporters would make.[27]

Public-interest groups had also begun a campaign to get the public more involved. The ability to file FCC comments via the Internet had potentially opened up the proceeding to many people outside the Beltway. Normally, primarily industry and its supporters along with a tiny handful of nonprofit groups file in these proceedings. But the Internet made filing easy to do. By early 2003, the *Wall Street Journal* reported, "Letters opposing media consolidation [were] flooding the electronic mail room of the Federal Communications Commission." The effort to rally opposition was paying off. Some observers, including a few reporters and elected officials, were beginning to notice that there was growing interest in what the FCC was doing. The opposition wasn't just the "usual suspects" anymore.[28]

While Powell refused to venture out of Washington, Copps was willing to travel anywhere. Copps believed that the public needed to be told about the proposed changes to media policy, including how they would affect news and entertainment. He wanted to hear directly from different communities across the nation about what they thought about the media. The small group of DC-based media advocates were regularly meeting with Copps and his senior staff to strategize how they could generate more attention about the FCC's plans. That's when a number of groups decided that they would organize their own "public hearings" throughout the United States.

Such hearings were urgently needed. The media lobby was applying even more pressure. With the new year of 2003, News Corp./Fox, General Electric/NBC, and Viacom/CBS formally filed at the FCC asking it to "scrap all of the government's media ownership rules." The rules, as a Fox spokesperson told the *Wall Street Journal*, were "simply outdated." The *Journal*'s Yochi Dreazen explained that while the networks had long argued for such policy changes, "what's different this time is that a changed legal and regulatory climate means the companies' request could become reality." Dreazen, of course, was primarily referring to the Powell FCC.[29]

Derailing the FCC

But Powell faced other powerful forces in his efforts to successfully have the commission change its rules. He was now being criticized by key members of Congress and *New York Times* columnist William Safire. Democrats still controlled the Senate in mid-January 2003, and Powell was raked over the coals by then Commerce Committee chair Hollings and Senator Bryon L. Dorgan (D-ND). Dorgan had been a leading critic of media consolidation and was concerned about its negative impact on the country long before Powell was in office. He was one of the few senators who voted against the 1996 Telecommunications Act. During the 2003 hearing, Dorgan challenged Powell, warning that the country was "heading in exactly the wrong direction. You should have your foot on the brake, not your hand on the throttle."[30] Powell dismissed this criticism, however, calling it a "melodramatic" description of what he intended to do. Once again, Powell's outright rejection of concern had not served him well. The senators didn't appreciate having their views abruptly dismissed.

But just a few days later, Dorgan and the anti-Powell forces would have a real-world example to illustrate the folly of what Powell proposed. One of the impacts of the act was a sharp reduction in radio news. With more stations under the control of large conglomerates, local news had virtually disappeared. To cut costs, stations automated their news and music from remote locations, as mentioned earlier. On January 18, 2002, around 1:30 A.M., a train derailed in Minot, North Dakota, releasing three hundred thousand gallons of dangerous anhydrous ammonia, a fertilizer. The Minot chief of police tried to use the emergency alert system that connected to the town's radio stations. Yet all six of the town's commercial radio stations were now operated by Clear Channel and were "programmed" by an automated system to play music. When the police called the stations, "no one picked up the phone." The incident was a stark reminder of the consequences of media deregulation. As news of the derailment spread, it attracted press attention. The police chief publicly complained that local news had suffered since Clear Channel had taken control of the Minot radio market. An outraged Dorgan told NPR that the Minot "accident ought to persuade us to be very concerned about absentee owner-ship, concentration of ownership." The incident in Minot soon be-came a symbol of the dangers posed by Powell's proposals. The Future of Music Coalition pointed out that the effects of consoli-dation in radio were like the coal miner's "canary," as radio was a harbinger of the problems we would have with newspapers and TV if Powell got his way.[31]

The Minot station owner, Clear Channel, would continue to be a lightning rod for critics. Among those speaking out against the ra-dio giant were rock musician Don Henley of the Eagles and Sena-tor Russ Feingold (D-WI). The company also attracted more unfavorable attention when a number of Clear Channel stations banned singer Natalie Maines of the Dixie Chicks for expressing opposition to the Iraq war. She was also no longer played on the 262-station network run by Cumulus Media. These actions would help spark even more protests against consolidation, especially among college students.[32]

Conservative *New York Times* op-ed columnist Safire had often been concerned with communications issues. Not surprisingly, the FCC's ownership review was on his radar screen. In the first of a series of columns, Safire criticized Powell and the media lobby's ownership proposals.[33] Safire called on GOP congressional leaders, including McCain, to oppose further consolidation. Conservative economics, said Safire, was based on protecting "small business and consumers" against monopolies. He chastised Powell while quoting approvingly from Copps, and lambasted the media's "conflict of in-terest" in not covering the commission ownership proceeding. In a subsequent column a month later, Safire accused Powell of being someone "who never met a merger he didn't like." Perhaps more than any other journalist from the mainstream media, Safire well understood how media consolidation was a serious threat to the mission of journalism. Widely read by GOP leaders, including the

Bush White House, Safire's series of articles illustrated the growing unhappiness with the Powell agenda from within its own conservative ranks.[34]

New York to Powell: Drop Your Proposals

The first independently organized public hearing against the Powell proposal was held in New York City in mid-January 2003. The sponsor was the prestigious Columbia University Kernochan Center for Law, Media, and the Arts. Advocates understood that the FCC and other opponents would merely dismiss an event they organized. So the organizations working to put on the meeting sought to have Columbia (and eventually other universities) serve as cover for its work. While the New York event appeared to have been organized by the university, the groups made most of the decisions about it behind the scenes. Three FCC commissioners, including Copps, Republican Kevin Martin, and newly sworn in Democratic commissioner Jonathan S. Adelstein, agreed to attend. Powell was invited as well, with everyone assuming that he would decline. But Powell agreed to come. His last-minute decision to "travel to Gotham," explained *Variety*, was made in response to the "pressure building" and a desire to avoid "a public relations problem."[35] Suddenly, the rump hearing was seen as an "official" event.[36]

One of the goals was to permit members of the public to hear for themselves what media lobbyists and executives actually said to each other and policymakers. Unless one is part of the industry or regularly reads the show business "trades," one doesn't have a good sense of the arrogance exhibited by many media executives. So it was highly informative to the audience when then Viacom/CBS executive vice president Dennis Swanson answered, in response to a question from the audience concerning what Viacom was doing to address the needs of the poor, that CBS had built a bigger, more powerful transmitter for its New York TV station. Swanson apparently believed that extending the channel's reach was a generous philanthropic gesture for those poor viewers who couldn't afford cable. It was an eye-opener for many in the auditorium, who saw clearly that the media industry was more concerned with serving itself than the public interest.[37] The hearing was seen as a success. Media reform advocates had been able to frame the debate outside the control of Powell and the industry. The coalition worked on having as many additional hearings as possible in the remaining months before the scheduled FCC vote in June.

In addition to the hearings, the groups had developed another strategy to galvanize opposition: the failure of the press to effectively report on both the run-up to the Iraq war and the invasion itself. Many in TV news had become cheerleaders for the war itself; newspapers had suspended analysis and criticism. Few among the critics of the war knew that the parent companies of the four TV networks and major newspaper companies were lobbying the White House, Congress, and the FCC to support new pro-consolidation policies. Through contact with the leading antiwar organizations, this inherent conflict of interest was pointed out. While media industry special-interest lobbying wasn't the only reason for the lack of critical Iraq coverage, many believed it was a factor.[38] It was also suggested to critics of the war that past consolidation had seriously undermined the ability of the media to engage in in-depth journalism, especially with international news. As a consequence, it was argued, the plan for further consolidation was a national security risk at a time when the country was engaged in many global conflicts.[39] Helping to further convince antiwar groups was the rejection by Comcast, Viacom, and Cox of TV ads criticizing the run-up to the war and other policies of the Bush administration. This also helped make vivid the dangers of media consolidation. If the FCC went ahead as planned, a few corporations would control many more major news outlets, harming the ability of groups to effectively engage in dissent.[40]

Meanwhile, Adelstein had joined the commission in December 2002. A former senior aide to Senator Tom Daschle, Adelstein worked closely with Copps as an effective team opposing Powell's media ownership plans. Their expression of concern about further media consolidation and the lack of meaningful public outreach by Powell gave opponents an almost official sanction of their effort.[41]

With the success of the New York hearing, advocates against the FCC rules began organizing their own hearings across the country. Either Copps or Adelstein was present, or often both. Through a donation from Philadelphia philanthropist David Haas, local media groups were able to quickly organize events in Chicago, San Francisco, Los Angeles, and Seattle. Hearings were also held in several other communities, including Atlanta, Philadelphia, Durham, North Carolina, and Tempe, Arizona. A standing-room-only crowd in San Francisco, at a city hall hearing organized by the Media Alliance, helped underscore to commissioner Adelstein that average people were concerned about the impact of any rule changes on how the media served their communities and the nation. Local city councils passed resolutions opposing the changes. City and national policymakers spoke out against the plan. While some media outlets underplayed or basically ignored the events (such as the *Chicago Tribune*, whose parent company was lobbying hard on the FCC rules), the hearings helped generate press coverage that otherwise would not have been possible.[42]

The vote for the FCC's rule changes was expected around June. By the spring, opposition was heating up. Groups such as Common Cause, Moveon.org, and the newly created Free Press generated tens of thousands of additional comments to the FCC opposing changes. The Free Press had been co-founded by scholar Robert W. McChesney and journalist John Nichols. The group would soon become a major force promoting communications policies in the public interest. Organizations concerned about the war in Iraq also weighed in, including the Code Pink and Global Exchange groups. Code Pink activists contended that Powell should be "pink-slipped"—fired—for not effectively supporting public-interest policies. Copps also reached out to more conservative groups concerned about cultural content issues, urging they participate in the FCC debate. As a result, the United States Conference of Catholic Bishops and the Parents Television Council (which then had around 850,000 members) each played an active role opposing further consolidation.[43]

But perhaps the biggest surprise that spring was the entry of the

National Rifle Association (NRA) into the fray. In an "Urgent NRA Bulletin: Media Monopoly Alert," members were implored "for the sake of your Second Amendment rights" to fight the "major anti-gun media corporations" and oppose the proposed "sweeping changes in the FCC that *prohibit monopoly ownership* of media sources in your community and across the United States."[44]

NRA executive vice president Wayne LaPierre asked NRA members to send in the five postcards attached to the bulletin—one for each FCC commissioner; three hundred thousand postcards were sent in. The group also gave out Powell's and the other commissioners' e-mail addresses and fax numbers (and asked for a special donation as well). Media ownership rule changes, LaPierre wrote, would mean that "your NRA would face a disastrous situation where—in a political crisis—a small group of top media executives could literally *silence your NRA and prevent us from communicating with your fellow Americans by refusing to sell us television, radio, or newspaper advertising at any price.*"[45]

Soon, papers such as the *Washington Post* were writing stories about the "Unlikely Alliances Forged in Fight over Media Rules."[46] As reporter Frank Ahrens noted, conservatives were split on the issue, with many now part of the anti-consolidation forces. Important Republican senators were also speaking out against the FCC, including Olympia Snowe of Maine and Lott of Mississippi.[47] For the first time in many years, a number of Democrats in Congress were also stating they were against FCC action on media ownership. They were stirred, in part, by a major TV, newspaper, and online ad campaign launched by Common Cause, the Free Press, and MoveOn.org that helped generate 170,000 e-mails and letters to the commission. In the TV ad, Fox's Murdoch is portrayed as controlling every TV channel and much of U.S. news, having benefited from Powell's upcoming media ownership decision.[48]

"Good Results"

Even as Powell tried to fend off the onslaught of public outrage, he continued to assure the industry of a positive outcome. Appearing in late April 2003 before the NAA, which represents almost every major newspaper company in the United States, the chair told the publishers that they were "likely to fare well. . . . I'm confident there's going to be a very good result across the board on June 2."[49] Needless to say, the publishers were overcome by Powell's promise that they soon could grow their companies by buying up newspapers and TV stations in a single community. Perhaps the greatest praise for Powell came from outgoing NAA chair William Dean Singleton, the CEO of MediaNews Group (the publisher of such newspapers as the *Denver Post* and the *Salt Lake Tribune*), who had aggressively lobbied to kill the cross-ownership rule. "I could have written the speech myself," he told *Editor and Publisher*.[50]

But Powell now faced a growing national revolt from media industry insiders, artists, and the general public against his proposals. The majority of public comments filed at the FCC were opposed to any rule changes. Powell had only a sliver of support—and that was from the very companies that stood to benefit.[51]

All along, Powell critics had said that he was fundamentally out of touch with what was going on in the news and entertainment industries. But emphasizing the perspective that media concentration had undermined competition and creativity were two media industry heavyweights. In a keynote address to the annual meeting of the NAB, veteran movie as well as TV and new media executive Barry Diller (who had launched the Fox Network) gave a blistering critique of media concentration. Consolidation had given oligopoly control over TV to five companies, he declared. In 2003, it was impossible to think of starting a new national network such as he had with Fox more than a decade before. "There are real dangers in complete concentration," Diller warned. "The conventional wisdom is wrong—we need more regulation—not less."[52]

Ted Turner, the founder of CNN, also spoke out. In a *Washington Post* op-ed appearing just prior to the June 2 FCC vote, Turner wrote that the proposed changes would "stifle debate, inhibit new ideas and shut out small businesses trying to compete." Echoing Diller, Turner reflected that "if these rules had been in place in 1970, it would have been virtually impossible for me to start Turner

Broadcasting, or 10 years later, to launch CNN."[53] Even though, he admitted, he was a major investor in one "of the five media corporations that control most of what Americans read, see and hear" (then known as AOL Time Warner), he opposed Powell's proposed changes.[54]

Powell's FCC was also rocked by a late May 2003 report from the Center for Public Integrity, which found that big media companies had been picking up the tab "for FCC Commissioners and agency staffers to attend hundreds of conventions, conferences, and other events in locations all over the world, including Paris, Hong Kong and Rio de Janeiro." Over an eight-year period nearly $2.8 million was spent, with payments made for travel by many industry trade groups, including the NAB, the NCTA, and the FCBA (whose members are primarily working to influence the FCC). Powell was singled out in the report as having "chalked up the most industry sponsored travel and entertainment," with nearly $85,000 spent on his forty-four trips. "The idea that the FCC can render an objective, independent judgment about media ownership is laughable," commented Charles Lewis, the center's executive director. Powell, who had a thin skin when addressing his critics, refused to speak to the center about its report.[55]

A vote had been scheduled for June 2, 2003, on the policy changes sought by Powell. Powell was urged by his fellow FCC commissioners Copps and Adelstein, as well as leading members of both parties of Congress, to publicly release his proposals prior to any vote. Many groups and scholars also went on record asking him for time to analyze his recommendations. While Powell and the industry charged that such requests were merely delaying tactics, the demand to review the rules prior to their enactment was driven by a greater concern articulated in writing by lawmakers from his own party "that it would be inappropriate to make significant changes that could have a sweeping impact on how our society engages in public debate without first having a complete public airing of these changes."[56]

Powell refused to release his new rules in advance, and was backed by other GOP lawmakers and the media lobby.[57] Despite Powell's claims of an open process, within the commission he operated along clearly partisan lines to negotiate the final rules, while keeping his Democratic colleagues out of the loop. When he finally shared his proposal with Copps and Adelstein, he gave them less than three weeks to review the plan for the June 2 vote.

In the meantime, to underscore the strange bedfellows working together against Powell, Copps and Adelstein held a forum just prior to the June commission meeting, inviting groups from across the spectrum to sit side by side and testify. Despite their widely divergent political perspectives, these organizations all shared concerns about how further media consolidation would harm journalism, reduce creativity in show business, and spur more indecent programming. As Parents Television Council head Brent Bozell, one of the speakers that day, commented, "When so many disparate organizations—groups ranging from the Catholic Conference to Common Cause, from the Family Research Council and the NRA to MoveOn, the Writers' Guild and NOW—when all of us are united on an issue, then one of two things has happened. Either the earth has spun off its axis and we have all lost our minds, or there is universal support for a concept."[58]

By this time, the commission had received 435,000 public comments about media ownership, nearly every one arguing against weakening the existing safeguards. Almost 150 members of Congress had also weighed in, either asking for more time for public review or opposing new consolidation efforts.[59] Shocked by the opposition to his proposed regulations, Powell launched a political counteroffensive, sternly warning that "if you don't do surgery on this patient, it is going to die. Free over-the-air TV is going to die. The [existing media ownership] rules are going to die."[60] The only way to save the gravely ill patient, Powell argued, was to allow the networks to own more stations.

June's Busting out All Over

The FCC's contentious deliberations ended in a three-to-two vote along party lines. The new media ownership rules permitted greater control of newspapers and TV stations by media companies both locally and nationally. Newspapers and TV stations would be able to merge in most communities. In the largest markets, a single entity would be allowed to own up to three TV stations. Many more communities would now see "duopolies," where two TV stations are jointly operated. The scenario that advocates had feared had come to pass: in a single market one entity could now scoop up the major daily newspaper, three TV stations, eight radio stations, a cable company, and the major Internet service provider.

Powell praised himself and his colleagues at the FCC, saying he was "confident and proud of the job" done. "We have embraced a challenge unparalleled in the FCC's history. We collected a thorough record, analyzed our broadcast ownership rules from the ground up, and wrote rules that match the times." He once again repeated that the commission had "most importantly—sought the views of our citizens."[61] The FCC released what it called a "diversity index," a new analytic measure that "reflects the degree of concentration in viewpoint diversity in local markets," as part of its rule making that day. The index was at the core of Powell's quest to find new approaches to media public policy. It attempted to create a framework that justified the further concentration that the new rules would bring, including greater cross-ownership of media outlets. But it was riddled, noted critics, with a bias that undermined its legitimacy.[62]

Both Adelstein and Copps delivered sharp attacks on Powell's plan. "[It is] a sad day for me, and I think for the country," Adelstein commented. "This is the most sweeping and destructive rollback of consumer protection rules in the history of American broadcasting. . . . This plan is likely to damage the media landscape for generations to come."[63] But even with the final outcome of the FCC vote, there was no doubt that the campaign against Powell had made an impact. In its official press release announcing the rules, the commission had to claim its order "Sets Limits on Media Concentration." The release's subtitles included phrases such as "New Limits Protect Viewpoint Diversity," "New Rules Promote Competition and Choice for Americans," and "Limits on Concentration Serve the Public Interest."[64] The commission also rejected eliminating the rule that would have allowed one of the four big TV networks to buy another—that would have been going too far in the political climate that its opponents had created.

Many of the big companies were disappointed that Powell and his allies hadn't been able to scuttle most of the rules. They had hoped, as *Variety* put it, "for more sweeping changes." Giants Viacom/CBS and General Electric/NBC could only publicly muster that Powell and his allies had delivered "a first step." Murdoch's News Corp./Fox termed it "an important step."[65]

Despite the public relations gloss that Powell tried to put on his decision, there was growing protest, not only from the diverse coalition of advocates that had opposed the rule changes but also from Congress. Legislation to overturn Powell's rules would be introduced. Advocacy groups appealed to the federal courts through the efforts of both the Media Access Project and the Institute for Public Representation at the Georgetown University Law Center. By early September, a federal appeals court in Philadelphia issued an emergency stay, suspending the implementation of the rules just one day before they were to take effect.[66]

By mid-July, a House committee approved a bill that ensured the broadcast networks could not benefit from Powell's new rules by owning many extra stations. Two weeks later, the House approved the measure, 400–21.[67] Momentum was building for a complete rejection of the Powell plan. In mid-September, with strong bipartisan support, the Senate approved by 55–40 a resolution of disapproval that completely reversed all of the new rules.[68] Media ownership was now a major issue in Washington, drawing the attention of presidential candidates and many members of Congress. Some Hill observers said that as Congress ended its first session in 2003, only Medicare had rivaled media policy as the most "discussed issue by constituents in 2003."[69]

Only through the intervention of President Bush and the GOP leadership was the House prevented from joining with the Senate to hold a vote on an override of Powell's rules. Two hundred and five House members, including eleven Republicans, wrote to Speaker Dennis Hastert (R–IL) asking him to allow a vote on an

FCC media rules override. Bush had threatened to veto any such proposal, and the Republicans were able to prevent an FCC roll-back from passing.[70] But the agreement was still a slap at Powell. His commission's new national ownership limit for networks had been revised downward.[71]

Ultimately, Powell suffered three rebukes. First, Congress clearly had sent a message through hearings and legislation that it was un-happy with his June 2 plan. Second, the U.S. Third Circuit Court of Appeals June 2004 decision suspending the implementation of his rules—sending them back to his commission for an overhaul—was a major setback. For now, the "old" pre–June 2 limits would re-main in place. Finally, it was evident that Powell had unleashed a torrent of public criticism toward the FCC—something that was unprecedented in the agency's history.

Powell now retreated into his more personally comfortable role as "new media guru." A year after the debacle of his media owner-ship decision making, Powell joined an elite Silicon Valley blog site to pontificate. He was "talk[ing] back" to members of the "Al-waysOn" network, many of whom were interested in revitalizing Silicon Valley's high-tech economic growth. We're engaged in a "digital migration," Powell assured his readers. Powell's blog was peppered with ads, including spots from KMPG, Accenture, Ban-ner Corporation, IBM, Yahoo!, and AOL.[72]

Powell submitted his resignation to President Bush on January 21, 2005, effective in March.[73] The FCC's release making the an-nouncement was accompanied by a document called "Policy Highlights of Michael K. Powell's FCC Tenure." Under each of seven roman numerals, Powell tallied his achievements. His first was for his "light touch to promote development" of broadband. He was next praised for work labeled "Revolutionary Wireless Re-form." Then it was for having "stopped unwanted telemarketing calls." Powell was lauded for giving "Digital Opportunities for Un-derserved Communities" and "Countering New Threats with New Technology" by helping protect Homeland Security. Only at the end of part VI, after a discussion of his work "Driving the Transition to Digital TV" and how he had "strengthened decency on the public airwaves" was there any mention of media owner-ship. At the end stood a single line, unadorned by the explanatory copy that had accompanied almost all of his other "highlights": "conducted most comprehensive review of media marketplace in FCC history."[74]

After he left the agency, Powell chose the career path of all the current living FCC chairs—work in the media and telecommunications industry. Like his immediate predecessor Kennard, Powell joined an investment firm, where he was a "senior advisor" helping the "preeminent private equity firm in the global media, communications, and information industries"—as Providence Equity Partners calls itself—make money. One of Powell's new duties was to "advise the firm on . . . regulatory issues in the media" industries.[75]

In many ways, the public has to be grateful to Powell. Because he believed so strongly in his own vision and did not seek out alternative perspectives, Powell helped galvanize a media reform constituency. He played a key role transforming a little-understood area of national politics—communications policy—into a raging issue that cut across party lines and helped make the struggle over our media future more public and ultimately more participatory. Powell became the perfect villain.

If Powell had chosen to have a serious debate on the issues, he might have prevented what became the largest public protest against the FCC and the media lobby. Thankfully, Powell did not.

Powell's arrogance helped lay bare a system that for decades has placed the interests of a few media companies over those of the public. While we need to be appreciative that Powell's bullheaded-ness attracted attention and opposition, the lesson ultimately transcended personalities. It revealed that if informed of the issues, the public is concerned about the quality of U.S. communications systems. Activism from across the political spectrum helped defeat a set of policies that had been considered unstoppable. Mergers, takeovers, and other plans by the biggest media companies had to come to a screeching halt. Only through such organized efforts can we hope to balance the special interests of a few media companies with the larger concerns more fitting of a democracy.

7

The Brandwashing of America:
Marketing and Micropersuasion
in the Digital Era

A "specially designed MRI machine with TV monitor" is flashed on the screen, followed by color scans of a brain watching ads for Coke and Evian. "Brain activation is strong for both commercials in the medial Prefrontal Cortex," it is reported. The audience is briefed about the range of neurologists, psychophysiologists, and other specialists working on the project. One of the goals of the effort, they are told, is to learn how we can more effectively engage the unconscious part of our minds. They are advised that "emotional responses can be created even if we have no awareness of the stimuli that caused them."[1]

It's 2005 "Advertising Week" in New York.

Backed by a consortium of leading industry groups, the Measurement Initiative: Advertisers, Agencies, Media, and Researchers (MI4) endeavors to help define the public's "emotional response to advertising" by studying how to engage emotions, memory, and other brain behaviors. "The industry needs new measures to capture unconscious thought, recognition of symbols and metaphors," ad executives are told. One of MI4's first investigations is to examine the relationship between beer ads and brain behavior.[2]

The policy debates concerning communications have principally focused on issues related to ownership and control of media outlets, including the broadband Internet. But there has been hardly any discussion about one of the key beneficiaries for the policies aimed at spurring the development of a high-speed digital highway: the U.S. advertising industry.[3] Much of the technology now being put in place to deliver the broadband Internet, digital TV, and mobile services has been designed to serve the needs of marketing. Advertisers have been at the forefront of plans to ensure that new communications technologies target individuals with sophisticated pitches, collecting lots of information about us in the process.

While there has been growing concern expressed over the loss of privacy in online communications, little has been said about the role advertising plays in helping create a digital future where our privacy is lost. The ad and marketing industries have been engaged in a largely behind-the-scenes role ensuring that the federal government doesn't protect our online privacy. Recent controversies over the government's data collecting practices, including its successful legal efforts to have AOL, Yahoo!, and Microsoft turn over consumers' Web surfing records, have overshadowed the expansive commercial data collection system that is emerging. Beyond the loss of privacy, we all should be alarmed about how interactive advertising is shaping the kind of programming and content available to us in the future.

It's an Ad, Ad, Ad World

Advertisers are developing increasingly sophisticated technologies designed to track, analyze, and persuade us in the Internet era. Throughout the digital landscape, an unprecedented system of data collection is already delivering more precise "targeting" with "personalized" advertising. Our online "behavior" is closely followed and then shared with many Web sites without our real consent. Marketers know more about us because they are connecting our cyberspace travels with information readily for sale by data-mining warehouses.

Powerful interactive video and animated images—what the ad industry calls "rich media"—beckon us to become emotionally involved with the advertising. Automated selling technologies seek to "convert" us, as the ad industry terms it, from online window-shoppers to active buyers. Talking, animated "ad bots" float across our computer screens to engage us in conversation about ads and brands. Online marketers understand, courtesy of Stanford University research, that these fictional characters are perceived by the more primitive part of our brain as real and trustworthy people. Practically every major media and online company is now using sophisticated online marketing software and techniques to track and target us.

We have grown up in a culture where advertising already plays a major role in our lives, shaping our elections, news media, and entertainment. Newspapers, radio stations, TV channels, and many Web sites are paid enormous sums to deliver us marketing messages. That's why TV networks sell our *eyeballs*, and why Google and Yahoo! sell our *search words*, to advertisers. Some $260 billion is spent on U.S. advertising annually. Online advertising revenues, now at $6.85 billion a year, are growing. While this is far behind what is spent on broadcasting and cable—some $68 billion—digital marketing will become even more important in the years ahead.[4] Advertisers plan to go well beyond what they already have developed for the Internet. They are working to create more powerful and ubiquitous commercializing technologies. Wherever we go, interactive marketing will be there. A system of micropersuasion is emerging, where the potent force of new media is being unleashed to influence our individual behavior. Today, it is commercial products such as soap, prescription drugs, cars, and popular culture. But it will also be used to sell religion, political ideas, and elections.

The ad industry likes to say that the public has more control over what advertising they see or whether they see it at all. The industry points to the increasing expansion of the media—everything from iPods to satellite radio to video on demand—and argues that advertising is now less powerful. Advertisers often characterize the industry as being at a disadvantage now that users can effortlessly fast-forward through commercials or create their own ad-free media.

But such assertions are disingenuous. An advertising technology "arms race" is underway to make digital marketing more effective and pervasive. Fueled by global media consolidation, content companies are now working even more closely with advertisers. The broadband Internet, digital TV, and new forms of wireless or mobile communications are all being shaped by the forces of marketing. Advertising is becoming more powerful, not less.[5]

Every Move You Make

Your legal concepts of property, expression, identity, movement, and context do not apply to us. They are all based on matter, and there is no matter here. . . . We will create a civilization of the Mind in Cyberspace.

—John Perry Barlow, "A Declaration of the Independence of Cyberspace," 1996

One of the greatest fears the advertising community had was that there would be no ads in cyberspace.[6] After all, the Net had initially developed as a noncommercial medium, where the informal netiquette of its early users discouraged selling. A popular tenet at that time suggested that online content would be available for free, distributed without advertisers playing a role. Some of these netizens even predicted that the Internet would make all big media and advertising extinct. But soon after the Internet was officially disconnected from its federal government roots as an academic network, all kinds of product pitches flowed in cyberspace.

The newly elected Clinton administration embraced the importance of what was then popularly called the Information Superhighway. A series of meetings with various industry and nonprofit groups was held as part of the administration's work to develop a national Internet policy agenda. At one meeting attended by national advertisers and their lobbyists, marketers expressed alarm at the prospect of any federal policy that endorsed an ad-free Internet. The message Procter & Gamble (P&G) and other heavyweights sent the administration was simple: don't do anything that hinders the role of advertising online. The Internet's potential would be irreparably harmed without commercial sponsorship, they said. There wouldn't be much content, they claimed, unless advertisers could do for the Net what they had done for radio and TV.

Forget too, they also said, about any legislation or regulation that would protect online privacy. It was too early for any privacy policy, they successfully argued. Any rules prescribing what information could be collected online would also harm the Internet's future. The Clinton administration got the message. Advertisers would have a free digital ride.[7]

Almost since the Web's introduction, the ad industry was working to advance its potential as a commercial medium. At a meeting of the Advertising Research Foundation (ARF) in 1994, there was a demonstration by cable channel USA Network of a "live, online focus group" exploring how the newly created "graphical browser" for the Web could be utilized. The cable channel Nickelodeon, always at the forefront of investigating methods to target kids, gave a presentation showing that the "Web was a suitable environment for doing market research on children."

But to make the Internet a more fertile environment for marketing, Silicon Valley would have to ensure that its technology was more compatible with selling. Netscape, then the leading online browser, helped lead the way. The company was concerned that its initial Web software "was not robust enough to support the implementation of commerce applications, such as shopping carts or pay-per-view services."[8] That's when cookies—a software "ID card" placed on one's personal computer that communicated information about the user to Web sites—appeared. In 1995, they were placed in version 1.1 of the Netscape browser, so multiple cookies could be sent to users.

Meanwhile, there was also a great deal of work to make Internet technology more suitable for online marketing. Intel, interested in an "Internet Advertising Ecosystem," played a crucial role supporting early experiments in rich media. The creation of the popular multimedia software Flash (and later Shockwave) helped make advertisements more vivid and was quickly bundled into basic software packages, including Microsoft's Internet Explorer and AOL. Both companies, of course, had a huge stake in the success of interactive marketing. Through commercial spin-offs from the MIT Media Lab and others, there was soon also so-called intelligent agents that learned about one's online behavior in order to make product recommendations. These technologies became the basis of "collaborative filtering," used by Amazon.com and many others.

The industry also began creating initiatives designed to both protect the role advertising would play online and also expand advertisers' influence over it. In 1994, two of the largest ad lobbying groups created the Coalition for Advertiser-Supported Information and Entertainment (CASIE). Its mission was "to ensure that advertising will remain a key funding source for information and entertainment services in the evolving world of telecommunications and the new interactive media."[9] Marketers also wanted to better understand how Internet advertising could influence consumer behavior. That's when P&G stepped in. In 1998, P&G helped create the Future of Advertising Stakeholders "to ensure that the basic necessities for an advertising market could be put in place for online media." A series of meetings was held around the world to help create "a set of unifying principles" for online media measurement.[10]

While many industry heavyweights supported early research in new media and advertising, the New York Times Company played a pioneering role. By 1996, the *New York Times* online had "the largest database of any news site."[11] Online tracking technology captured "highly reliable data on behavior," including a user's operating system, the site they had been on prior to the *Times*, any purchasing they had done at the site, and a user's "click through activity." All this online data gathering was amplified by the personal information given by subscribers and *Times* online users, including zip code, gender, and income. Martin Nisenholtz, a former academic and ad executive who had been recruited in 1995 to run the New York Times Electronic Media Company, was an avid supporter of digital advertising. He believed that "the ultimate promise of the web for advertisers" was one-to-one marketing. Nisenholtz was critical in urging his ad industry colleagues to "exploit the unique power of digital media on behalf of their clients. . . . [N]ew media communication" can help to foster "an emotional bond in the consumer . . . by being a part of the brand itself, not a distinct and separate commentary."[12] The *Times* would remain at the forefront of digital marketing in the years to follow.[13]

Big Brother Lives on Madison Avenue

The rise of digital marketing has been built on decades of research designed to better understand and manipulate consumers. Databases are overflowing with updated information about ourselves, our families, and our communities, including credit card spending, auto purchases, real estate transactions, occupations, and family size. "Geodemographic" tools provide marketers with "lifestyle" and location information that can target us down to the "census block" (the immediate area where we live). Advertisers can type in a "zip code plus four" to learn what kind of marketing identity (or cluster) we're assigned, based on our income and purchasing behaviors. Are we part of the well-to-do, big-spending "Winner's Circle" group? Do we better fit in as part of the "Gray Power" types who reside in comfortable retirement communities? Or perhaps we're listed in what they call "Sunset City Blues"—at the "end of their careers" working in blue-collar occupations? There are also innumerable research "panels" where millions of consumers allow advertisers to learn about what they buy, watch, listen to, read, and do online.[14]

Practically since the first static online banner ad appeared in 1994, advertisers recognized that the Internet had the characteristics of an ideal commercial medium. Two-way communications permitted marketers to interact directly with consumers. Information about an individual user's interests could be captured, stored, and shared through voluntary methods such as filling out forms and more stealthlike data collection practices. This was a "revolutionary . . . new marketing paradigm," claimed two marketing aficionados, Don Peppers and Martha Rogers. Their 1993 book, *The One-to-One Future*, helped influence the evolution of online advertising. Ads could be created and then delivered to individuals. This freed the industry from the "limitations" of mass marketing, they said. Internet-savvy advertising agencies quickly sprang up, alongside technology companies selling "Web analytics," software that helped track and deliver personalized ad messages.[15]

Much of the euphoria of the 1990s' dot-com boom was based

on the belief that the Internet would become a powerful marketing engine, delivering tens of millions of consumers who could be individually influenced by one-to-one advertising. Such predictions revealed the greed of marketers who thought they could instantaneously change our behavior. But the one-to-one digital marketing vision was merely premature, waiting for greater public acceptance of the Internet and the maturation of online selling technologies.

Ironically, the dot-com bust helped spur even greater focus by marketers on perfecting tools that would pinpoint and influence individuals. What was needed more than ever, interactive ad experts said, were techniques that could make ads more "intelligent." They wanted to develop a deeper understanding of our consumer behavior, predicting in "real time" what we might do, and motivating us to do it, and following us throughout the digital landscape. That's what the advertising industry is engaged in today.[16]

We are being "shadowed" online by a slew of software-driven digital gumshoes working for Madison Avenue. Our movements in cyberspace are closely tracked and analyzed. Real-time collection of our Internet behaviors is closely followed. They know how we get to a site and where we go after we've visited. They analyze what we click on and how we relate to it. They know what content leads us to advertising (and what kind of content doesn't turn us from visitors to buyers). Did we take our mouse and scroll over some of the content? How long did we interact with an ad? Did we drag some of its content? How long did we view its videos or animation? Did we pause or stop it?

All this and much more concerning our online behavior is collected, stored, and utilized. Long-standing ad industry "metrics" that are used to determine the effectiveness of advertising are now applied to our digital lives. Our responses to online ads are routinely reviewed to determine whether we are more aware of the product, known as *brand lift*; have our responses helped *raise purchase intention* or improved *image perception*? Perhaps the interactive ad's *emotive brand attributes* have resulted in driving us to feel more positively about that prescription drug, fast-food product, or TV show?

The Whole World Is Watching You

Although highly competitive, the ad industry has a well-organized and coordinated effort to advance its business and political interests. A network of not-for-profit groups, both in the United States and abroad, is helping ensure that evolving digital technology facilitates the goals of advertising. One key group is the Advertising Research Foundation, ARF, established in 1936. The ARF's members come from major advertisers and media companies, ad agencies, research organizations, and universities. One of its roles is to make sure that the industry benefits from the latest academic and professional insights. A dozen ARF research "councils" regularly meet to focus on such topics as youth, multicultural, and online media marketing. Every year the group organizes a major "Convention and Trade Show" that displays the latest research findings. For example, at its fiftieth such show in 2004, the ARF panels included "A Collaborative Journey to Deep Consumer Understanding—Driving Kitchen to Kitchen Connections" featuring a representative from Campbell Soup, and "Proof That Online Advertising Really Moves Product" with a "category development officer" from Yahoo! A workshop on "Insight Mining" gave participants "hands-on experience with psychological techniques that bring fun, creativity and understanding, as you learn to unleash the buying power of your target's unconscious."[17]

The ARF's "Online Media Council" works to develop an industry-wide approach to expanding the role and impact of interactive marketing. It closely tracks the latest research involving new media and the brain, for example, and is playing a leadership role in advancing the ad industry's use of brain research. The ARF's "Emotion Team" is now exploring "the neuro-psychological underpinnings of the subconscious response to advertising."[18] One of the academics working with the ARF is Harvard University's Gerald Zaltman and his "Mind of the Market Laboratory." Zaltman, now an emeritus professor, is helping explain to advertisers "how the brain processes the icons, metaphors and stories that are the essence of most successful advertising campaigns."[19] All of this research will be applied to the techniques of online advertising.[20]

There is also a tremendous global effort to advance the impact of digital marketing. The international ad research network known as ESOMAR (the World Association of Research Professionals) is helping develop what it calls the "Gold Standard" for measuring the impact of interactive advertising. It gives awards to the best paper that advances digital marketing research and holds an international conference that focuses on the latest online-related research. (Another one of ESOMAR's projects is the "Global Legislative Initiative," designed to ensure that "the freedom to perform market and opinion research" is unhindered by any law or regulation.)[21]

The U.S.-based Interactive Advertising Bureau (IAB), founded in 1996, is another leading group helping to advance online marketing. Its many committees and task forces strive to expand the impact of new media advertising, including with video games, broadband, and Spanish-language content. For example, the IAB's "Search Engine Committee" works to enhance the role that advertising and marketing play with that medium. Members include AOL, *Business Week*, Comcast, Google, MSN, Disney, and Yahoo![22]

The IAB helps influence technology design to enhance the impact of advertising. For example, in its guidelines to designers of online content with advertising, it urges that player buttons be enabled (such as stop/start) "*with the exception of Fast Forward*" (its emphasis). The group helps build industry consensus about interactive ads, including techniques for measuring their impact on consumers. The IAB has also created standard definitions for the size (dimensions) of such online ads as the "square pop-up," "microbar," "wide skyscraper," and "floating unit."[23]

Two national lobbying groups, the American Association of Advertising Agencies (AAAA) and the Association of National Advertisers (ANA), play a key research role as well. The ANA represents "more than 300 companies with 8,000 brands that collectively spend over $100 billion annually in marketing communication advertising." Its "New Media Committee"—whose more than eighty members include Philip Morris, Coca-Cola, Burger King, and Merck—regularly meets with Silicon Valley and other high-tech experts, including academics. The group helps ensure that the latest technology breakthrough is thoroughly vetted for its branding and marketing potential.

The ANA and the AAAA have created a single system, called Advertising Digital Identification (Ad-ID), that will assign a twelve-digit "unique identifying code" to *every* ad from every medium. Ad-ID is more than the equivalent of the bar codes we see on products. It is also part of the industry's effort to learn about our behavior. That's one reason why the creation of Ad-ID in 2003 was heralded by industry insiders just as epochal as "when Ted Turner went live on satellite with CNN; when Wozniak and Jobs first introduced the Apple; when Marc Andreessen created the browser. . . . Ad-ID will provide advertisers with micro-intelligence for tracking consumer exposure to advertising messages."[24] Ad "guru" Peter Sealy told one new marketing publication that Ad-ID "will result in the ability to track advertising consumption down to the household and individual level. . . . Marketers will know who is viewing, when they are viewing and where they received the message from."[25]

Marketers have also significantly expanded their own research efforts to closely study the public's relationship with the Internet. Panels composed of millions of consumers have voluntarily permitted marketers to track all their "surfing and buying behavior." ComScore, a major marketing research firm, tells potential clients that it has a two-million-member panel that can "capture all Internet activity . . . including where they visit, what they buy, how they react to ads and other online stimuli, and more." ComScore is able to download information about "every site visited, page viewed, ad seen, promotion used, product or service bought, and price paid." Nielsen/Net Ratings, part of the network of companies that compiles TV ratings, also has panels that measure Internet use, both at home and in the workplace. Nielsen is now deploying an "Anytime, Anywhere Media Measurement" service that will track our use of audio and video "on the Internet, outside the home, and via mobile media." The entire range of new media behavior from wireless and AOL to instant messaging and games is tracked.[26]

Measure for Measure

Exactly the right ad at exactly the right moment.
          —*CEO of When U, quoted in* Release 1.0

In late July 2004, just as the Democratic National Convention was entering its second day and interest online in political issues was high, users had major problems accessing some of the Internet's "most highly trafficked Web sites." Hackers had launched an attack—known as a "Denial of Service"—where a "flood of bogus Web page requests" overwhelms servers and causes a serious disruption. On that day, the hackers' target was the company known as DoubleClick. Some of the Internet's "40 most-visited Web sites," according to the *Washington Post*, were severely disabled as a result.

DoubleClick is little known outside of online ad circles. But it's a major pipeline for a great deal of online advertising. Many online users may not be aware that the advertising they view on Web sites is actually sent to our computers by an online ad company. Content providers send you the news, entertainment, and other information, leaving the advertising that appears on their Web pages to an online ad specialist like DoubleClick. All of DoubleClick's nine hundred customers suffered Web site problems that day, including the *Washington Post*, CNN, the *New York Times*, NASDAQ, and the *Wall Street Journal*.[27]

DoubleClick would tell you that its principal job is to send your computer an online ad, known as "ad serving." But it is really just one of the many online ad companies that track you on the Internet. DoubleClick and many other "adware" companies have developed a bundle of online tools designed to make Web sites more effective in promoting branding and sales. Web analytics tracks your navigation through an individual Web site and on the Web itself. It analyzes how you are relating to the content, and whether it is working effectively to connect you to the ad. A system like Double-Click's has automated the advertising campaign process. The system tracks what ads you've seen and how you've interacted with them. It determines whether to send you a particular ad at a later date, when it thinks you would be more receptive to a pitch or theme. Ad sizes and shapes can change, as the system recognizes your online behaviors and interests. It may think you are a good candidate for an "upsell" and try to get you to spend more.

In addition to ad-serving companies, there are also many "ad networks." These ad networks can consist of many Web sites, from both large and small companies. They work together to target you, often sharing information about you with each other. That's one reason why you might see an ad for a similar product or service on many different sites. Often, the same company that serves the ad also operates an advertising network. DoubleClick operates two such ad networks.[28]

Founded in 1996, DoubleClick is credited with recognizing that you could share information collected by cookies across many different Web sites. Cookies, as mentioned earlier, are tiny files placed on your computer. They help Web sites recognize you online, so you don't have to retype (or recall) such things as your user name and password. But they also contain extensive profiling information about you, thereby informing both the Web site and the online ad network about your interests, shopping habits, and behaviors.

Pressure from public-interest groups such as the Electronic Privacy Information Center has forced Internet companies to better explain on their "privacy" page how they collect their data. Unfortunately, too often the privacy page is ignored.

Each cookie given to you by DoubleClick has a "unique" set of numbers. It's called a "marketing score" that reflects "your recent Web surfing" on sites that DoubleClick works with. This score also has information about recent search terms you used, and whether you clicked on any of the ads sent to you. In an example that DoubleClick provides, say that "in the past 10 days, [you've] searched on women's fashion sites, floral sites, home/gift sites, and even more bridal sites," and have searched the words "weddings" and "bridal registry." You are given a unique cookie tied to a marketing score that would look something like this:

COOKIE	Sports	Autos	Wedding	Fashion	Business	Technology
123	0	0	19	10	0	0

"The fact that this computer's browser has been searching these categories may indicate that this Internet user is planning a wedding. Many companies wish to advertise to people during the specific time that they are planning a wedding. This means that this Internet user may see more ads for gifts, vacations, and home furnishings than other Internet users during the same time period or even when visiting the same Web sites."[29]

DoubleClick places marketing scores on our computer for dozens of areas. While acknowledging that the list changes "frequently," here's what it tracked in 2005:

Art/History; Automobiles; College & Education; Comedy/ Comics; Computer Games; Consumer Electronics; Diversions (crosswords, puzzles, etc.); Domains; Entertainment; Family; Fashion/Beauty; Finance/Mortgage/Loans/Funds; Food/Wine; General Business; Home & Garden; ISP/Portal Users; IT Professionals; Investment; Careers; Law; Literature; Luxury Goods; Movies; Music; News/Current Affairs; Online Auctions; Online Radio; Pets; Photography; Real Estate; Science; Small Business; Sports; Sweepstakes; Technology; Telecommunications; Television; Travel; Weather; Web Technology; Weddings.[30]

Another form of data collection used by DoubleClick and many others is called either a "Web beacon," "Clear GIF," "Web bug," or "spotlight tag." Your browser is tagged by the ad you clicked on by a tiny and generally invisible file. This Web bug, like the character E.T., "phones home" by sending back information about your online behavior, including clicks.

Every computer, as it goes online, generally has a special number called an Internet Protocol (IP) address. An IP address is like a combined area code and telephone number for our computer when we go online. It not only permits content to arrive to our computer, it is also part of the tracking process used by marketers to learn more about us. Our IP address is a key data point for marketers to collect many facets of information, helping them engage in what DoubleClick and others call "Advanced Geo-Targeting." This provides them with "precise demography" about online users, including "income levels, ethnicity, and personal interest." They know our zip code, and through a database containing "400,000 mapped networks," can identify where we live and thus our marketing cluster. Geo-targeting is used by most of the major Web sites, including Google, AOL, Microsoft, and Disney.[31]

DoubleClick feeds all this information to its ad-serving system, known as Dynamic Advertising Reporting and Targeting. More than sixty billion ads a month are sent to us via this system. (The company says it has "the capacity to serve more than 100,000 ads per second.") Personally targeted ads can be sent to you in milliseconds.[32]

Online "social networking" communities such as Myspace.com (now owned by Murdoch's News Corp.) and Friendster.com rely on DoubleClick's ad technology. So do MTV and AOL. When AOL and DoubleClick signed a "milestone" agreement in 2005, both companies promised that there would be "enhanced" technologies for delivering "more complex ad campaigns and promotions."[33]

Watch Your Behavior!

It's much more intuitive for a marketer to buy a person than to buy a keyword.

—*Dave Morgan, CEO of Tacoda Systems*

Today, the online industry has added tools to its arsenal of data collection and profiling that extend way beyond cookies. A new form of Web advertising called behavioral marketing has emerged. This technique can do "laser targeting," sending an ad that reflects actual online behavior. Sites such as the *New York Times,* the *Wall Street Journal,* and *Business Week* are using these techniques to target their online readers. Much of this information comes from the real-time collection of information from the use of some search engines and thousands of Web sites that target users this way.[34]

There are several methods used by behavioral marketers to gather this information. In some cases, in exchange for free software users may knowingly or unwittingly download behavioral adware. This is sort of an electronic spy in your computer that tracks all your online activity. All this information is placed into a profiling database that also contains such information as your zip code. So they know when someone is looking at travel or auto sites, for instance. Soon a pop-up or other ad appears for airfares or a new car, following you on many sites that are members of the behavioral network. The ads may change as the adware figures out whether you are just researching or actually in the market to buy.[35]

Online ad networks are big business. Time Warner's AOL acquired one of the biggest, Advertising.com, in 2004 for $435 million in cash. The Web sites that make up its ad network attracted nearly 70 percent of all U.S. users. Part of the attraction for AOL was Advertising.com's "ad decision" technology called AdLearn. Composed of "complex mathematical algorithms," AdLearn helps AOL and other Web sites better understand our online behavior to more effectively target us.[36] Companies like Time Warner's Advertising .com use behavioral targeting by identifying "highly concentrated behaviors" through the thousands of Web sites working with them. Its "Advanced Targeting" tracks your real-time Web site activity, analyzes it, and combines it with a host of other data such as where you live and your marketing characteristics (demography) to offer advertisers pinpoint accuracy, including "as you travel on other Web sites." Ad performance is also "continually" analyzed. Like other online marketers, including DoubleClick, Advertising.com boasts of its ability to follow a user online and eventually get them to engage in some action, such as filling out an online registration form.[37]

The NYTimes.com site also provides advertisers with the ability to target via online behavior, including what it calls a "Surround Session." According to *Times* online executive Martin Nisenholtz, "The advertiser owns the user during his entire experience with the *Times* online site."[38] The *Times* also has access to "an extensive database of reader-supplied information" that can be used by its advertisers for targeting, including age, gender, and household income.[39]

Rich Media, Poor Consumer

If you can get someone to watch your ad, you can get them to feel.
—Tom Jenen, director of marketing at Eyeblaster

Rich media has been designed to make online marketing even more effective. These multimedia ads rely in particular on broadband's ability to deliver interactive video, animation, interactive graphics, and sound. "With rich media," explains DoubleClick in one of its many industry reports, "online ads approach television in dynamic terms: they can float above content, animate, integrate video, a jingle and even go beyond television to include interactive elements like pull-down menus for more information."[40] Rich media ads can also be created with games and other devices so you are persuaded to fill out a user profile or actually make an instant purchase.

Advances in technology will only make such multimedia advertising more compelling. The goal is to immerse you in the ad. So-called immersive advertising is designed to give consumers a virtual reality experience, surrounding them with powerful images and other content that encourages people to surrender their normal conscious awareness. Undoubtedly, research into brain behaviors, including stimulating a reaction from the unconscious part of our minds, will help shape rich media's evolution.[41]

Come Spy with Me

DoubleClick and practically every Web site will state on their privacy pages that they don't collect "personally identifiable information" unless you give your consent. This information includes such things as your name, e-mail address, and phone number. Online marketers had hoped to be able to easily merge off-line and online information to better target us. But public concern over privacy online and the threat that legal safeguards would be passed forced Web marketers to beat a retreat. Now they all claim that they don't really collect information that reveals who you are.

But in reality, they are compiling a great deal of data about you, combining information obtained both online and through other sources such as databases. They know about your interests, and can track your Web visits and online behavior. All this is placed in an invisible profile, so you can be manipulated by online ads later.

"Goog," as the stock symbol is called, is well-known for its fast and efficient online search results. But at the heart of the search venture is advertising. Yahoo!, Google, MSN, and other search engines are all developing sophisticated ways of better targeting us. These companies sell keyword search terms to marketers, who may be charged on a pay-per-click basis. For example, with Google's AdWords program, the advertiser only pays when their ad, which appears at the top or to the right of the search results, is actually clicked through. For Yahoo!, which has an aggressive approach to search advertising, advertisers who pay the most show up at the top of your results.

Google's initial public offering of its stock generated much interest, especially because it offered potential buyers a little-used approach to acquiring shares, in a "Dutch" auction. But while the company proclaimed in its initial public offering that it was "a global technology leader focused on improving the ways people connect with information," Google was ultimately devoted to making targeted advertising more effective and ubiquitous. "We generate revenue by delivering relevant, cost-effective online advertising," it told potential investors. Among the "risk" warnings to potential investors was the concern that "new technologies could block our ads, which would harm our business."[42]

Google and others plan an expansion of their online advertising capabilities. They want to move beyond what is known as contextual advertising, where your search term triggers a related ad. In late

2005, Google filed for a patent that will allow it to develop profiles of individuals. The profile "describes interests of the user, and can be derived from a variety of sources, including prior search queries, prior search results, expressed interests, demographic, geographic, psychographic, and activity information."[43] Your past search questions and results, including Web sites you may have gone to as a result, will be part of the data in the profile as well. Advertisers will have to pay significantly more to Google if they are to benefit from all its new data-mining user insights. Google's growing power to deliver sophisticated pinpoint advertising was one reason why Time Warner's AOL wanted to become its partner. Google acquired a $1 billion, 5 percent stake in AOL in late 2005. Now the two online giants will be working together to enhance each other's advertising goals. It is expected that AOL content and services will become more prominent on Google's search engine.[44]

To help make Yahoo! the "Largest Global Player . . . [in] Internet Advertising," it acquired commercial search technology giant Overture in 2003 for $1.6 billion. Overture's "world-class monetization platform," said Yahoo! CEO Terry Semel, would help increase "branding, paid placement, graphical ads," and other forms of advertising.[45]

Not to be outdone by its rivals, Microsoft's MSN network also increased its ability to target online, including behaviorally. Now MSN allows advertisers to gain access to the information that its four hundred million users have provided (through such products as Passport, Hotmail, or Messenger). This includes so-called demographic information such as their location (work or home), age, and gender. MSN told marketers that it could also "overlay additional data rented from database marketing companies, such as wealth index and psychographic information, to target more specifically."[46]

Guys and Dollars

Director Steven Spielberg's 2002 film *Minority Report* depicts a futuristic world of interactive advertising. Robots and other technologies, including animated characters who run around on a cereal box, pitch and sell to customers. Spielberg turned to MIT futurists to gain insights into how our world will look in 2054.[47] But much of what was predicted for tomorrow is already here today. Take, for example, the emergence of a "virtual host" (Vhost). As you access one advertising technology Web site, a brown-haired young person stares at you, says "Good Morning," and remarks that "there are only two more days to the weekend." They can speak English, Korean, Japanese, Hebrew, Portuguese, and other languages. They tell you that they are a Vhost, a "lifelike conversational character" that "intelligently interacts" to promote brands, e-commerce, and advertising. The Vhost informs you that Stanford University research shows that interactive online characters can improve "click-through and conversion rates," making marketing more effective for all kinds of products.[48]

Vhosts are an instance of "socially intelligent interfaces." A whole new generation of automated persuasion technologies, designed to influence our behavior, is emerging. Marketing robotics "create new potential to persuade at the right time and place," notes B.J. Fogg, who helps run Stanford University's Persuasive Technology Lab.[49] Fogg and his mentor, Stanford professor Byron Reeves, understand that these computerized agents can be perceived as trustworthy friends.

Reeves, whose research paper "The Benefits of Interactive Online Characters" is promoted on the Vhost Web site, boasts that "social intelligence in automated interactions is good business." These characters can help companies "gain control" over online users, he claims, because our brains believe a real social interaction is taking place. That's because even if we live in the early part of the twenty-first century, our minds, says Reeves, still act as if we are engaged in a real-life social encounter.[50]

Of course, the ad industry has used both real personalities and cartoon characters for decades, from Lucille Ball promoting tobacco products to Charlie the Tuna selling cans of fish. But the new line of empathic and emotional agents—programmed to work on one's subconscious predilection for social engagement and armed with a smooth-talking script—works on a more profound level. These adbots are designed to have winning personalities, encouraging us to have a close relationship with them. Companies have lined up to use Vhost and other animated sales agents. Among them are ESPN (Disney), McDonald's, the Discovery Channel, MTV, and the Black Entertainment Network.[51]

Clearly, the Internet is more than a marketing machine. It has revolutionized access to information, greatly enhanced free speech and communication, and given us tools for creative expression. New forms of ad-free independent media are flourishing. It appears that the hold by a few media giants has been broken.

But adware is rapidly evolving on Internet time. As we develop a more seamless environment between the physical world and computing, the nature of advertising will change. Computerized objects will sense our personal world, and surround us with marketing messages that resonate deep within our emotions and unconscious. Major corporations are backing research at universities to help accomplish this goal. Ever ready for a corporate handout, scholars at Stanford University, the MIT Media Lab, the University of Southern California, the University of California at Berkeley, and others are working to advance interactive marketing.[52]

To further hasten the development of interactive advertising, Microsoft announced a new state-of-the-art lab based in Beijing called adLab. Specialists in the fields of data mining, information retrieval, statistical analysis, artificial intelligence, auction theory, and other technologies have been assigned to expand the ability of digital media to target consumers.[53] Yahoo! has also opened up similar labs in Spain and Chile.[54] The successful experience that marketers have had online, moreover, is now being used to develop the next generation of TV.

TV That Watches *You*

There is nothing wrong with your television set. Do not attempt to adjust the picture. We are controlling the transmission. If we wish to make it louder, we will bring up the volume. If we wish to make it

softer, we will tune it to a whisper. We can reduce the focus to a soft
blur, or sharpen it to crystal clarity. We will control the horizontal. We
will control the vertical . . . we will control all that you see and hear.
                    —Introduction to 1960s' Outer Limits *TV series*

The coming of digital TV is supposed to usher in a world that gives
us greater choice. But those with a stake in the TV business—and its
ability to deliver $60 billion a year in revenues from commercials—
have no intention of letting the public really be in control. Programming and marketing executives have been working together
to make TV advertising more influential and ubiquitous. A TV profile will be created so they can send you targeted and personalized
ads and pitches. They will collect and analyze your TV viewing behavior on a second-by-second basis. Ad executives are eager to
unleash a marketing vehicle that combines the power of video, with
its ability to tap our emotions, with interactive technology. It's
a medium destined to become, they suggest, the "Internet on
steroids."[55]

None of this is fantasy. Comcast, News Corp., and Time
Warner, among many others, have made significant investments so
they can bring us our brave new world of TV—now. Plans for the
future of digital TV are already being laid out. Yes, there will be
more channels and programs, but most will be heavily branded and
directly shaped by advertisers. So-called ad-skipping digital video
recorders (DVRs), such as TiVo, will actually "push" more advertising to us, often without our consent.

The first wave in the United States is known as "on-demand" and
"enhanced" TV. Comcast delivered one billion video on-demand
programs in 2005, demonstrating that its new technology readily
enables customers to download a program with a simple click.
Disney/ABC and other networks have been providing so-called
enhanced viewing, where a TV show and a Web site have been
synchronized to work together. Enhanced or two-screen programming, as it's sometimes called, is seen as a testing ground for
the networks before TV itself becomes a fully interactive medium.
The Academy of Television Arts and Sciences has already awarded

one of its new Emmys to an enhanced program for "Outstanding Achievement in Interactive Television." There will soon be more Weblike features available on our TV sets, including interactive games, video "chat," and on-screen voting.[56]

You Are the Target

Media executives have long dreamed of the day when TV could deliver personalized ads, also known as "addressable" advertising. But the success of Internet marketing catalyzed the industry into action. Starting in the late 1990s, a host of companies developed interactive advertising systems for TV based on the one-to-one on-line model.[57]

Today, cable TV "advertising management systems" can digitally "splice" in personalized pitches to viewers. A commercial you see on your favorite show may not be the one seen by your neighbor next door or others living in your town—who the sponsors believe may not have enough money to actually buy the product. Fairly soon, we will be urged to click on interactive objects flashing on our screen, which transport us into a crazy quilt of commercial formats. The already-battered wall separating programming content and advertising will be further damaged, if not obliterated. We are heading far beyond product placement, where advertisers pay to have shows feature items in the script, or even plot placement, where an entire series is built around its relationship with a sponsor. Marketers and programmers have entered into an even stronger bond to marry more seamlessly the relationship of editorial content and advertising. They hope, of course, to unleash digital TV's power to further direct our behavior, sending us on a shopping spree for their foods, video games, prescription drugs, and politicians.

Three adults watch the TV screen, transfixed, with the lone male firmly holding the remote control. In another room, two young children are watching their own digital programming. But this is not just some family and friends gathering by the electronic hearth for leisure viewing. Their behavior is being closely observed on video, streamed back to advertisers and programmers miles away.

We are in iBurbia, a West London research facility, whose studios are filled with TVs, computers, and the latest home entertainment technology. Interactive TV advertising has already taken hold in the United Kingdom, with many U.S.-based companies embracing it, including Disney, Viacom, and News Corp. They seek to exploit, as data-mining firm Claritas calls it, interactive TV's ability to track "the viewing habits of every single household . . . every channel, every programme, every switch of the channel, of all viewers."[58]

In the United States, there are coordinated industry initiatives to advance digital TV advertising, including in the promotion of new technologies and interactive commercial formats. Many of these groups are the same ones working to expand Internet marketing, including the ARF, the AAAA, and the ANA. But there are also many other research and marketing organizations focused on perfecting digital TV advertising, such as the new Interactive Television Alliance. Already, many have joined together to ensure that digital TV embraces the Ad-ID.[59]

The almost ninety million subscribers in the United States to either cable or satellite TV generally pay little attention to the set-top box. That's the device that delivers channels to your set, and for those with digital boxes, enables the purchase of pay-per-view and on-demand programming. But this box is also designed to serve as a spy in our homes, recording viewing behavior.

Digital set-top boxes are now being given added intelligence, called middleware (a software-based operating system). As TV offers greater interactive features, viewers will rely on middleware to run such things as built-in DVRs and update TV schedules (via electronic program guides). But middleware is also part of the advertising management system that will be tracking viewers and sending the information back to media companies. Powerful monitoring tools are now being placed inside the set-top box. They will help create what the industry calls our "digital silhouette" or TV "thumbprint," giving companies "improved insight into [our] viewership habits." They know that the middleware and set-top connection can "record every click of the remote control by every digital subscriber."[60]

"Don't Touch That DAL!"

You watch an ad, click, and then are transported into a "long-form" commercial. Thirty-second spots are about to become a portal—a digital gateway—to a larger commercialized video universe. That is what's being planned by various media industry groups for the digital TV era. Innovations in Digital Advertising (known as ID!A) was launched in 2002 to help pave the way for supercharged interactive commercials. ID!A is a another *Who's Who* of the industry, including Walt Disney, Grey Advertising, Time Warner, Viacom, and the ARF.

ID!A wants to make sure that the basic digital TV ad encourages us to interact. Programs are to be embedded with what they call "hotspots," "triggers," "bugs," and "tickers," urging us to click our remotes. Some of these will serve as "attract icons," "cycling through colors . . . or rotating in some way in order to grab the viewers' attention." Once we click on, the program will pause while we are sent to a dedicated advertiser location (DAL). Virtual channels, DALs are part of the new electronic real estate that will be populated by advertisers and marketers. DALs store the advertising, which might be a long-form "telescoped" ad such as an eight-minute commercial. At this sponsor-run channel, viewers will be able to ask for a product trial, receive a discount coupon, or engage in a viewer poll. They will be able to bookmark ads and watch them later. One digital TV ad technique is known as a screen overlay, literally a commercial on top of another ad or the program itself. The overlay will encourage viewers to engage in some form of transaction. ID!A's other proposals suggest that the bottom one-fifth of our TV screens will become more like a marketplace, with all kinds of interactive gimmicks flickering for our attention.[61]

The media industry recognizes that to make interactive TV marketing a success, it must ensure it effectively measures our responses. Programmers know that they can demand higher prices from advertisers to deliver commercials targeted by zip codes, neighborhoods, and even individual subscribers. For their part, advertisers are also demanding more precise delivery of their ads, including documentation of whether and how the ads are viewed.[62]

These new ads for TV are part of a comprehensive tracking and measurement system. Digital TV "ad units" are to serve in consumer profile development, collecting both personally identifiable and other data. Ads will be sent that target us as closely as they can, based on our profile, similar to what is regularly practiced online. Like cookies, data about our viewing behavior, including where we live (zip code plus two or four), our age, ethnicity, household size, income, and other lifestyle information, will be gathered and stored. Advertisers also intend to know how we dealt with the ad, including with what they call "trick play." Did we rewind it or pause it? Did we watch it live or recorded? To ensure that the first and last frame of the ad was actually delivered to our set-top box, the Ad-ID is to serve as a "watermark" or "timestamp."[63]

This BUD Ad Really Is for You (Fill in Your Name Here)

The delivery of commercials based on the collected data of individuals, noted *Broadcasting and Cable* magazine, is a "tectonic" shift in the TV business.[64] Relying on U.S. census data, outside databases, and the set-top box information, the media industry will have a powerful picture of our TV-related behavior. Companies making TV tracking technologies predict "unprecedented accuracy" in understanding us for targeted advertising. They will know what we are watching, and whether we've ignored the ad or bookmarked it. They will even know when we are actually viewing something we recorded on a DVR.

The TV industry claims that personalized advertising will benefit the public. The ads will be relevant, interesting, and informative, it suggests. Why would someone want to have to sit through an ad for a compact car, when advertisers know you need a larger vehicle to hold all your kids, or that you can't really afford the model they are pitching?

The industry also says that it respects privacy, and besides, all the information it plans to collect may not be personally identifiable. But the industry is being duplicitous and self-serving. While it is simultaneously claiming that all this information about viewers is anonymous—meaning that your actual name isn't linked to the data collected about you—it is telling advertisers and investors that it can deliver a precisely targeted commercial to an individual in a home.

Yet even if the industry didn't actually add your name to its TV viewing profile, it will include vast amounts of information about you, including your neighborhood, "ethnic makeup," and "if your household is upscale or downscale."[65]

The online marketing industry and now the TV industry have both been hiding behind the terms anonymous and not personally identifiable to prevent the passage of privacy legislation. But the public shouldn't be fooled into believing that because your profile may not contain your name that you can't be identified. First, since they know so many of your behaviors and characteristics, the computerized advertising system can pretty much determine what will work with you. Second, as Carnegie Mellon professor L. Sweeney has noted, "In general, few characteristics are needed to uniquely identify a person." Her research has shown that most of the U.S. population (87 percent) could be uniquely identified by knowing only their zip code, gender, and date of birth.[66]

No matter what they claim, the cable and satellite industries are striving to perfect their ability to target individuals. Comcast tells sponsors that its capacity to deliver pinpoint interactive marketing messages is "growing more sophisticated every day." Comcast's Spotlight service "provide[s] advertisers with the ability to customize messaging to target audiences." The cable giant relies on what it calls two "sophisticated segmentation products": Adtag™ and Adcopy™. These technologies enable marketers to create and simultaneously deliver targeted commercials in a single community, aimed at various subgroups. For example, in Los Angeles, Comcast and other cable companies can send multiple versions of a commercial at the same time to various neighborhoods. So people in

Beverly Hills or some other wealthy community will see the sport utility ad, while those less economically favored are pitched the subcompact car. Not surprisingly, companies such as General Motors have been major users of Adtag and Adcopy.

A huge amount of data about us is compiled to make Spotlight work, including "thousands of data points based on . . . key . . . profiling attributes such as product usage patterns [and] auto registrations." On its Web page promoting Spotlight, Comcast assures marketers that the latest in research is used to "more accurately target audiences for advertisers," enabling them to collect the following data:

- Target audience identification/confirmation
- Purchase behaviors of your target
- Lifestyle activities of your target
- Viewing habits of your target by geographic region
- Advertising activity of your competitors

More than forty popular TV networks now help Comcast deliver this "exciting evolution of ad-supported television," including CNN, Comedy Central, ESPN, Lifetime, and MTV.[67]

But Comcast wants to go far beyond Spotlight. In 2004–5, it acquired two major interactive TV technology companies that help create personalized commercials: Liberate and MetaTV. It also made major investments in "the next generation in digital advertising" systems that enable it to send scores of different ads to different channels.[68]

Comcast is also working with one of the leading companies involved with the delivery of one-to-one TV ads: Visible World. That company's "Intellispot" creates "dynamic customized advertising messages targeted to zip code clusters or individual households." It promises advertisers that thousands of customized video pitches can be developed, relying on "marketing data" to make them "more relevant to consumers."

Once the personalized ads are made, they are delivered through "intelligent addressing," placed in an electronic envelope addressed to your set-top box. As with many other interactive ad services, Visible World says that commercials can be easily updated "on the fly," quickly changed based on the latest marketing information or a new approach to targeting you. So a commercial you'd seen a few days ago might suddenly appear saying that the bike you clicked on is now at your local retail store—but only a few are left, so hurry. In 2005, Fox TV also began using Visible World.[69]

> *Make viewers an active part of your ad . . . turning their remote into your response mechanism.*
>
> —*Open TV*

John Malone, once the nation's most powerful cable operator, now rivals Comcast and Murdoch for title of king of interactive TV advertising. Malone owns OpenTV, whose "Spot-on" technology "can be used to get your target market to say 'yes' to free offers, opt-in to receive targeted follow-up information, complete a survey or poll giving you rich information about their preferences, make instant purchases—whatever objectives you choose and limited only by your imagination." The key to its effectiveness, says OpenTV, is its ability to incorporate household data in its targeted ads, through its relationship with "Experian, the world's largest information provider."[70]

OpenTV can segment viewers by such things as ethnicity, age, household income, household size, presence of children, and location. And, the company notes, in describing its audience-measurement capabilities, our "TV click stream data" is automatically collected and processed second by second. Timestamps reveal when we use an electronic program guide, search for the weather, or play a game. All this is part of its OpenTV's "Interactive Advertising Platform."[71]

Rupert Murdoch has invested heavily in interactive advertising, which is featured on his Sky satellite TV service in the United Kingdom. He is now bringing both his technology and marketing strategy to the United States, through his set-top box software company, NDS. The NDS Audience Measurement System™

"records subscriber viewing habits so operators know who is watching their content, and how," says the company, "including TV viewing, electronic program guide usage, interactive applications and time-shifted viewing."[72] The largest satellite service in the United States, DIRECTV, which Murdoch owns, is just beginning to use the NDS system.

No Ad Hop, Skip, or Jumping Allowed

One of the myths perpetuated by the media industry is that new technologies empower consumers to bypass advertising. DVRs such as TiVo are said to be commercial-busting devices. But advertisers and programmers have been working to prevent DVRs from effectively playing that role. DVRs have now become ad friendly, with industry leaders advising marketers that the recorders can help them learn when "viewers watch a personally selected program, how long they watch, whether they keep it and watch it again, even when and where they pause, fast-forward and rewind it."[73]

There are two strategies to ensure DVRs don't dampen advertisers' clout and the TV industry's big profits. First, independent DVR companies have been tamed by the media industry through tactics ranging from co-ownership to legal intimidation. Second, a new generation of DVRs is coming directly from the cable and satellite industry as part of the set-top box. These digital recorders will be programmed to push TV shows and advertising to viewers.

TiVo is the best-known DVR service, enabling its 3.6 million customers to conveniently record programming. But TiVo's list of "equity investors" looks like something out of the pages of *TV Guide*: Comcast, Time Warner, Viacom/CBS, General Electric/ NBC, Fox/DIRECTV, and Disney/ABC, among others. TiVo's official advertising partners also include many of the TV networks operated by its investors. So it shouldn't come as a surprise that in its annual Securities and Exchange Commission report, the company describes itself as "a platform for advertisers" and "audience measurement research."

In 2003, TiVo named an NBC executive as president, who quickly reassured marketers that his service was an "advertiser's dream." "We have the exact combination advertisers want," Marty Yudkovitz told *TV Week*. "We can measure how long [or if] a viewer watches a certain program or commercial. . . . We are measuring it on a super-granular basis."[74] Murdoch's NDS has also assured advertisers that "our technology tags the commercial. It can be set so that the commercial cannot be skipped."[75]

DVR manufacturers know that they had better not mess with the forces of advertising and marketing, or they may end up like bankrupt Sonic Blue. That company manufactured the Replay DVR and promoted the device's ability to quickly zap ads. Replay's threat to advertising was one reason that many of the biggest media companies filed a lawsuit in October 2001. Disney, NBC, Viacom, Time Warner, and Fox, among others, seethed at Replay's "Auto-Skip" feature that encouraged viewers "to watch recorded programs totally commercial-free."

In their suit, the media companies complained that the "removal of commercial messages by itself robs the advertisers . . . depresses the value of such advertising time, and undermines the economic models by which television programming is provided." The media companies were also alarmed that Replay was suggesting that its customers could send their recordings over the Internet.[76] Soon Sonic Blue was spending a million dollars a month in legal fees and filed for bankruptcy. It was forced to sell off its Replay device to another company. While Replay is still sold as a DVR, it no longer promotes its ad-skipping potential.[77]

Not-So-Hidden Persuasion

Our secrets, great or small, can now without our knowledge hurtle around the globe at the speed of light, preserved indefinitely for future recall in the electronic limbo of computer memories.

—Associate Justice Joyce Kennard,
Shulman v. Group W Productions, *1998*

Nearly fifty years ago, Vance Packard warned about the power of advertising to manipulate us, stealthily shaping our attitudes and behaviors. The goals of marketers are much the same as they were when Packard published his critique. But we are now surrounded by a much more sophisticated advertising system. All the tools of our contemporary media culture are in service to the idea of life-long branding. We are to be encouraged to admire a product and the consumer lifestyle from childhood to old age.

It is clear that in our current digital media era, there's a no-holds-barred philosophy when it comes to the practices of the advertising industry. The system of interactive TV and online marketing—where our personal information is routinely fed to cable, telephone, satellite, online, and advertising companies—requires immediate state and national safeguards. More than privacy is at stake. This new media marketing system has been created without the public's consent. No doubt, some may prefer receiving more personalized advertising, but many will not. It will take courageous state attorney generals, as well as legislators to oppose these fast-moving media industry developments. I address what can be specifically done to protect us from such practices at the end of this book. But we also need to debate what kind of interactive TV system we require as a democracy, and whether we need to tear down the system now being built for us.

8

Cable Costra Nostra:
Why You Should Never Believe What the
Media Industry Promises

Although an older media, cable controls a key gateway to both video and Internet communications as one of two wires that serve almost all Americans who have online access (the other is run by local phone companies). Today the cable industry is in the midst of an ad campaign, loudly proclaiming its efforts to bring us the benefits of high-speed, broadband Internet service. But the real purpose of the blitz is to help persuade policymakers to award the cable industry favorable policies. Yet more than thirty years ago, the same cable industry also promised the nation it was building an information superhighway. It was going to be, cable said at the time, an interactive medium overflowing with an endless array of programming and public services. Yet that highway was never built. If it had been, why would the cable lobby—which has contributed more than $20 million to federal candidates since 2000—now be asking for new federal favors to build another one?[1]

The broken promise of a data highway is just one example of a theme in modern U.S. media history. In exchange for favorable corporate policies, companies claimed there would be countless benefits. In the 1930s, radio station owners vowed a vibrant system of civic and educational programming. They repeated that pledge as broadcasters expanded into TV. In the 1960s and 1970s, the cable industry swore its wires would provide TV to help empower community voices. Phone, cable, and online companies alleged in the 1990s that they would quickly connect everyone to a low-cost data highway. None of these media industries ever intended to live up to these public commitments, which instead served as convenient political ploys to neutralize critics.

Once a media industry had achieved its political goals, including the elimination or weakening of any public-interest requirements, the promises were quickly forgotten. Now, once again, there are promises hurtling around congressional committee rooms, through FCC hallways, and in costly TV and newspaper ads. That's why as lawmakers prepare to create new legislation to govern digital communications, it is useful to revisit how the country was conned by cable. For much of today's rhetoric about how broadband will shower the public with untold riches once new laws are enacted can be found in what has been called the "cable fable." As those concerned with ensuring a democratic communications system prepare to fight for the public welfare in the broadband era, there is much to be learned from what happened with cable.

Cable's Xanadu

The Cable Center is the industry's showcase, paying homage to its astounding success. Located at the University of Denver, the center is a symbol of cable's prominence and power.[2] With annual revenues of almost $70 billion a year and climbing, cable's humble business roots are now a dim memory. Long the industry's political and financial base, Colorado is now where cable touts its legitimacy. Visitors to the center enter to face a video tower, a wall of ninety-eight TV sets continuously showing famous cable brands. One can easily spot Nickelodeon, HBO, C-Span, CNN, and Discovery. Interactive learning stations explain how cable has made a contribution to our culture. "Cable television has changed everything about the way we learn, listen, laugh, and communicate," the center reminds its supporters.[3]

A *Who's Who* of industry heavyweights contributed more than $60 million to fund the center's construction and initial operations.[4] And why shouldn't cable's leaders be generous—to an institution dedicated to promoting their own personal and collective glory? America's love affair with TV helped many of cable's "pioneers" find "rags-to-riches" success. A quick look at the 2005 *Forbes* magazine's list of the "Richest 400 Americans" illustrates the immense wealth that was derived from the cable business:

112. Amos Hostetter (Continental Cable, MediaOne)
125. Charles Dolan (Cablevision)
133. Ted Turner (Turner Networks, Time Warner)
153. John Malone (TCI/AT&T)
235. Frank Batten Sr. (Landmark Communications/Weather Channel)
258. Alan Gerry (Cablevision)

There are those among the *Forbes* 2005 list that have invested in cable to generate further wealth:

1. Bill Gates (Comcast)
3. Paul Allen (Charter)
12. Barbara Cox Anthony and Anne Cox Chambers (Cox Cable)
26. Donald and Samuel Newhouse (Advance/Newhouse Communications)
133/153. Members of the Hearst family (A&E, Lifetime, etc.), one at no. 133, others at no. 153

Many others on the list have achieved a great deal of success from their dealings with cable:

25. Sumner Redstone (Viacom, MTV, Nickelodeon, etc.)
32. Rupert Murdoch (Fox News, Fox Sports, FX)
78. Haim Saban (Fox Family Channel)
258. Barry Diller (QVC)[5]

Cable's success has come at a price to consumers, viewers, programmers, and citizens. The industry claimed that with the end of video gatekeepers, there would be an explosion of creativity in programming. Cable would give voice to those marginalized by the

U.S. media system, especially people of color and low-income Americans. These commitments and more were used as cable sought to help sell itself to the public. But even while it was making such commitments, cable was building a powerful political machine to undo them. Over the last thirty years, cable has used its clout to largely avoid having to fulfill any meaningful public-interest role. A medium that was to provide community communications is now primarily a national entertainment service run by a few monopolies. There is neither diversity nor competition in programming, especially from minorities and independent programmers. Rapacious business practices bring skyrocketing rates to consumers.

Today, cable is the leading provider of TV in the United States, serving seventy-three million subscribers (about 70 percent of all homes). It's also number one in broadband, with more than twenty-one million households relying on it for high-speed Internet access. Once an industry with hundreds of small companies, just two—Comcast and Time Warner—now control more than half of all cable TV customers.[6] Comcast alone basically has veto power over the creation of any new cable channel. Potential programmers who fail to secure the blessing of the Roberts family, which runs Comcast, are quickly out of business.[7]

Community Communications: Cable's Promise

Four decades ago, it was clear that the cable wire that brought broadcast TV into the home would also deliver many channels and services. Local governments were promised the benefits of a wired city. Experts and media activists at that time had high expectations. Cable's potential was seen as a force to address concerns about poverty, especially among inner-city communities of color. It would be a medium, said civil rights advocate Charles Tate, more "responsive to and reflective of the differences in culture, language, history, experience and race." Assessing cable's potential more than thirty years ago, Tate envisioned that "control, ownership and operation of cable systems by minorities could provide economic and political leverage. . . . Imagine television and radio systems where blacks could program for blacks; Chicanos for Chicanos; Indians for Indians and Puerto Ricans for Puerto Ricans—a system that can give the community a communications voice as well as the income and profit that the system receives for providing this service."[8]

From the late 1960s to the early 1980s, when cable companies actually competed with one another, each would outbid rivals in what were called the "franchising wars."[9] Each company promised to fulfill cable's potential, offering, for example, to build local TV studios and provide a score of channels along with funding for public access TV. New interactive technologies would enable viewers to easily access information.[10] Schools would be wired to computer databases. Parents were assured that there would be an ad-free channel for children called Nickelodeon.[11]

The industry understood that promoting the democratic potential of cable was an effective marketing strategy. What better way to sell a franchise to local officials—a contract that might extend up to twenty-five years and was already considered lucrative—than to speak to that vision? Thus cable leaders described in glowing terms how cable would help positively transform the country.[12] Today, cable leaders employ "blue skies" as shorthand for what, they claim, was unfairly demanded by local officials during the cable franchising rush. They dismiss as science fiction the reports and studies that focused on cable's potential. But cable's increased capacity was no fantasy.[13] Cable viewed itself as the perfect medium to deliver the emerging computer revolution. Even as cable companies negotiated contracts promising to deliver the electronic village, however, they were also plotting strategies designed to undo these deals.

As *Broadcasting* magazine revealed at the time, cable was engaged in cynical practices transparent to industry observers: "Cable operators also talk about 'bait and switch,' a game played by some cable companies that 'promise anything and then cry for relief.' Because once franchises are made, they're hard to take back, the temptation is there to promise extraordinary services at below ordinary rates in an attempt to secure the initial award. Companies feel that once the award is made, they later can apply for relief—and are likely to get

it because few cities or towns relish taking on the job of finding another franchisee."[14]

Echoing present-day debates about broadband communications,
cable advocates understood the need for policies that would democratize video-based communications. Cable was seen as a form of
utility, a basic public resource like electricity, sewers, and highways.
The United States would enjoy the benefits of "the wired nation,"
as writer and advocate Ralph Lee Smith put it, only by ensuring
that cable could "exercise no judgment on TV programming or any
other service that goes over their cables." It would be essential to
prevent cable from becoming a video gatekeeper, since it would
use this to control programming. Cable would need to be regulated
as a "common carrier," requiring the medium to fairly serve all
programmers.[15]

A range of advocates supported this policy, including the American Civil Liberties Union. But in what would be an early example
of the cable lobby's tactics, it launched effective campaigns to kill
any utilitylike policies. Cable also began to build the political power
that would free it from ever having to deliver on its commitments.[16]

Rent a Citizen, Legislator, Local Leader, or Member of Congress

Cable leaders understood they needed to work together effectively
to influence policymakers and break any regulatory hold. Like
broadcasting, cable organized its political operations to mirror U.S.
politics. Cable would be able to influence each of the 435 congressional districts. There would be local lobbyists at the city or country level; state associations to handle the legislature, governor, and
utility commission; and a national trade group that represented cable's
interests in Washington, including Congress and the FCC. Cable
would offer politicians appearances on the local public affairs programs it controlled. C-Span itself was a product of cable's work to
influence policymakers. Cable hired former public-interest "activists"
and prominent ex-officials to influence the outcome of policy de-

bates or franchising decisions. Contributions were doled out to political campaigns, nonprofit groups, and lawmaker associations.[17]

Cable pressed lawmakers, relying on many political ploys still
used by cable and other media to this day. When media and
telecommunications industries seek favorable policies, they claim
new technologies are present that are challenging them in the marketplace. There's no need for regulation because there's competition. Such technologies now make monopoly status a relic of the
past. Using a well-worn refrain, cable told Congress in the early
1980s that such new media "enjoy a competitive advantage. They
don't pay franchise fees, they don't have to give away service, they
don't have to underwrite various local ventures." But such new
technologies were largely in the planning stage and not a serious
threat to cable. The cable lobby knew that, but since many lawmakers are out of touch with media developments, they fell for
such arguments.[18]

Cable's political ace in the hole was its alliance with Rep. Tim
Wirth (D-CO). As chair of the House Subcommittee on Telecom-
munications, Wirth became one of the industry's most strategic advocates. Cable lobbyists spotted him early on in his political career.
After all, Wirth's district was part of cable's domain, Colorado.[19]
Wirth originally rebuffed an alliance, but cable decided to make
him take notice by helping reelect him to his second House term.
As Thomas Wheeler told the Cable Center's oral history project,
"We were going to let Tim Wirth know that we knew how to organize his constituency. And if we knew how to organize his constituency, we knew how to organize anybody's constituency. . . .
Your toughest election is always your second election. . . . So we
decided that we were going to make ourselves very visible in that
race. It was touch and go. It was really touch and go. . . . And that
was part of the message that 'You're a player, we're a player. Let's go
do something together.'"[20]

The Cable Communications Policy Act of 1984 was a major
victory for the industry. Ironically, while the purpose of the law
was to "assure that cable communications provide and are encour-

aged to provide the widest possible diversity of information sources and services to the public," it did so by seeking to "minimize unnecessary regulation that would impose an undue economic burden on cable systems."[21] The act helped create the consolidated ownership and anticonsumer industry we have today. Cities had little authority over cable companies. There was no guaranteed support for public-interest programming. Without real oversight, cable could readily raise its rates for service.[22]

One of cable's great failures was to ensure ownership by persons of color. There is a lack of nonwhite ownership of media outlets and programming services today—a development that might have been corrected decades ago with action. In his call to action in 1972, Charles Tate asked, "Why should the community settle for the privilege of buying time or being allowed free time on a system that it supports through its monthly fees, when it has the right and opportunity to operate and control the system and serve as the administrator of the public access guarantee?" There were tremendous financial opportunities that would spur community development. There was "gold in the ghetto," said Tate.[23]

But the cable industry viewed minority programming as a means to an end. Initiatives to serve diverse audiences have been driven by strategies designed to secure the support of politically powerful allies and neutralize potential opposition. That's one reason why cable industry giant TCI backed the creation of BET, acquired in 2000 by Viacom/CBS. It was also a key factor in why Comcast supported the new African American channel in 2003 called TV One.[24] Many of the channels specifically serving Hispanics and African Americans are primarily controlled by the biggest media companies, including Time Warner, Fox, and NBC.[25] In the controlled world of cable TV, substantive minority programming is off-limits.[26] A proposal by BET that it launch an African American public affairs channel, according to press reports in 2000, was swiftly nixed by the industry.

Consolidation, Fraud, and Consumer Rip-off

While it was generally reported as a personal financial indiscretion, few made the connection that the bankruptcy of Adelphia Communications, one of the country's largest cable companies, revealed something more. The tremendous profits derived from cable have contributed to a corrupt cable industry culture. This illustrates how neither Congress nor the FCC can be counted on to protect the public from illicit industry practices. Nor should we expect politicians—unless there is real reform—to ensure Americans reap the social and economic benefits from the country's communications system.

On July 24, 2002, John Rigas, a man who had just been given many of the industry's highest awards, was arrested. Rigas had to do the "perp walk," handcuffed by federal law authorities in a well-photographed public display. Also arrested were his sons, Timothy and Michael, and two other top executives. The Rigases were accused of engaging in "one of the largest schemes of self-dealing and financial wrongdoing in American corporate history." "Billions of dollars" had been "looted," which eventually forced Adelphia's bankruptcy. For more than a decade, said the U.S. attorney, the Rigas family had been using Adelphia "as a private ATM."[27]

Barely a year before he was whisked away by federal authorities, Rigas had been inducted into the Cable Television Hall of Fame. In 2000, he had received the Vanguard, Operator of the Year, and Kaitz awards—the industry's highest honors. He was serving his third term on the board of the industry's trade association, NCTA, as well as on C-Span's board.[28] Rigas was described in 2000 "as 'the' person to whom the cable industry looks these days to where the cable industry will be going in the years ahead."[29]

Founded in 1952 by Rigas and his brother Gus with only $300, Adelphia was typical of how many of cable's pioneers ran companies. The family controlled the key company positions and had a voting majority of the stock. Such was true at Comcast and Cablevision. At Adelphia, Rigas was chair, president, and CEO; his son Timothy was the chief financial officer, the chief accounting officer, an executive vice president, and the treasurer as well as a board member; and his son Michael was an executive vice president and a director. Another son, James, served as an executive vice president and a director. There were plush jobs for Rigas's wife, daughter, and son-in-law.

After his arrest, Rigas was an embarrassment to the industry that had moments before praised his leadership and business acumen. But it's highly unlikely in the close-knit and financially connected world of cable that the major firms were unaware of the Rigas machinations.[30] The cable costra nostra code of the industry evidently kept everyone silent, though.

With many of the world's leading banks and financial institutions complicit, the "Rigas family directors" of Adelphia, as they are called in various lawsuits, created a financial flimflam. Huge amounts of money were borrowed by the family and deposited into a web of outside companies they controlled. But their loan collateral was Adelphia, not their own personal wealth. Unbeknownst to shareholders and financial regulators, these loans were adding billions of dollars in debt to Adelphia. The family also manipulated Adelphia's books, falsely inflating the revenues, and submitted "materially inaccurate" financial statements to the Securites and Exchange Commission, according to the complaint filed by the SEC.

For a while, the Rigas family's investments, purchasing $2 billion worth of additional shares, helped make Adelphia shares skyrocket. Investors believed that if they were committing their own cash, Adelphia was sound. But Adelphia was piling up debts that would total $18.6 billion. There was also an Adelphia-funded deluxe lifestyle for the Rigases.[31]

So sure were they of cable's steady influx of subscriber cash, many of the largest investment banks kept lending money, even though they knew about the Rigas scheme. The banks had a keen understanding of and a close relationship with cable and the entertainment business. Their loans would be safe, said a lawsuit from creditors, because Adelphia's cable customers could be counted on to cover the bill, regardless of default.[32] There was another reason the banks kept loaning the money: they "earned hundreds of millions of dollars in investment banking and other fees" from Adelphia.[33]

The whole charade came apart in March 2002. Soon the stock was worthless and the company was in bankruptcy. In 2005, Rigas was sentenced to fifteen years in prison—likely a life sentence for the ailing eighty-year-old.[34] Both he and son Timothy were convicted on eighteen felony counts for conspiracy and fraud.[35] Meanwhile, under new management, Adelphia sought additional financing. Cable's steady lucre attracted plenty of banks, including some that had lent the Rigas family money.[36]

The Rigas affair wasn't the only financially related problem roiling the industry. Time Warner, Cablevision, and Charter all had been under investigation. Comcast was accused of having a board controlled by its Roberts family founders. Cable's business dealings hurt the investors of AT&T when the phone giant got mixed up with the industry.[37]

Today, cable is a close-knit industry that ensures that none of the companies engage in serious competition with each other. Less than 2 percent of the nation's cable customers have a choice of more than one provider. A few companies have carved the United States into what the industry calls clusters and superclusters. These are vast tracts of cable systems comprising towns, counties, states, and regions.[38]

The public is still largely unaware of how cable operates and why oversight is necessary. For decades, the industry has reaped the benefits of a business model that was based on not paying any federal taxes. All the while, cash poured in each month from cable customers, enabling the cable companies to buy more cable systems, movie studios, and overseas media properties, and to create or acquire programming channels. The consolidation of the communications industry was paid for by this practice. Cable customers have been socked with rate increases three or more times the rate of inflation; they are now paying at least double what they paid just a decade earlier.[39]

Cable remains hostile to fulfilling what's left of its community obligations, including supporting public access TV. It has fought proposals that would enable communities to benefit from its high-speed Internet connections. Cable companies have lobbied to prevent the creation of publicly operated high-speed Internet networks, including wireless. Such competition, they fear, would undermine their own plans for the broadband market. Cable has become, in the words of journalist John Wicklein, an "electronic nightmare."[40] It also serves as a valuable history lesson as the country embarks on a policy debate about the future of digital media.

9

The Golden Wire

Over the next few years, much of our media and telecommunications will be coming from the country's largest cable and telephone companies. Comcast, AT&T, Verizon, and others are in hot pursuit of what they call the triple play: the profitable set of services—telephone, video programming, and high-speed Internet access—that all can flow over their cable or wire, or be sent wirelessly through the air. Executives dream of untold revenues as consumers depend on a single company to handle all their communications needs, both in the home and via mobile devices. The cable and telephone industries know they are unlikely to face any real competition, now that the government has ruled they can extend their monopoly businesses into broadband.

At the core of their vision for our media future is convergence, but not necessarily the kind that will better inform us and bring real programming diversity. The cable/telephone company vision is rooted in what has reliably worked in the past to generate profits. Ultimately, these industries wish to use their power over the digital wire to bring us a world where TV programming and Internet merge. It will be a place where advertising and interactive content will travel to us at fiber-optic speeds, offering what will undoubtedly consist of appealing offerings of commercial programming. One of the pioneers most responsible for helping the cable and telephone industries envision how they could benefit from a marriage of TV with the Internet was AOL.

Today, AOL is not the twenty-first-century media monopoly its founders dreamed it would be and its competitors feared it would become. Once it arrogantly viewed itself as ruler of the digital universe. But now, as we know, it no longer even shares equal billing with merger partner Time Warner. AOL is just one of a number of divisions operated within the vast Warner empire. Steadily losing subscribers who want high-speed connections instead of slower dial-up Internet access, AOL's future is in doubt in the broadband era.

The emergence of the Internet during the 1990s raised fundamental questions about the future of our media system that are still at the core of our concerns now. How was the nation going to ensure that all Americans, especially those earning low incomes, have meaningful access to the new medium? Could we really permit only the well-to-do in our society to have Internet access in their homes and at their community institutions while millions had little or no online service? Many also wanted to ensure a strong role for noncommercial public service and educational online communications through federal rules that would continue the tradition of reserving resources for nonprofit media. How could we also protect privacy, now clearly more at risk due to both technological innovation and the emergence of electronic commerce? Groups pressed the Clinton administration, the Congress, and the FCC to enact policies that would help strengthen the Internet's potential as a democratizing force.[1]

But for AOL's just-turned-forty CEO Steve Case, hailed by the press as a new media "*wunderkind*," such policy proposals for the Internet were unwarranted. The Internet, he and allies argued, was just too new and "self-correcting" to require the imposition of public safeguards. Besides, everything was now happening on "Internet time," Case claimed, making irrelevant any rules lawmakers might consider. In a speech at the National Press Club in Washington, DC, during fall 1998, Case even stated that the worldwide growth of the Internet had transcended the ability of nations to create policies. "This new global medium challenges us to create a new model for the industry to govern itself—one that's based on a new partnership among government, industry, and consumers," he said. Case warned policymakers not to imagine rules developed for other media, such as public-interest policies for TV, because they would threaten the economic and social benefits of the Internet. "The Internet is different from any previous medium," explained Case. It has "no center and no edges." Corporate "self-governance," he asserted, was the governing principle everyone should endorse.[2]

At the time Case made that speech, AOL and other major media and telecommunications companies profiting from the Internet were opposing policies that would protect privacy online and enable states to impose sales taxes on electronic commerce. Although Case denounced calls for Internet regulation, he was in fact seeking government help.[3] Even as he condemned public policies for the online medium, Case also argued for one, telling the press club audience that "government has a responsibility to preserve an open playing field—to preserve the openness, innovation and competition that are at the heart of the Internet, so that it can deliver fully on the promise it holds for improving the lives of individuals and benefiting society."[4]

What Case meant was that AOL as well as thousands of other Internet service providers were only in the online business because of public policies regulating the telephone. Local phone companies were required by FCC rules to seamlessly connect AOL's (or any other provider's) customers online. Such common carrier policies were part of a series of safeguards designed to keep the telephone network an open and nondiscriminatory public communications highway. The success of the Internet as a medium for both expression and commerce was due in part to this regulatory scheme. As Stanford professor Lawrence Lessig has explained, one of the core characteristics of the Internet's architecture was a principle known as "end to end." Communications and applications flowed freely from one end—the sender—to the other—the receiver. The Internet had been designed with the knowledge that the phone company was not permitted to censor traffic on its lines, such as by slowing down or blocking a phone call or e-mail. Since the telephone company, unlike the cable network, owned no content it could favor, so much the better. The end-to-end and nondiscrimination principles were also know as "open access."[5]

Case, however, understood that the online medium was rapidly evolving, ushering in new forms of multimedia content. The dial-up phone service AOL relied on was slow, and thus unsuitable for delivering video, animation, and colorful graphics. There was only one high-speed pathway capable of delivering to the majority of U.S. homes a video-friendly broadband connection. Without federally mandated access to cable broadband, Case knew, AOL wouldn't survive. For despite all of his talk about the Internet's potential to transform global society, Case's real focus was on what made AOL money: online advertising and subscriber-pleasing entertainment. He and AOL's other leaders, such as MTV co-founder Robert Pittman, shared a vision. They wanted to combine the instantaneous interactivity and one-to-one marketing capabilities of the Internet with the visually compelling and emotionally powerful branding of TV. An "AOLTV," they believed, would be the perfect selling medium.

Cable quickly rebuffed AOL as it sought access to its wires. Cable had a different vision for the future, one unencumbered by the very policies that had played a vital role in the development of the Internet itself. If openness was in the Internet's DNA, as experts such as Lessig reminded us, the opposite was true of cable's. The cable industry planned to extend its monopolistic TV distribution practices into the new broadband market. Operators would use their control of the cable pipeline to give their digital content first-class, high-speed delivery, while relegating competitors to the slow lane or worse. Already, by the late 1990s, cable-controlled broadband ventures such as @Home and Roadrunner dominated the high-speed Internet access business. These services placed stringent restrictions on the downloading of streaming media to ensure there wouldn't be any video programming competition to cable. Non-cable-affiliated Internet service providers could not offer their customers cable modem service at all.

A number of public-interest organizations also sought to require open access for cable independently of AOL's campaign.[6] They feared that without such safeguards, the online medium's potential was threatened. The policies underlying the dial-up Internet had helped develop a powerful medium of information and communications independent of the media giants. But there was no guarantee that the Internet would operate so freely once it was under the control of the cable industry. Advocates recognized that the phone companies would begin to press policymakers to eliminate open access requirements for their own broadband services, demanding a "level playing field" with cable.

AOL fought cable by relying on Beltway tactics. When one is in political trouble or has a policy goal in Washington, the first instinct is to reach out, hire extra lobbyists, and create public-interest front groups. Aside from employing a former network TV lobbyist as its chief political fixer, AOL also brought in a former public-interest media advocate. Suddenly, a new organization called No Gatekeepers was working to mobilize nonprofit allies for a cable broadband policy. Controlled by AOL, the group was operated out of the offices of still another ex-public-interest leader and now AOL consultant. But it was clear that despite all its open access rhetoric, AOL was more committed to its own survival than to ensuring that broadband continue the Internet's end-to-end structure. AOL, advocates understood, would do anything to gain access to cable's wire.[7]

Clinton FCC to Big Media: We Feel Your Pain

> *Government is too slow to keep up with the digital environment. The industry should remain unregulated. Our role in government is to provide a consistent environment for buyers and sellers.*
>
> —*Clinton administration Internet policy chief*
> *Ira Magaziner, 1998*

The Clinton administration itself supported a corporate "self-regulatory" policy regime for the Internet. It was convinced that the most effective way to ensure the development of the new medium was for industry to take the lead. The administration wanted to position itself as the champion of new media, in part because Clinton had befriended as well as raised money from a host of high-tech investors and marketers. Clinton officials responsible for what they called the National Information Infrastructure policy dismissed concerns posed by media advocates. Senior administration aides insisted that only executives from the major telecommunications companies or technologists could really comprehend how the Internet was making the concerns about any public policy safeguards obsolete.

The FCC chair during the late 1990s, as discussed earlier, was Kennard. Public-interest groups worked to pressure Kennard's FCC to pass a nondiscriminatory requirement for cable broadband. They had given to Kennard what they believed was a revealing blueprint for the cable industry's plans for the Internet.

Each year, cable's leaders gather for the NCTA convention. Booths and exhibits pitching the latest programming and money-making cable-related products fill a stadium-size hall. As the 1999 NCTA trade show, a white paper was discretely handed out to a few insiders from technology manufacturer Cisco Systems. "Controlling Your Network—A Must for Cable Operators" explained all the new opportunities the cable industry now had to make more money in the Internet business. New technologies permitted cable (and other) broadband network operators to have control over the flow of data going in and out of their subscribers' homes and businesses. Like a form of digital air-traffic control, cable operators would know what kind of content was being transmitted and could impose a raft of business policies designed to monetize the entire Internet experience.[8]

Cable companies, said Cisco, could use their new power over Internet traffic to "police and monitor" all content flowing over its broadband network. They could "prioritize" content they owned by giving it faster speeds, while discouraging subscribers from "accessing content that is not favored by the network, including video content from outside parties." Cable operators would be able to continually observe and collect data about everything a user did online. Armed with such information, cable could more effectively market additional services to individual customers. Cisco urged cable to begin "metering" online usage in order to impose different fees and charges, recognizing that this was similar to the way cable ran its TV business.[9]

But Kennard appeared fearful of alienating Congress. His administration didn't support any online-related policies. He took a position that would help him in his post-FCC career. Speaking to a receptive audience of cable operators, Kennard said that "if we learned anything about the Internet in government over the last 15 years it's that it thrived quite nicely without the intervention of the government."[10] Declaring that it was the marketplace that should determine Internet access, Kennard's FCC opposed any open access policy for broadband cable.

Rejected by Washington, AOL recognized that it would have to become part of the cable monopoly if it wanted to gain broadband access. It found a suitable partner in Time Warner, the second-largest cable company. Case and Warner CEO Gerald Levin also shared a belief that the future of the Internet required it to be connected to TV. But the price of admission to cable broadband was that AOL had to give up its efforts on open access. Accordingly, its campaign came to a screeching halt. At the January 2000 press conference announcing the merger deal, Levin said, "We're going to take the open access issue out of Washington and out of City Hall, and put it into the marketplace and into the commercial arrangements that should occur to provide the kind of access" for multiple Internet service providers.[11] In other words, there might be Internet connections for other providers only if they agreed to the onerous financial terms imposed by a new AOL Time Warner.

The price for AOL's access to broadband had been the largest media merger in U.S. history. The fate of broadband regulation was now more in doubt, given that its principal corporate proponent had joined the cable lobby. There were also new and dramatic concerns over media consolidation, given the potential clout an AOL Time Warner said it would have over digital communications. As Mark Cooper of the Consumer Federation of America observed, the Clinton administration's and chair Kennard's refusal to support open access had ultimately forced the $160 billion marriage of AOL and Time Warner.[12]

Let My Media Merger Go

The operating system for everyday life.
    —*Merrill Lynch statement on the AOL*
        and Time Warner merger, 2000

The AOL and Time Warner merger was not simply a matter of increased individual corporate power. It was also emblematic of how media mergers would now combine and operate both old media assets and new media properties. An AOL Time Warner would become the second-largest cable company, a TV programming powerhouse, the nation's largest provider of online services, and an important source of print and electronic journalism (*Time* and CNN, for example). AOL Time Warner was also staking a considerable part of its future on the development of interactive TV. Opposed to a nondiscrimination policy for broadband, the company would try to limit competition and programming diversity, both online and with interactive TV.

AOL and Time Warner's "Public Interest Statement" to the FCC about the benefits of the merger was a discussion of potential products and digital gadgets, reflecting the two companies' vision for the role of interactive communications. "This merger offers consumers so much: it will generate new, enticing next-generation products and services as a natural by-product of the melding of the two companies' cultures and expertise," the statement explained.[13] The two companies told the FCC that there were only "public-interest benefits" stemming from the merger. There wasn't, they said, any "anticompetitive impact."

Wall Street Lays Another Egg

The merger of American Online and Time Warner creates a new media powerhouse that can set the agenda for how the media industry will participate in the new digital age as the Internet evolves into a mass communications medium.

    —*Paine Webber, 2000*

A phalanx of Wall Street firms bolstered the merger and its business model, which included closed broadband access. The endorsement of media mergers by financial institutions is another time-honored lobbying technique used to limit critical questioning and opposition from federal officials. The future financial success of the to-be-merged companies is often the paramount policy concern of lawmakers and regulators. So when a form of monetary mumbo jumbo from Merrill Lynch predicts, as it did with AOL and Time Warner, that the merger will help "develop pockets of value that have heretofore been locked within vertically integrated value-chains," it's seen as an oracle of truth.[14]

Among the Wall Street investment houses supporting the merger and its financial prospects were Salomon Smith Barney and Morgan Stanley and Co. In a document submitted to the FCC, the two companies said that they had each reviewed the deal and had "held discussions . . . with certain senior officers" of both companies. They had also "examined information relating to some of the strategic implications and operational benefits anticipated from the merger," and conducted their "own independent evaluation of this information."[15] Not surprisingly, they said that what AOL and Time Warner promised as a financial boon for the company and the national economy was consistent with their own analysis. Of course, buying such valuable letters of merger approval "transit" does not come cheap. Salomon Smith Barney and Morgan Stanley would each receive $60 million from AOL and Time Warner to help them consummate the deal.[16]

Many other Wall Street heavyweights also rushed in to help. AOL Time Warner submitted these investment analyst reports as evidence that their merger was in the public interest. Given to the FCC were a trio of documents, including Merrill Lynch's "AOL Time Warner: You've Got Upside," Paine Webber's "AOL Time Warner: A Merger That Defines the New Digital Age," and "America Online/Time Warner: Perfect Time-ing" from Goldman Sachs. Merrill Lynch predicted that AOL Time Warner would become the new "Microsoft . . . by owning the branded consumer interface, the 'front screen' around which consumers organize their entertainment, information, and communications activities." Among the authors of Merrill Lynch's report was its star media expert Henry Blodgett, who would soon be permanently barred from working as an analyst because of his deliberately misleading advice to investors.[17]

Closed Access

We didn't spend $56 billion on a cable network to have the blood sucked out of our veins.

—*AT&T executive*

Most media and telecommunications mergers in the United States must pass two federal regulatory hurdles: an antitrust review and a public-interest test. On antitrust, either the Department of Justice (DOJ) or the Federal Trade Commission (FTC) has jurisdiction. The FCC must also see if such mergers are in the public-interest, since it has to approve any change of ownership of licenses for broadcast stations, cable systems, or broadcast satellites.[18]

Antitrust review is usually an ineffective method for dealing with problems stemming from media mergers. Deals can be stopped if, for example, the two biggest shoelace manufacturers or grocery distributors want to merge. If the DOJ or the FTC finds that significantly less competition will lead to higher costs for consumers or advertisers, then the agency may reject the transaction. But our antitrust laws, such as the Sherman Act, regard communications companies the same way they do office suppliers, even though the product in question is the creation and distribution of information and ideas. If a media company is going to get bigger, then usually the antitrust regulators won't bat an eye, as long as there are two or three other giants doing business. Never mind that there's been a further loss of an independent outlet for information.

But if enough political pressure is applied from competitors, Congress, and public-interest groups, then occasionally some safeguards will be imposed.[19] Such was the case when a group of advocates, including scholar Larry Lessig, joined with media giants to persuade the FTC to impose open access requirements on AOL Time Warner as a condition of approval. The FTC understood that some form of competitive Internet service provider access for broadband, however modest, was important to protect the emerging high-speed Internet market, and thus required AOL Time Warner to connect at least three unaffiliated providers. Disney as well as NBC was particularly concerned with how AOL Time Warner would operate its interactive TV networks, fearful that non–AOL Time Warner programming would be banished to some broadband hinterlands. As NBC general counsel Richard Cotton urged in a July 24, 2000, letter to the FCC, "The ability of the merged entity to favor its affiliated content in both television and the Internet . . . raises serious public-policy issues regarding competition, the free flow of information, and consumer access to diverse voices and content."[20] A safeguard was added by the FTC that required AOL Time Warner to operate any interactive TV systems in a nondiscriminatory manner.[21]

While the AOL Time Warner merger ultimately failed, its vision for a broadband and TV hybrid, controlled by a handful of behemoths, became a model for others. To secure this scheme, the big cable and phone companies are again knocking on Washington, DC's door.

10

Supermedia Monopolies

The leaders of the nation's largest cable and telephone companies are telling lawmakers something familiar. New national policies are required to connect everyone to what they call a "superbroadband" Internet highway. If Washington supports their political agenda, the companies vow that the nation will benefit from advances in health care, improvements in the quality of life for senior citizens, and major boosts for jobs and the economy. But, say corporate executives, we are stymied by rules, regulations, and local and state policies. Congress, the FCC, and the White House must get government out of the way. They claim that the emergence of the Internet has set the stage to remove most of the public policies and safeguards that now govern media and communications—everything from limits on media ownership, to rules governing equal time for political candidates, to requirements that communities receive public-service programming. Competition, we are assured, will address any problem once handled by law or regulation, and also bring us the promised digital cornucopia.

To help win their goal of privately controlling what will be the most powerful media and communications system ever developed, Comcast, Verizon, AT&T, and others have unleashed teams of lobbyists. A large war chest doles out campaign cash; companies say they will spend whatever it takes. To help ensure success, they are bankrolling a major public relations campaign. Bucolic and reassuring images of American families, happily satisfied as their children connect swiftly online to an educational Web site or they all sit down to watch an on-demand program, are shown on TV, in print, and online. It's a not-so-subtle message to lawmakers: all you have to do to bring everyone this miraculous digital future is to quickly act on our behalf. Supporting their call for what they label "new rules" is a loud chorus of allies, part of a long chain of academics, think tanks, and nonprofit "consumer" groups. Newly minted front groups, flush with industry cash, go state by state to help the big media win even more favorable policies.[1]

Going, Going, Gone?

The rush to get government assistance is a standard reflex of the communications industry. But now, securing favorable treatment has taken on an urgency. Phone and cable giants fear that if the online medium is permitted to continue to offer a vast, unlimited array of content and services, such as video programming or low-cost telephone connections, their revenues will wither. They have built their businesses as government-sanctioned monopolies, with the Baby Bells dominating telephone and cable controlling multichannel TV. Now the Internet poses a fundamental challenge, since it permits practically anyone to also offer what these giants do. So the cable and phone companies are relying on their lobbying and financial prowess to seize control over the Internet's future, especially now that it has become the high-speed, always-connected medium called broadband. Since they provide the more than 90 percent of such broadband connections in the United States, the cable and telephone industries believe they are in a prime position to become the key Internet gatekeepers. Their clout over broadband has recently been made more secure by a series of favorable decisions, all of which they heavily lobbied for, by the Bush FCC.

Their vision for the Internet is a turbocharged selling machine, sending us a never-ending lineup of digital entertainment, interactive advertising, virtual gambling, and data-collecting forms of online social networking.

Also up for grabs are many of the nation's broadcast radio and TV stations and daily newspapers. The few remaining limits on media consolidation will likely be severely weakened or eliminated by the FCC. Consequently, there will be a further shrinking of the number of conglomerates dominating our local and national media. Soon, larger media monopolies will emerge, as the cable and phone companies that control vast expanses of online communications seek to also acquire newspapers, broadcast stations, and TV networks. Such deals, the media lobby will declare, will be the only way to save journalism, deliver public-interest programming, and ensure new and innovative services. Eventually, the owners of the so-called competing broadband Internet wires of the cable and telephone industry will likely consolidate as well. Instead of having a communications environment that promotes freedom, creativity, and expression, we could witness a dwindling number of major corporations controlling the most powerful media outlets.

The Bush presidency, the GOP-controlled Congress and FCC, and too many corporate-prone Democrats have endorsed such a scenario. It was FCC chair Powell, and then his successor Kevin Martin, that led the commission to approve policies in 2002 and 2005 permitting cable and phone companies to gain greater leverage over the broadband Internet. With these new rules, the cable and telephone industries can operate their broadband service without regard to what had made the Internet a vibrant medium of expression to begin with. Under the regulations governing the old Internet, using dial-up connections, the medium was required to treat all content in a nondiscriminatory manner. Formerly, the FCC required that the public have a choice of Internet service providers, which had numbered in the thousands. Yet the cable and phone industry now have been given near-monopoly status as broadband providers. They can deny any competitor access to their lines. More disturbingly, there are no federal regulations preventing cable and telephone companies from discriminating against any online content they compete with or dislike.

That the self-serving interests of a few giants could end up threatening the potential of the Internet to serve democracy and fair competition illustrates the corruption and intellectual bankruptcy of U.S. communications policymaking. Industry and its political supporters have hijacked the policy process, using the rhetoric of deregulation, to relegate the public into the passive role of consumers, reduced to whether they might have more channels to watch or pay a few cents less for them. In Congress and at the FCC, the economic welfare of the owners of media and telecommunications outlets regularly trumps the interests of citizens. Instead of policies that benefit average Americans and serve the nation as a whole, broadcasters, cable, phone, and new media companies have been showered with federal favors so they can maximize earnings.

Repetitive Promises Syndrome

Much of what is now being touted as rewards for Americans once Washington approves industry's broadband agenda are the same commitments made by the same interests only a few years ago. Our lawmakers frequently forget about such past promises from corporate lobbyists. Perhaps that's because federal candidates since 1990 have been given more than $183 million in campaign contributions by the communications lobby—$115 million of that since the 2000 election. The phone, cable, and broadcast industries have spent $344 million for lobbyists since 2002 alone. As the media and communications industries aggressively push for favorable legislation, their spending significantly increases at the local, state, and federal levels.[2]

Essential to the plans of both the largest cable and phone companies is ensuring that they can operate their broadband Internet systems as private networks. These giants don't want any government role overseeing the rules of the digital road. That's because they want to make sure that their content and that of their highest-paying customers receives first-class treatment as it's sent via their wires or wireless servers to digital TV sets and personal computers. Those who can pay the most will see their programming or applications travel in so-called fast lines; those who can't pay the tab will be relegated to less optimal online thoroughfares. Under this plan, the United States is to have a digital medium where all Internet content is regarded as varying forms of commercial-paying freight.

Blueprints for how both cable and phone companies plan to operate their broadband networks are reflected in numerous white papers written by many of the leading Internet technology firms. Through their power as controllers over the flow of data coming into our homes, say these documents, phone and cable companies can run a system optimized to generate revenues from every transaction, monitor our online habits, and pick and choose which content and applications are to be favored. Since everyone's online usage can now be accurately metered, Comcast, BellSouth, and others are urged to create "Bronze, Silver, and Gold" service plans that will limit how much content one can download as well as the speed of a connection.[3]

Now also rolling off the assembly line are both hardware and software permitting "deep packet inspection" of users' content. They have names such as "SmartFlow," "NetEnforcer," "NetPure," "NetRedirector," and "IP Control System." All Web and other broadband communications can now be monitored, classified, and controlled in real time to give broadband providers granular control over service. Companies behind these products make a point to remind their potential cable and telephone clients that they can be used to limit unprofitable peer-to-peer applications or even ban them. Peer-to-peer technology offers Internet users the ability to participate in the creation of potentially more democratic forms of communication. Independent content, including video programming, can be easily and inexpensively distributed to millions of users through such software. Consequently, peer-to-peer technology is seen as a potential competitive threat to the phone and cable companies that seek to impose new revenue-generating business models for broadband. The companies will claim that disabling peer-to-peer distribution will prevent illegal copying of music and movies; their real motive, however, will be to use NetEnforcer-style technologies to eliminate as much competition as possible to their own and allied ventures.[4]

Quality of Disservice

Such plans by cable and the Bell companies have alarmed several leading new media companies, including eBay, Amazon.com, Google, and Microsoft. They each recognized that their ability to do business has been based on an online architecture where all content is permitted to travel freely. Now they face interlopers who plan to change the rules of the Internet and become everyone's not-so-silent partner or, worse, potent competitor.

Their growing concern over a fundamental change in how the Internet serves Americans prompted Vinton Cerf, considered one of the co-founders of the Internet for his work on its basic protocol and now Google's "Chief Internet Evangelist," to write Congress in 2005 warning that "allowing broadband providers to segment their IP offerings and reserve huge amounts of bandwidth for their own services will not give consumers the broadband Internet our country and economy need. Many people will have little or no choice among broadband operators for the foreseeable future, implying that such operators will have the power to exercise a great deal of control over any applications placed on the network."[5] Cerf's Google, other leading new media companies, and public-interest media groups such as the Free Press, Common Cause, and Public Knowledge called on Congress to pass a "network neutrality" safeguard. This would prevent cable and telephone companies from exiling unaffiliated content or slowing users down who go to competing sites. It would also require a broad, open lane for everyone to use.

Cerf would get his reply in the form of a candid expression from the CEO of then SBC (now AT&T), Edward Whitacre, who told *Business Week* in November 2005, "Why should they be allowed to use my pipes? The Internet can't be free in that sense, because we and the cable companies have made an investment and for a Google or Yahoo! or Vonage [an online company selling telephone service] or anybody to expect to use these pipes [for] free is nuts!"[6] Whitacre's sentiments were loudly echoed by other executives from Verizon, BellSouth, and the cable industry.

But obscured by these battles among the country's Internet giants was the reality that they all shared the same goal. They each wanted to perfect a digital media system that would allow them to target content and advertising to individuals—all to assist in the delivery of personalized pitches and to "keep . . . and monetize eyeballs." While communications company executives regularly offered up litanies that the public had greater choice today to pick and choose content and even bypass advertising, they were collectively engaged in ensuring that an all-encompassing interactive marketing system would play a defining role in digital media.[7]

Community Broadband

As cable and telephone companies rushed to operate private broadband networks, communities began to recognize that they should provide their residents with Internet service. Not a "red" or "blue" state issue, cities in states such as Louisiana, Wisconsin, Tennessee, and Pennsylvania created what's known as community or municipal networks. There were a number of reasons driving interest in wired cities. For some, it was to build a high-tech infrastructure that would attract business and help keep young people from looking for opportunities elsewhere. For others, it was a way to assist education or the most inexpensive method of making Internet affordable, especially for low-income residents. A few recognized the importance of community bandwidth—broadband assets controlled by the public—that could provide a wide range of services. Unlike the cable and phone industries, where decisions were made by private fiat, here would be a form of communications service more accountable to local residents.

But in a clear indication of their interest to oppose all forms of competition, phone and cable companies launched an attack on such efforts. Whatever form such networks took, including "fiber-to-the-home" wired networks or wi-fi, major cable and phone companies declared, as Groucho Marx told the college faculty in *Horse Feathers*, "Whatever it is, I'm against it!" The phone companies fought all the way to the Supreme Court in one case, successfully undermining the ability of local governments to create their own broadband facilities. Comcast and Verizon lobbied side by side in 2004 to pass legislation in Pennsylvania, so alarmed were they by the city of Philadelphia's community wireless plans. Now any other city in that state will find it impossible to do the same. In three small neighboring cities in Illinois—St. Charles, Batavia, and Geneva—SBC and Comcast fought plans by groups such as the Chamber of Commerce and the Jaycees to build a community fiber-optic network. The citizens' group backing the "Fiber for Our Future" referendum went down to political defeat twice, in 2003 and 2004, after a well-funded advertising and misleading public relations campaign.[8]

Meanwhile, as they entered the broadband video business, the phone companies also laid siege to the only policy left that helped ensure that communications networks served the public-interest of the communities in which they financially prospered. Having to negotiate a contract—known as a franchise—with local officials to make certain that broadband addressed specific community needs such as health, education, or public safety would delay the creation of a national superbroadband network, claimed AT&T to the FCC in 2006. Verizon pledged to spend whatever it took to get Congress to junk oversight by local government, saying "it's the cost to get into the market."[9]

As all of this was occurring, the United States has slipped further down the list of countries with the most penetration of broadband to homes, ranking sixteenth in 2005. Korea and Canada, having regulatory regimes permitting serious broadband competition along with a more proactive governmental role, were able to offer higher broadband transmission speeds at much lower costs than in the United States.[10] The United States, which was where much of the Internet innovations had taken place, was now trailing Iceland, Belgium, and Finland.[11]

But the Bush administration rejected the notion that the United States is falling behind or offering Internet users a slower and more expensive network than other countries. It claimed that all was rosy, especially now that cable and phone companies were being given the incentives to quickly roll out broadband. Broadband "deploy-ment," as it is called, was the key overall concern for U.S. Internet policy. Based on Section 706 of the Telecommunications Act, phone and cable companies had been able to successfully argue that nothing else really mattered other than helping them to make as much money as possible so they could deploy their broadband fa-cilities.[12] Neither Congress nor the FCC appeared worried about supporting policies that placed broadband deployment before any concern related to broadband democracy. Sadly ignored as a conse-quence of laying wires out at any cost were the needs of tens of millions of low-income Americans who couldn't afford Internet service at all.

Not Fit to Print

Most of these issues and debates have been ignored by the news media. One of the consistent themes about media ownership and communications in general has been the failure of the press, espe-cially TV news, to report and explain the issues to the public. As discussed earlier, the print press has generally exiled such stories to its business pages, away from the view of many readers; broadcast and cable TV news has largely engaged in a press blackout. These practices continue today, even as Congress prepares a major new communications law. But since practically every media company is lobbying for some form of special provision, such self-censorship and outright censorship is viewed as a form of job and wealth preservation.

The role that the mainstream media plays in our lives is fre-quently mocked by commentators across the political spectrum. One of the most potent criticisms is that they are largely irrelevant. Digital technology, it is claimed, has now made nearly everyone a publisher. Citizen journalists, the blogosphere, never-ending inno-vation producing low-cost technologies, and the endless informa-tion resources available to the public have fundamentally changed the media equation. There is a long tail, it is said, that opened up and made potentially profitable new outlets for distribution. There is an also understandable skepticism, if not disagreement, that the big media and communications companies will make a dent in the Internet's ability to further challenge and undermine the dominant media system.

But the lessons of U.S. media history tell us we shouldn't take for granted that technological innovation will win the day. As this book discusses, commercial media culture has been working to become stronger and more relevant in the digital age. Big media will use all the resources at their disposal to take advantage of a political system where money and power go hand in hand. Technologies and the goodwill of many people will have to square off against the most successful and entrenched interests on the globe. We have already seen Congress bend to special interests in the form of legislation awarding the so-called dinosaurs of old media greater control over copyright, look away as music and movie companies launched an attack on peer-to-peer networks, champion the interests of marketers by refusing to pass online privacy safeguards, and now hand phone and cable companies the keys to the broadband kingdom. It's no wonder that some netizens are saying that it is time to issue a new "Declaration of Independence in Cyberspace," just as they did back in the mid-1990s.

Such a call is timely. Our communications system is at a crossroads, and the country's digital destiny is at stake. The long-awaited convergence of digital media with the older media of radio, TV, and newspapers has arrived. That's why those who care about having a media environment that nurtures a democracy should fight to create a different media future. The giants from our commercial media and telecommunications industries will bring us a wondrous, interactive, intelligent, and personalized distribution system for entertainment, advertising, and marketing. But this system will not meaningfully foster civic expression, robust journalism, and diversity of ownership, and it will no doubt reflect the race and class divisions that haunt the United States. Our foremost commitment should be to ensure this system reflects our highest aspirations as a society. That's why it's crucial to recall our recent media policy past and try not to permit communications history to repeat itself.

11

A Policy Agenda for the Broadband Era

Despite what appear to be gloomy prospects for change, the transition from the old media world to one dominated by digital broadband communications offers a critical window of opportunity. There is time to organize and engage in a serious fight for a media system that can better sustain a democracy. Broadband business models have not yet been fully perfected. Laws and regulations will still need to be enacted. More important, the public is still uninformed about what the consequences are for their families, communities, the nation, and the rest of the world if the corporate media vision wins the day. What follows are some specific recommendations for consideration and action.

Organizing and Activism for Media Reform: Over the last several years, what was once a relatively small group has blossomed into a potential major political movement. It is essential that everyone who cares about a more representative, responsive, and diverse media system join in the fight to determine the country's digital destiny. We must challenge the corporate and political status quo that dominates the communications policy debates. There are opportunities for organizing and action throughout the country, including at the community, state, and federal levels. The movement requires people who can develop new approaches to legislation and regulation, work to change how mainstream journalism covers media issues, and help ensure that the media reform movement becomes more reflective of race, gender, and class. One of the most critical contributions can come from those who are knowledgeable about the potential of new technology to positively transform our media system. We must continue to expand the range of products and services, such as open source video and peer-to-peer applications, that further democratize the way we produce and share information.

There is now an array of groups providing leadership for the movement. National groups such as Common Cause, the Free Press, the Future of Music Coalition, and the Prometheus Radio Project have joined such longtime activist stalwarts as the Media Access Project, the Consumers Union, the Consumer Federation of America, the FAIR, the Alliance for Community Media, the U.S. Public Interest Research Group, the United Church of Christ, and the Media Alliance. There are also local organizations fighting to improve the quality of media in communities across the nation such as Seattle's Reclaim the Media and the Philadelphia-based Media Tank. Many of these nonprofits are part of the new Media and Democracy Coalition operated out of Common Cause in Washington, DC. More groups and individuals are recognizing that if the United States is to evolve as a civil society, it will require a media system that promotes the interests of the many over a privileged few.

The Media and Democracy Coalition and the other activist groups need to be supported, politically and financially. Most of these organizations depend on philanthropic foundation support. Unfortunately, funders have not played the kind of role that could help spark a change in how the country governs its communications system. Most foundations, as they say, don't fund media projects. Yet the core mission of many foundations dovetail with many of the values of media reform: ensuring an informed and educated society; redressing social, political, and economic inequities; and supporting the creativity of artists, writers, and other talented individuals. The fate of the not-for-profit sector in general is also tied to its ability to use new digital media effectively.

Socially responsible investment funds also need to play a supportive role. Responsible investors have already expressed concerns about the threats to Internet access by repressive regimes such as China. Responsible funds should use their wealth and influence to ensure that what they fear from abroad doesn't also happen here. It's time they recognize that most U.S. media and telecommunications stocks are not reflective of their values—all they have to do is examine the company's lobbying agenda. Funds should either divest themselves of communications holdings where companies are opposed to, for example, an open Internet, privacy protection, municipally controlled networks, or press for meaningful change at shareholder meetings. Investment firms and other persons and institutions of wealth should also back inno\ilot ventures that demonstrate how digital media can serve the interests of a civil society.[1]

Community Broadband: Broadband access is a necessity, and we need to make sure it's readily available, robust, and cheap. It must above all serve the public as citizens and community members, not just as consumers. But this won't happen if our networks are totally under the control of private, commercial enterprises that lack a public policy obligation to serve anyone other than their investors. Every community should have the right to build its own broadband network, whether municipally owned or operated by a public group. That will mean passing legislation that ensures communities have the right to do so, and repealing laws that now prevent or restrict such networks. There is a growing community broadband movement that can offer inspiration and practical advice.

Local government should also have the legal right to impose a contract on any broadband provider. For decades now, as discussed earlier, cities and counties have been empowered to authorize and benefit from such cable services. The growing perversity of phone companies and their political supporters, who claim that such a notion is unnecessary, outmoded, and inefficient, is a smoke screen. They don't want anyone requiring them to share control over what they see as their private network. But citizens in towns, cities, and counties are in the best position to help determine what is required in terms of community bandwidth. Such local bandwidth— supported through relatively modest technological and financial resources—can ensure the public the range of information they need to be informed, engaged, and safe (such as via alert systems for natural and other disasters).[2]

Equitable Access to Broadband: There was a compact made long ago that residents of the United States would have access to affordable communications—a policy known as universal service. Through various federal and state regulations, including lower-priced phone charges, and via free, over-the-air radio and TV broadcasting, Americans received a range of electronic media services. It's evident that the Internet has now become, like the telephone, an essential service for the public. Anyone who has a child in school and has helped them with homework knows the importance of a fast, in-home Internet connection. From e-mailing teachers, to looking up prescription drugs and their effects, to the voting records of officials, to renewing motor vehicle licenses, ready access to the Internet is crucial. As all forms of Internet-based communications incorporate more multimedia content, having a high-speed connection will become a necessity. Income is the most critical factor in determining whether the Internet is available in the home.

We should subsidize access to broadband for low-income Americans through a revamped universal service policy. This would include charging those more fortunate to help pay for those who are not, including those that economically benefit from communications such as cable, telephone, and major online ventures. Such an investment will pay off for our society in many ways, including helping families build a better future and supporting future generations of online users who will help advance all our interests.

Nondiscriminatory Internet: The Internet must remain a robust, open medium. But it is likely that phone and cable companies will attempt to use their ownership of the lines to impose business schemes that favor their own bottom lines. This will certainly be true as they deliver interactive video that includes some form of Internet content. Expect to see companies such as Comcast and Verizon push their own programming into the foreground by sending it at superfast speeds compared to their competitors and independent sites. Cable and phone companies will also likely bundle together online access, TV service, and their own content into financially unbeatable packages for consumers. What would you prefer to watch, a network news program for free or an independent news show where the digital meter is running up your credit card?

A multiple system of checks and balances is required to make sure our Internet providers don't discriminate against applications, protect privacy, and stay technologically up to date. That's why it's important for federal legislation to require all broadband providers to manage Internet traffic fairly, without regard to who owns the content. That means sending everyone's content in an unbiased manner. Phone and cable companies must also be required to regularly upgrade their pipelines so they grow in capacity, reflecting what will be continued technological innovations. That's why oversight is essential. One approach is to create public boards that can monitor the operation of an area's broadband networks. Made up of local experts and community advocates, these bodies could publicly report on such things as whether the network is state of the art, being used to favor certain content, and meeting the needs of education and civic affairs. Similar efforts should also occur at the state and federal levels. We should not allow only corporate executives along with their lobbyists and hired experts to determine the technological and business parameters of what is a public resource.

Noncommercial Commons: A well-organized system fostering noncommercial communications is required within what some call a "commons" or public-interest "sphere." Residing within the commons and distributed to all at no cost will be civic-related information necessary for public participation and a host of noncommercial programming services. While the Internet has an endless source of such nonprofit information, it is important to make such content readily accessible and easily locatable. It is also necessary to provide the public with access to quality information for free, without having to pay for fancy subscriptions, being forced to watch interactive ads, or give up personal information as a quid pro quo. As part of this effort, we need to reenvision public broadcasting. Both public TV and radio stations have expanded capability to transit additional programming and other content. This is due not only to digital technology but also to policy decisions that helped public TV stations gain access to digital cable TV channels. Public broadcasting is also engaged in a number of promising experiments to make its content more available, including online and on-demand programming via such devices as iPods.

But if public broadcasting is to play a significant role in the commons, it must insulate programming decisions from both politics and an ever-growing commercial orientation. Recent attacks on news and public affairs programming by Congress and conservative critics underscore the need for safeguards to ensure that PBS produces hard-hitting journalism and other programming genres. For decades, there have been calls for a public broadcasting trust fund or some other permanent funding scheme. A trust fund should be created that is run independently, with a diverse group of commissioning editors, programmers, and advisers who are unaffiliated with the stations or the network. Funds should be earmarked to guarantee that member stations, the PBS and NPR network, and independent producers can regularly create news, investigative reporting, culture and the arts, independent productions, and children's content. These funds should be designated to support a diverse schedule of programming as well. This will help prevent the entire budget for PBS going for such safe things as "Barney Reads to Bill Bennett" or "Antiques Roadshow Cooks Cajun." It is unlikely in the short term that Congress would approve such funding, so our largest media corporations should be publicly pressured into contributing.

Beyond public media, there will be many new approaches to providing the public with noncommercial content, including so-called citizen journalism. Such programming, as discussed below, should qualify for free distribution and meaningful promotion on all broadband platforms, including cable and phone networks.

A key factor for the growth of a commons is having sufficient access to the digital highway. More of the public airwaves or spectrum needs to be available outside the control of private interests such as broadcasters and phone companies. Open airwaves where anyone can easily distribute their content to all are also critical for both innovation and programming independence. Groups such as the New America Foundation have been fighting against corporate spectrum "squatters" who desire to make private what belongs to all of us.

Electoral Communications: This should be one of the initial areas for political action. Our political system has been held hostage for too long by both incumbent lawmakers who can raise enormous sums of money and the TV industry that takes it all to run political advertising. If we fail to act now to change our political communications system, we will extend the corrupt system into the interactive TV era. It could take even larger sums to buy access to broadband or digital TV services. Consequently, we will face an electronic media system that makes even more unaffordable the ability to inform voters about critical issues. The commercial TV industry will want to continue the business of campaign advertising; after all, it generated $1.6 billion in TV revenues during the 2004 presidential election. The capabilities of both digital TV and broadband will be the preferred method for sending political communications. The ad of choice will be personalized and interactive, precisely delivered to individuals in the home or at work based on data collection and profiling. TV and broadband companies such as Comcast and AT&T will be able to gain enormous revenues from their ability to individually target homes and discrete segments of viewers and users. Broadband providers will also be able to sell candidates access to eye-catching space on home page portals and electronic program guides. They will sell the opportunity to download messages directly onto the hard drives of personal video recorders—a technology that will increasingly be part of our TV experience. There will also be extra fees charged to ensure that viewers and users can readily request further information or engage in opinion surveys.

The cable industry has already shown that it opposes any policy that would require it to offer federal candidates free or low-cost access. It understands how much money is to be made in the new era of interactive political ads. Cable, phone companies, and the broadcast TV industries will spend whatever it takes to maintain the system where the highest bidder has the most access. But there is no need to continue this system.

There is also no shortage of TV capacity; given digital technology, it's practically limitless. Broadcast stations, cable TV, satellite systems, and major broadband providers should be required to transmit all electoral-related speech for free as part of comprehensive campaign reform. Such content should be prominently featured on electronic program guides, and readily downloaded to personal video recorders and set-top boxes. Electoral communications should also be assured first-class delivery, without surcharges or other fees being imposed.

If we act swiftly and decisively, we may be able to open up a new era in politics—one that is more reflective of the kind of democracy we deserve.

Privacy: Online and interactive communications require meaningful safeguards to protect our privacy, including financial, health, voting behavior, and other information. The communications industry wants to maintain the commercial market that permits it to harvest our personal data for use and sale throughout the digital and non-virtual landscape. Online information firms such as Google and Yahoo!, among others, depend on such information as the core of their business. That's why direct marketers and others from the media industry have long opposed a simple proposal that would require members of the public to affirmatively "opt-in" (give permission) before any personal data are collected. Such approval should also include the use of nonpersonal data, which the marketing industry calls anonymous information, but which can provide specific details about our behavior and location as well. No information should be collected or used without our consent. We should also regularly be informed about what information is being collected, how it is to be used or sold, whether it's part of a profile of our activities, what psychological or other behavioral attributes have been identified, and so on. Consumers should be in control—

not the advertising or media communities. Such a proposal would require congressional approval. The privacy community, led by such groups as the Electronic Privacy Information Center, needs our help if we are to protect ourselves from more sophisticated encroachments on our identities.

Commercialism: Interactive technologies of persuasion, including increasingly refined data-mining techniques, will make marketing more effective. Much of our new media system is being shaped to enhance the ubiquitous presence of marketing: from wireless devices such as cell phones to digital TVs to the Web. Digital advertising will be melded together with other approaches, such as viral marketing and product placement, creating a system that will play an influential, but largely invisible, role in helping us construct our lives. (This is especially clear with children, who are beyond the scope of this book.)

Advertising has an important place in our media system. But there need to be limits, alternatives, and safeguards—especially in this era of interactive marketing.

First, many of the techniques being used and developed for online advertising require intense public scrutiny and debate. State attorney generals and consumer advocates should pursue formal complaints to watchdog agencies such as the FTC. One area prime for investigation is the emerging field of immersive advertising, which uses new technology to "place" the viewer inside or as part of a commercial. Such ad strategies may be ruled illegal or, as the FTC terms it, considered an unfair marketing practice.

Journalists and muckrakers should also seize the fertile ground offered by this issue. This book has only skimmed what is a quickly changing field of global proportions. Reporting should be routinely done on the new mechanisms of marketing, its societal implications, and the ad industry's lobbying apparatus. It will require biting the hand that feeds many reporters, as many of our old and new media rely on the same questionable advertising practices. Groups such as Commercial Alert will likely continue to play a key role raising public awareness.

We will never live in a world without advertising, and it will, as I said, only get stronger. But the combination of a strong noncommercial commons along with an effective privacy policy and redress for the worst practices can help address some of these concerns.

Media Ownership: How do you put the ownership genie back in the bottle? You likely can't, and we have to face this. If the media lobby has its way, there will also be fewer owners who control more radio, TV stations, and newspapers. There will eventually be cross-ownership of newspapers and TV stations in the same market as well. Since broadcasters can now also merge with cable TV, expect deals to be announced that bring together more broadcast-cable and newspaper combinations.

We need multiple responses to media consolidation, ranging from proactive legislation to strategies designed to foster the vitality of both mainstream and alternative journalism. At the moment, it's unlikely that Congress would be willing to enact a law ensuring meaningful ownership limits. Even if the Democratic Party were in charge of both Congress and the White House, the hold that the media lobby has over them is too great. Yet that doesn't mean we can't frame the debate by developing and building support for a new "media ecology diversity" law. Such legislation would prevent the further merging of cable, telephone, and broadcast networks with each other. It would also address what will be mergers between our largest media outlets such as Disney/ABC or Time Warner with a major online entity such as Microsoft or Google. Under a new media diversity law, each merger or alliance would undergo a multiple media "environmental impact" test, conducted by both the FCC and an antitrust agency. But we should also create an outside team of independent evaluators to conduct such a review. These evaluators could come, for example, from the consumer protection, journalistic, academic, and entertainment communities. People working in the media industries know firsthand how media consolidation has negatively affected their ability to serve the public. Yet they are regularly ignored by both Congress and the FCC. Such experts must play a larger role in helping shape the debate about how to address further concentration. These recommendations from the independent evaluators would have to be broadly publicized, so the public could better understand what was at stake. As was demonstrated in 2003 in the effort to overturn the FCC's new media ownership rules, there are many people who are concerned about the direction of the country's media policies. This constituency will be essential in the battles to come.

There must also be efforts to help redefine First Amendment jurisprudence. Media companies such as Time Warner, General Electric/NBC, and Viacom/CBS have continually argued in federal court that public-interest media policies violate their corporate First Amendment rights. It's time to assert that the public's right to a diverse and equitable media system is paramount to business interests. Through an expanded research agenda, we can help to strengthen the legal and economic rationale supporting the public-interest in the digital era.

The academic community must do some soul-searching as well. Too many scholars are more interested in cashing handsome checks from the media lobby than in addressing the needs of the public. The frenzy of fund-raising by major universities has helped create an atmosphere where selling out to the highest corporate bidder is viewed as acceptable professional behavior. Universities and scholarly organizations should encourage professors to work pro bono on public-interest projects. Foundations should support public-spirited research, such as what the Ford Foundation is now attempting to do with academics.[3]

Finally, it's important to underscore why broadband communications, including the Internet and digital TV, should be required to operate in an open and nondiscriminatory manner. Even as the remaining mainstream media are likely to acquire each other and merge, the Internet must continue to serve as a powerful means for sending an array of content.

The Public Interest, Convenience, and Necessity: The pact between our electronic media system of TV and radio, as embodied in the "public-interest, convenience, and necessity" section of the 1934 Communications Act, has never served as either a serious or reliable means of ensuring public-service programming. As with media ownership, too much has happened to hope that we can require our major media to put the interests of the public before their self-serving financial focus. It would be ideal if we could pass legislation or FCC rules that specified how each radio and TV station, cable system, and broadband provider had to regularly provide public service. There could be, for example, a menu of options that a station could choose from. That would help address concerns about balancing the First Amendment interests of both the audience and a media company. For many years, there has also been a call that broadcasters pay a yearly fee to offset their free use of the airwaves. While today cable companies pay annual franchise fees to each local government they serve (around 5 percent of gross TV revenues), such funding is in jeopardy. Some of these funds have been used to support community TV. But cable and phone companies delivering TV through broadband connections will try to undo having to make such payments.

We need to develop other strategies and policies that reflect the principles and values of the public-interest, but in the context of today's digital communications system. That means an open Internet, expanding an information commons, reforming the public broadcasting system, and doing what we can to foster the vibrancy of journalism and independent media. If we are able to accomplish even part of such an agenda, we would have made a valuable contribution to balancing a media system that daily influences our lives.

The Future of Journalism: Media consolidation and lax FCC oversight have helped make a great deal of our news media incapable of effectively serving the public. As we witnessed with 9/11 and after, Americans are sadly underinformed about many issues from foreign affairs to domestic concerns such as health care, retirement, the environment crises, and so on. The country deserves to have a range of reliable, in-depth information and analysis on TV and radio, in print, and online. I'm not talking about media that spews forth ideological perspectives from the Left or the Right. There's an important place for such commentary. But even in the age of blogs and citizen journalism, it's still vital to protect the role that many reporters, editors, and producers want to play: providing the facts with as much context as possible. That requires having both the time and resources to do so.

Today, news organizations are largely trapped within a commercially oriented system primarily set up to sell products, including entertainment. A company devoted to theme parks, movie studio tours, or defense contracts cannot be relied on to intellectually and financially sustain the environment necessary for news, public affairs, and civic discourse. That's why we need to explore the creation of journalistic institutions that are not dependent on or required to be part of larger, nonnews companies.

We should call for the separation of the news operations of the existing TV networks from their parent companies. The news departments of ABC, CBS, NBC, and CNN should be working for the public. These companies should be encouraged through both legislation and public shaming to set up public trust funds for their news services. Their former parents should give these newly independent operations the adequate funding and whatever programming distribution they require. They could be operated as either for-profit or nonprofit concerns, with boards composed of journalists and public-spirited individuals.

Not all news companies need to be not-for-profit, as long as safeguards are in place. But for-profit news organizations should not have the fiduciary responsibility other corporations have to reward investors by making the most profit. Congress must pass legislation that in the words of the authors of *Taking Stock*, brings "changes in tax and securities laws that would encourage long-term investment" for both newspapers and other news organizations. Nonprofit holding companies running newspapers and other outlets should be also encouraged—and managed by journalists too. More minority-owned and minority-controlled news operations are also essential.[4]

We must ensure that all news organizations, large and small, have unfettered and free access to the key communications pathways, including cable, satellite, telephone, and broadband. Today, powerful gatekeepers get to decide, for example, who has access to cable channels and on what terms. The public was denied twenty-four-hour programming from BBC News during the 1990s because it competed with cable-industry-owned news programming. If a news organization can't afford to transmit programming because of the high rates or other conditions imposed by the owners of cable and satellite, than the public is being denied access to an essential resource. Congress must pass a Freedom to Report the News Act that requires free "carriage" of news programming on all distribution outlets, regardless of whether it's a one-hour special or an around-the-clock channel.

As mentioned previously, both PBS and NPR have new local and national digital platforms that could be a crucial part of a renaissance for journalism. Public TV should serve as an important producer and distributor of news and public affairs programming. We also need to have a greater awareness of the role that public policy plays in shaping our media system. Much more emphasis by the nation's media critics must be on both revealing what the media lobby is doing and what its implications are for the public. This will require a more candid critique of what their own employers are doing. Missing, for example, from *Washington Post* editors Leonard Downie Jr. and Robert G. Kaiser's lament about the state of the news, *The News about the News*, was how the political goals of the media companies—including the Washington Post Company—have played a major role in contributing to the field's decline.[5]

News organizations should also empower their ombudsman or designate a journalist who will regularly monitor and report on the political dealings of their employer. It's time that some trust and credibility were restored by ensuring the media report on itself. Stories about media policy, especially those involving the company, should be placed on the front page or at least the "A" section of newspapers. Radio and TV newscasts should also produce a media beat segment to take a closer look at how media companies, including their own, are part of the fleecing of America.

The FCC: This agency requires serious reform. It should serve as the public's communications watchdog—not corporate lapdog. Congress needs to reform the process of choosing FCC members. Only persons who are unaffiliated with corporate media and telecommunications interests should be considered for nomination. Indeed, commissioners should be politically independent, unaffiliated with either major political party. It's also time to stop relying on lawyers to serve as commissioners. Nominees should be chosen from such fields as consumer protection, education, social welfare, and other professions dedicated to serving the public. No matter what they say, it doesn't require the background of a legal expert or technological whiz to be a commissioner. What's really required is someone who combines basic intelligence with a compassionate heart.

The current federal rules that are supposed to protect the public from the undue influence of former employees lobbying their agency, such as the FCC, are totally inadequate. There are loopholes that allow former federal employees to take advantage of their inside information and contacts to help advance the interests of their new media industry employer. While there are policies allegedly restricting federal employees from lobbying on proceedings or issues they were involved with, we know they are allowed to schmooze with former co-workers, who are likely to be the people they once hired or supervised, or with whom they are friends. The safeguards also don't stop former employees from providing assistance to their new employers concerning the best way to achieve their political and corporate goals. There are short, one- and two-year prohibitions against lobbying the federal government on issues one may have worked on.[6] These are totally inadequate.

I recognize that the passage of laws restricting the future employment of former federal officials would be difficult, given that many members of Congress themselves cash out as lobbyists when leaving office. But the revolving door between the FCC and the media and telecommunications industries is a problem. Laws should be enacted that would prohibit senior federal personnel from representing outside interests related to their public employment for at least five years. Moreover, professional organizations should create standards of conduct that enforce such safeguards, including rules that would make former commissioners think twice about working for the media and telecommunications industry after their term of office.

The commission should also be required to seek research and analyses from experts who are independent of the industry and public-interest groups. Moreover, there needs to be a division in the commission itself whose job it is to defend the interests of viewers and users. The commission has long had a bureau of consumer affairs that has been so low-key that one would never know it's there. It needs to be revitalized, so consumers are served by ensuring communications services are affordable and respect the public's rights.

An office of public ombudsman should be established to force the FCC to examine all its decisions in the light of how they affect the public-interest for the average American. This position should be independent of the commissioners and rotate regularly so it cannot be captured by the media and telecommunications companies. This person should not be from industry but instead have a background in serving consumers and citizens.

Without such reforms, it is likely that decisions made by the chair and commissioners as well as senior staff will always be connected to their thoughts and interests about their future media industry employers.

Technology and Programming Initiatives: While policies are a key issue, we also have a moment to engage in a form of digital bypass surgery. Whatever the harmful plans of cable or telephone companies, the new digital communications system has already provided us with the tools to create more content, especially from independent perspectives. It will likely take many years for the media reform movement to achieve a democratizing agenda. We need to decisively take advantage of the Internet and digital TV to boldly stake out as much territory in cyberspace as we can. As we look back a few years from now, much of our digital destiny may have been determined by how we have knitted together new projects that enhance civic discourse throughout what will be a ubiquitous electronic media system.

Notes

Introduction

1. Robert W. McChesney, *Telecommunications, Mass Media, and Democracy: The Battle for Control of U.S. Broadcasting, 1928–1935* (New York: Oxford University Press, 1993).
2. Erik Barnouw, *The Golden Web: A History of Broadcasting in the United States, Vol. II, 1933–1953* (New York: Oxford University Press, 1968).
3. James Surowiecki, "Net Losses," *New Yorker*, March 13, 2006, http://www.newyorker.com/printables/talk/060320ta_talk_surowiecki (accessed March 14, 2006).

1. Really "Meet" the Press

1. See, for example, "In the Matter of Cross-Ownership of Broadcast Stations and Newspapers, MM Docket No. 01–235, Comments of Belo Corp," December 3, 2001; "In the Matter of 2002 Biennial Regulatory Review, MB Docket 02–277, Cox Enterprises," January 2, 2003. The Tribune Company, Fox, the New York Times Company, and many others also filed at the FCC around that time and during the subsequent months. See also "FCC Initiates Proceeding to Review Newspaper-Broadcast Cross-Ownership Rule," press release, FCC, September 13, 2001, http://www.fcc.gov/Bureaus/Mass_Media/News_Releases/2001/nrmm0109.html (accessed March 7, 2006); "FCC Begins Reviewing Cable Ownership Limits," press release, FCC, September 13, 2001, http://www.fcc.gov/Bureaus/Cable/News_Releases/2001/nrcb0113.html (accessed March 7, 2006).
2. Pamela McClintock, "Nets See Regs as Best Relief," *Variety*, October 14, 2001, http://www.variety.com/article/VR1117854257?categoryid=14&cs=1 (accessed February 13, 2006). One of the most aggressive companies was Viacom/CBS, which sought regulatory

"relief" in the context of September 11. Although Viacom trumpeted its public interest programming service, Viacom president Mel Karmazin also sought to have insurers pay the company millions of dollars because it had to fulfill "its public-interest responsibilities" following the 9/11 attacks. See Dan Trigoboff, "Viacom Presses Claim for 9/11 Business Interruption," *Broadcasting and Cable*, January 13, 2003, http://www.broadcastingcable.com/article/CA270111.html?display=Top+of+the+Week (accessed February 13, 2006).

3. Project for Excellence in Journalism, "Gambling with the Future," Journalism.org, 2001, http://www.journalism.org/resources/research/reports/localTV/2001/future.asp (accessed February 13, 2006). See also "Supplement," *Columbia Journalism Review*, November–December 2001, pp. 2–16.

4. The Center for Media and Democracy has done excellent work tracking this issue. See, for example, Diane Farsetta, "Video News Releases: The Ball's in the FCC's Court," June 24, 2005, http://www.prwatch.org/node/3790 (accessed February 13, 2006). See also "Canned News: What Does It Mean When Local News Isn't Local?" *Columbia Journalism Review*, November–December 2003, http://www.cjr.org/issues/2003/6/comment.asp (accessed February 13, 2006).

5. James T. Hamilton, *All the News That's Fit to Sell: How the Market Transforms Information into News* (Princeton, NJ: Princeton University Press, 2004), chapter 6; Project for Excellence in Journalism, "The State of the News Media 2004," http://www.stateofthemedia.com/2004/narrative_overview_newsinvestment.asp?media=1 (accessed February 13, 2006).

6. Charles Geraci, "Watch Dog Is Asleep: Report Hits Media Coverage of Terrorism before 9/11," *Editor and Publisher*, July 22, 2004.

7. Susan D. Moeller, "Media Coverage of Weapons of Mass Destruction," Center for International and Security Studies, University of Maryland, March 9, 2004, http://www.cissm.umd.edu/documents/WMDstudy_short.pdf (accessed February 13, 2006).

8. "Bush Advisor Meets Hollywood Execs," BBC News, November 12, 2001, http://news.bbc.co.uk/1/hi/entertainment/showbiz/1651173.stm (accessed February 13, 2006).

9. Cassidy and Associates, "About Us," http://www.cassidy.com/about/biodetail.asp?Id=91 (accessed February 13, 2006).

10. Ted Hearn, "Sachs Players," *Multichannel News*, June 28, 2004, http://www.multichannel.com/article/CA430695.html (accessed February 13, 2006).

11. Quoted in Johnnie L. Roberts, "Media Mogul Maelstrom: The Via-

com CEO Endorses George Bush and Sets off a Debate about Political Partisanship," *Newsweek*, October 4, 2004, http://www.msnbc.msn.com/id/6173187/site/newsweek/ (accessed March 11, 2006).

12. Jeff Chester, "Gerald Levin's Negative Legacy," Alternet.org, December 6, 2001, http://www.democraticmedia.org/resources/articles/levin.html (accessed March 11, 2006).

13. Robert D. Leigh, ed., *A Free and Responsible Press: A General Report in Mass Communication: Newspapers, Radio, Motion Pictures, Magazines, and Books, by the Commission on Freedom of the Press* (1947; repr., Chicago: University of Chicago Press, 1974), 3.

14. Erik Barnouw, *The Image Empire: A History of Broadcasting in the United States, Vol. III* (New York: Oxford University Press, 1970), 177–207.

15. Gilbert Cranberg, Randall Bezanson, and John Soloski, *Taking Stock: Journalism and the Publicly Traded Newspaper Company* (Ames: Iowa State University Press, 2001), 1–15.

16. Ben Bagdikian, *Media Monopoly*, 6th ed. (Boston: Beacon Press, 2000).

17. Eric Boehlert, "The Big Blackout," *Salon*, May 22, 2003, http://www.salon.com/tech/feature/2003/05/22/fcc_blackout/index_np.html (accessed February 13, 2006). Boehlert lists the following papers as failing to cover the lone public hearing by the FCC on media ownership: *Boston Globe, Providence Journal, Hartford Courant, New York Times, New York Daily News, Philadelphia Inquirer, USA Today, Baltimore Sun, Atlanta Constitution, Miami Herald, Dallas Morning News, Houston Chronicle, Arizona Republic, San Diego Tribune, Portland Oregonian, Denver Post, Kansas City Star, Indianapolis Star,* and *Detroit Free Press.*

18. Quoted in Jeff Chester, "Strict Scrutiny: Why Journalists Should Be Concerned about New Federal and Industry Media Deregulation Proposals," *Harvard International Journal of Press/Politics* 7, no. 2 (2002): 110–11, http://hij.sagepub.com/cgi/content/abstract/7/2/105 (accessed February 18, 2006).

19. The Center for Public Integrity has done commendable work in this regard. See "Well Connected: Tracking the Broadcast, Cable, and Telecommunications Industry," http://www.publicintegrity.org/telecom/ (accessed February 13, 2006).

20. That such stories were about the future of their industry, journalism, and corporate accountability wasn't often said to them, since journalists hate to be chided. One always had to be aware that if there were going to be coverage down the line for the next deal, inside move, or policy debate, then these journalists would be needed.

21. "In the Matter of Cross-Ownership of Broadcast Stations and Newspapers, MM Docket No. 01–235, Comments of the New York Times Company," December 3, 2001.

22. In one its first editorials on the FCC ownership issue, the *Times* failed to acknowledge that the Times Company had asked for the rule to be eliminated; see "Protecting Media Diversity," *New York Times*, February 23, 2002.

23. As of February 2002, The Times had also invested $75 million in a cable TV sports service, New England Sports Ventures, LLC (NESV). That month NESV purchased the Boston Red Sox and other properties. See Russell Lewis, "Forward-Looking Statement for the Period Ended June 30, 2002," New York Times Company, December 11, 2002, http://www.nytco.com/investors-presentations-20021211a.html (accessed February 13, 2006); New York Times Company 10 Q, SEC, November 8, 2002. The Times Company continues to expand its media industry presence, including new media. See "The New York Times Company to Acquire About.com; Provides Compelling Strategic Benefits for Future Growth," press release, February 17, 2005, http://www.corporate-ir.net/ireye/ir_site.zhtml?ticker=NYT&script =411&item_id=676519&layout=23 (accessed March 7, 2006). In April 2006, the Times Co. announced plans to sell back its stake in the Discovery Times channel to Discovery Communications. "'New York Times' to Sell Back 'Discovery Times' Channel," *Marketing Vox*, April 16, 2006, http://www.marketingvox.com/archives/2006/04/ 17/new_york_times_to_sell_back_discovery_times_channel/ (accessed May 31, 2006). John Malone's Liberty Media Corporation owned 49.8 percent of Discovery Communications. In Liberty's annual report to the SEC, the company spelled out how it and its cable industry partners, including Cox Communications and Advance Newhouse, had agreed not to support any channel that would compete with Discovery—in essence dooming any potential competition. Liberty Media Corporation, "Annual Report 10K," U.S. Securities and Exchange Commission, March 25, 2003.

24. FCC, "In the Matter of MB Docket No. 02–277, 2002 Biennial Regulatory Review—Review of the Commission's Broadcast Ownership Rules and Other Rules Adopted Pursuant to Section 202 of the Telecommunications Act of 1996." Comments of the Tribune Company, January 2, 2003. See also the Tribune Company's Reply Comments, February 3, 2003.

25. Quoted in Cynthia Gorney, *The Business of News: A Challenge for Journalism's Next Generation* (New York: Carnegie Corporation, 2003), 37, http://www.carnegie.org/pdf/businessofnews2.pdf (accessed February 13, 2006).

26. FCC, "In the Matter of MB Docket No. 02–277, 2002 Biennial Reg-

ulatory Review." See also "Tribune Company Annual Report," February 2004; Gorney, *The Business of News*, 37.

27. Jeff Madrick, "The Business Media and the New Economy," December 2001, http://www.ksg.harvard.edu/presspol/Research_Publications/ Papers/Research_Papers/R24.PDF (accessed February 13, 2006). See also Jeff Madrick, "Enron, the Media, and the New Economy," *The Nation*, April 1, 2002, http://www.thenation.com/doc/20020401/ madrick (accessed February 13, 2006); Geraci, "Watch Dog Is Asleep"; James Bamford, "The Man Who Sold the War," *Rolling Stone*, November 2005, http://www.rollingstone.com/politics/ story/_/id/8798997?pageid=rs.Home&pageregion=single7 (accessed February 13, 2006); Michael Massing, "Now They Tell Us," *New York Review of Books*, February 26, 2004, http://www.nybooks.com/ articles/article-preview?article_id=16922 (accessed February 13, 2006).

2. Consolidation Dance

1. "Remarks by the President in Signing Ceremony for the Telecommunications Act Conference Report," February 8, 1996, http://clinton4 .nara.gov/WH/EOP/OP/telecom/release.html (accessed February 10, 2006).

2. White House, Office of the Press Secretary, "Remarks by President Bill Clinton and Vice President Al Gore at Signing of Telecommunications Reform Act of 1996, February 9, 1996."

3. Quoted in "Clinton and GOP: Telecom Law Will Create Jobs," CNN, February 8, 1996, http://www.cnn.com/US/9602/telecom_ bill/ update/index.html (accessed March 11, 2006).

4. Tomlin knew the business much better than Gore, understanding that his vaunted "information superhighway" would likely be the perfect medium for interactive advertising. See "Remarks by the President in Signing Ceremony for the Telecommunications Act Conference Report." As evidence that they were to share in the spoils of the new law were guests such as Ted Turner, Donald Newhouse (of Newhouse/ Advance, a holder of substantial cable TV holdings), Ray Smith (CEO of Bell Atlantic), and Motion Picture Association of America chief Jack Valenti. Librarian of Congress James Billington paid homage to these visitors, declaring that "Jefferson, were he here today, would [be] . . . glad to see many entrepreneurial forces gathered together with national political leaders in the building that bears his name." See Guy Lamlinlara, "Wired for the Future," *Library of Congress Information*

Bulletin, February 19, 1996, http://www.loc.gov/loc/lcib/9603/
telecom.html (accessed February 10, 2006).

5. "Remarks by Vice President Al Gore at National Press Club, December 21, 1993," http://www.ibiblio.org/nii/goremarks.html (accessed February 10, 2006).

6. "Remarks by Vice President Al Gore at National Press Club."

7. Electronic Frontier Foundation, "Gore Endorses EFF's Open Platform Approach," press release, December 21, 1993, http://www.interesting-people.org/archives/interesting-people/199312/msg00095.html (accessed February 9, 2006).

8. The Information Infrastructure Task Force, http://www.ibiblio.org/nii/NII-Task-Force.html (accessed February 10, 2006).

9. State of the Union address by the president, January 25, 1994, http://www.multied.com/Documents/Clinton/ClintonStateofUnion1994.html (accessed February 10, 2006).

10. "Executive Summary," Computer Systems Policy Project, http://www.cspp.org/Reports.asp?FormMode=Call&LinkType=Text&ID=0021715504 (accessed February 10, 2006).

11. Mike Mills, "Telecommunications Bill Passed," *Washington Post,* February 2, 1996.

12. Quoted in John Heilemann, "The Making of the President 2000," *Wired*, December, 1995, http://wired-vig.wired.com/wired/archive/3.12/gorenewt.html (accessed February 9, 2006). As Heilemann explains, Gore's comment was also a "shot at Gingrich." The two men were engaged in a feud over who would be seen as the country's leading politician and technology expert. Gingrich had referred to Gore as "totally Second Wave," saying that "the model Gore is trying to build is a futurist version of the welfare state. He's repainting the den; I want to build a whole new house." Both Gore and Gingrich did contribute to advancing new media infrastructure. While speaker, Gingrich played a key role in establishing Thomas, the federal service that places congressional legislation online. Ironically, overshadowing the debate about the impact of the Telecommunications Act on media ownership and communications were two provisions dealing with what some called "harmful content." The first was the so-called Communications Decency Act amendment that was focused on cyberporn, but would have prevented access to a wide range of online material. Second, a provision requiring all TV sets to have a "V-chip"—a technology that would help filter out violent and other programming content—was also in the bill. Despite the fact that the telecommunications bill was supposed to offer a vast new expanse of video and online programming, Congress was fixated on what it assumed would be problematic

content. The press was able to focus more on these two provisions than on what was actually in the bill because it was a simpler story to tell. It was also a way they could avoid reporting on what their own media companies were doing in lobbying for the bill.

13. In 1997, SBC purchased Pacific Telesis and Bell Atlantic merged with Nynex. SBC took over Ameritech in 1999. When Bell Atlantic acquired GTE, another phone company, in 2000, it changed its corporate name to Verizon. That same year, Qwest Communications ended up in control of U.S. West. Much more was needed to be done to ensure equitable access to communication services, especially for low-income Americans, than what the E-Rate accomplished.

14. The deals continued. Comcast became the largest U.S. cable company when it purchased AT&T Broadband. What was left of Ma Bell's phone business became part of SBC. General Electric/NBC purchased Universal. Even when companies choose to split up, such as Viacom/CBS, the deal didn't put a dent in the overall consolidation of control.

15. See, for example, "Biggest Media Mergers," CNN *Money*, September 7, 1999, http://money.cnn.com/1999/09/07/deals/media_mergers/ (accessed February 10, 2006); Geraldine Fabrikant, "Television Stations, Always Lucrative Ventures, Are Suddenly Hotter Than Ever," *New York Times*, August 19, 1996; Bill Carter, "Communications Reshaped: The Broadcasters, the Networks See Potential for Growth," *New York Times*, February 2, 1996; "How Clear Channel Became the Biggest," *Cincinnati Enquirer*, March 19, 2000, http://www.enquirer .com/editions/2000/03/19/fin_how_clear_channel.html (accessed February 10, 2006); Mark Landler, "To Infinity and Beyond: Is a Radio Deal Too Big? Westinghouse Would Own 32% of Top Markets," *New York Times*, June 22, 1996; Jeannine Aversa, "FCC Approves AT&T-TCI Deal," *Washington Post*, February 17, 1999, http://www.washington post.com/wp-srv/washtech/longterm/att_tci/att_tci.htm (accessed March 11, 2006); "News Corp./Chris-Craft Merger Finalized," July 25, 2001, http://www.pbs.org/newshour/media/media_watch/ july-dec01/chriscraft_7–25.html (accessed March 11, 2006). Anticipating the passage of the law and its pro–big media orientation, the Walt Disney Company took over the ABC Network (and its parent Capital Cities) in 1995 for $19 billion. See John R. Wilke, "Tribune Co. Deal Puts Regulatory Ban on Cross-Ownership in the Cross Hairs," *Wall Street Journal*, March 14, 2000.

16. Common Cause Education Fund, "The Fallout from the Telecommunications Act of 1996: Unintended Consequences and Lessons Learned," May 9, 2005, http://www.commoncause.org/atf/cf/

%7BFB3C17E2-CDD1-4DF6-92BE-BD4429893665%7D/FALLOUT
_FROM_THE_TELECOMM_ACT_5-9-05.PDF (accessed February
10, 2006).

17. Common Cause Education Fund, "The Fallout from the Telecommunications Act of 1996."

18. Common Cause Education Fund, "The Fallout from the Telecommunications Act of 1996." See also "Testimony of James Cullen,
Communications Reform Act of 1993, House Committee on the Ju-
diciary, Economic and Commercial Law Subcommittee, February 2,
1994," http://www.eff.org/Infrastructure/Govt_docs/hr3626_ jc-ecls
.testimony (accessed February 10, 2006); Patricia Aufderheide, *Communications Policy and the Public Interest: The Telecommunications Act of
1996* (New York: Guilford Press, 1999).

19. George Gilder, "The Freedom Model of Telecommunications,"
Progress and Freedom Foundation, March 1995, http://www
.pff.org/issues-pubs/other/950301freedommodel.html (accessed February 10, 2006). This article was adopted from Gilder's Senate Commerce Committee testimony of March 2, 1995. See also George
Gilder, "The Shattering of the Cable TV Monopoly," *American Civilization*, February 1995.

20. Heilemann, "The Making of the President 2000." Gilder was one of
the co-authors, along with Esther Dyson, George Keyworth, and
Alvin Toffler, of "Cyberspace and the American Dream: A Magna
Carta for the Knowledge Age," August 1994, http://www.pff.org/
issues-pubs/futureinsights/fi1.2magnacarta.html (accessed May 31,
2006). See also George A. Keyworth II, Jeffrey Eisenach, Thomas
Lenard, and David E. Colton, "The Telecom Revolution: An American Opportunity," Progress and Freedom Foundation, May 1995,
summary at http://www.pff.org/issues-pubs/other/950501telecom
revolution.html (accessed February 10, 2006). A chorus of conservative think tanks, including the Heritage Foundation, Citizens for a
Sound Economy, and the PFF, weighed in, along with the editorial
page of the *Wall Street Journal*.

21. Mike Mills, "Meeting of the Media Giants; Executives and Republicans Trade Views on Telecommunications Law," *Washington Post*, January 21, 1995.

22. Ken Auletta, "Pay Per Views," *New Yorker*, June 5, 1995, http://
www.kenauletta.com/payperviews.html (accessed February 10, 2006).
At the time, Gingrich was under fire for accepting a $4.5 million book
contract advance from Murdoch's HarperCollins press. Gingrich was
forced to turn down the advance. During the controversy, Gingrich
helped organize what was supposed to be a stealth meeting with me-

dia CEOs. See Michael Ross, "Gingrich Defends Book Deal," *Pitts-burgh Post-Gazette*, January 20, 1995.

23. Dean Alger, *Megamedia: How Giant Corporations Dominate Mass Media, Distort Competition, and Endanger Democracy* (Lanham, MD: Rowman and Littlefield, 1998). See also J.H. Snider, *Speak Softly and Carry a Big Stick: How Local TV Broadcasters Exert Political Power* (New York: iUniverse, 2005), 439.

24. The author talked to numerous reporters while working to get coverage of the Telecom Act. A number of journalists were candid about their conflicts due to their own outlet's involvement with the bill. There was also concern about what ownership changes might bring, including a perceptible anxiety that a potential new owner might disapprove of their now-new employees having written critically of the proposed law.

25. Mike Mills, "Convergence of the Data Highway; Gingrich Echoes Some Themes at Technology Conference," *Washington Post*, January 11, 1995; Mills, "Meeting of the Media Giants."

26. The increase in corporate political cash "reflects what was among the most expensive and contentious lobbying wars ever waged on Capital Hill." Findings from a study conducted for the *Post* by the Campaign Study Group in 1998 reported that "the nation's local, long-distance and wireless phone companies have spent $166 million on legislative and regulatory lobbying since 1996—more than the tobacco, aerospace and gambling combined." As noted by *Post* reporter Mills, "Lobbying spending and campaign-giving levels only rose higher after the Telecommunications Act became law on February 8, 1996." Mike Mills, "Telecom's Lavish Spending on Lobbying," *Washington Post*, December 6, 1998. The big cable and broadcast companies, of course, also piled on the cash. To help win deregulation for the cable industry during the 1994 and 1996 election cycles, cable giant TCI, the NCTA, Turner Broadcasting, and Comcast poured money into the coffers of federal candidates for office and the political parties. They gave mostly to the GOP, now in control of Congress. Cable's totals were more than $7 million. For the 1994 and 1996 cycles, the NAB and companies holding TV and radio stations doled out $3.7 million; the NAB alone contributed $1.1 million. During the same period, the top contributors from the TV, motion picture, and music businesses gave nearly $30 million. Contribution figures are from the Center for Responsive Politics, http://www.opensecrets.org/ (accessed March 12, 2006).

27. See the congressional testimony from broadcasting officials for an illustration of their agenda to eliminate media ownership limits. See, for

example, "Statement of Ron Loewen, Cosmos Broadcasting Corporation, before the U.S. Senate Committee on Commerce, Science, and Transportation," March 17, 1994; "Testimony of Bertram Ellis, Ellis Communications, before the Committee on Commerce, Science, and Transportation," March 21, 1995; "Testimony of John Siegel, Senior Vice President, Chris-Craft United Television, before the U.S. Senate Committee on Commerce, Science, and Transportation," March 17, 1994.

28. Ownership by persons of color of broadcast outlets had been, and still is, insignificant. Larry Irving, "The Big Chill: Has Minority Ownership Been Put on Ice?" September 11, 1997, http://www.ntia.doc.gov/ntiahome/speeches/91197nabob.htm (accessed February 10, 2006). See also National Telecommunications and Information Administration, "Minority Commercial Broadcast Ownership Overview," August 1997, http://www.ntia.doc.gov/reports/97minority/overview.htm (accessed February 10, 2006).

29. Henry Geller, "Multiple Ownership Policies and the Public Interest," Center for Digital Democracy, October 2002, http://www.democraticmedia.org/issues/mediaownership/multipleOwnershipPolicies.html (accessed February 10, 2006).

30. Brian Lamb, "An Accidental Victim: Greed Is the Culprit—Effects of New Telecommunications Law on C-SPAN and C-SPAN2, Nonprofit News and Public Affairs Television Networks," *Washington Monthly*, March 1997, http://www.findarticles.com/p/articles/mi_m1316/is_n3_v29/ai_19189452 (accessed March 11, 2006). Disney relied on retransmission consent to help it launch ESPN 2 and its SoapNet channel. Marianne Paskowski, "NCTA 'Neutered' on Retrans Debate," *TV Week*, May 22, 2006, http://www.tvweek.com/article.cms?articleId=29855 (accessed May 31, 2006). Fox used retransmission consent to ensure cable carriage for its Fox Movie Channel. Testimony of James Robbins, Cox Communications, Hearing on Media Ownership, U.S. Senate Committee on Commerce, Science and Transportation, May 6, 2003, http://commerce.senate.gov/hearings/testimony.cfm?id=749&wit_id=2017 (accessed May 31, 2006). Instead of merely ensuring that local cable monopolies couldn't arbitrarily wreak havoc with a local TV station's signal, Congress was roped into a policy that made media concentration worse.

31. Steve Behrens, "Broadcasters Float Other Uses for HDTV Frequencies," *Current*, February 28, 1994, http://www.current.org/dtv/dtv404.html (accessed February 11, 2006). The third part of the strategy had to wait until 2005, as the NAB and others advanced digital must-carry proposals.

32. Dennis Wharton, "Fritts Predicts at NAB Meet: B'Casters Here to Stay," *Variety*, March 22, 1994; Dennis Wharton, "B'Casters Cut in Front on Infopike," *Variety*, March 11, 1994.

33. "Statement of Ron Loewen"; Charles Lewis, "Profiteering from Democracy: Broadcast Corporations and Their Capitol Hill Allies Killed President's Bid to Have Campaign Ads Air Free," Center for Public Integrity, August 30, 2000, http://www.publicintegrity.org/report.aspx?aid=478 (accessed February 11, 2006).

34. "Statement of Ron Loewen."

35. "Testimony of John Siegel."

36. No one raised the "bleed, it leads" newscasts, the handful of seconds station gave to local and statewide political coverage, let alone the lack of in-depth and investigative reporting that made much of local TV news a vast wasteland.

37. "Testimony of Bertram Ellis."

38. U.S. Census Bureau, "Communication Industry's Revenues Surpass $288 Billion in 1995, Census Bureau Reports," press release, December 11, 1996, http://www.census.gov/Press-Release/cb96-208.html (accessed February 11, 2006). Broadcasters also wanted Congress to protect them from competition from telephone company video services, and they wanted unfettered access to all electronic program guides and other "navigation" devices offered by cable and satellite services.

39. Edmund L. Andrews, "Digital TV, Dollars, and Dissent: The Political Battle Grows over the Use of New Broadcast Technology," *New York Times*, March 18, 1996.

40. "Statement of Decker Anstrom, National Cable Television Association, before the Committee on Commerce, Science, and Transportation, U.S Senate," March 21, 1995, cited in "Testimony of Gene Kimmelman, Co-Director, Consumers Union, before the Senate Committee on Commerce," June 19, 2001, http://www.consumersunion.org/telecom/localdc601.htm (accessed May 31, 2006).

41. The National Republican Congressional Campaign even held a seminar for new House members titled Seven Steps in Liquidating Your Debt and Building for the Future. David Maraniss and Michael Weisskopf, "Speaker and His Directors Make the Cash Flow Right," *Washington Post*, November 27, 1995, http://www.washingtonpost.com/wp-srv/politics/special/campfin/stories/cf112795.htm (accessed February 11, 2006).

42. Guy Gugliotta, "Sen. Pressler's Rise to Power Is Marked by PAC Generosity," *Washington Post*, September 21, 1996, http://www.washingtonpost.com/wp-srv/politics/special/oncall/stories/oc092196.htm (accessed February 11, 2006).

43. Edmund Andrews, "Big Guns Lobby for Long-Distance; Insiders Are Trying to Influence Bill," *Raleigh News and Observer*, March 28, 1995. Then House Telecommunications Subcommittee chair Jack Fields (R-TX) "collected nearly $100,000 in PAC contributions alone from telecommunications industry PACs." Overall, according to the *Washington Post*, the telecommunications industry became "one of the top sources of congressional and presidential campaign funds. Among the key telecom companies in such a generous mood were AT&T, Bell Atlantic, SBC, BellSouth, and Ameritech." Gugliotta, "Sen. Pressler's Rise to Power Is Marked by PAC Generosity." Senators John McCain and Ernest Hollings, the two top members of the Commerce Committee at the time, received the largest telecom donations. The Telecommunications Act was a full-employment bonanza for lobbyists. Michael Oxley (OH), a senior Republican member then of the House Commerce Committee, told the *New York Times* that "everybody in this town who has a pulse has been hired by the long-distance coalition or the Bell operating companies." Quoted in Edmund L. Andrews, "Phone Bill Brings out Big-Name Lobbyists," *New York Times*, March 20, 1995. For example, Gingrich raised $20,000 at the home of the Pacific Telesis CEO just two weeks before the House passed the bill that now aided Telesis and the other Bell companies. Maraniss and Weisskopf, "Speaker and His Directors Make the Cash Flow Right"; Mike Mills, "Telecommunications Industry Is More Politically Active Than Ever," *Washington Post*, December 6, 1998, http:// www.washingtonpost.com/wp-srv/politics/special/oncall/oncall.htm (accessed February 11, 2006).

44. Bill McConnell, "How to Win Friends and Influence People," *Broadcasting and Cable*, March 21, 2005, http://www.broadcastingcable .com/article/CA511779.html?display=Special+Report (accessed February 11, 2006); Neil Hickey, "TV's Big Stick," *Columbia Journalism Review*, September–October 2002, http://archives.cjr.org/year/02/ 5/hickey.asp (accessed February 11, 2006); Charles Lewis, "Relaxing Media Ownership Rules Conflicts with the Public's Right to Know," Center for Public Integrity, January 16, 2003, http://www .publicintegrity.org/telecom/report.aspx?aid=96 (accessed May 31, 2006).

45. I also played a role, as executive director of the Center for Media Education, helping to muster whatever press coverage we could generate to pressure the administration to act more responsibly.

46. Alexandra Starr, "The Stiff Man Has a Spine," *Washington Monthly*, September 1999, http://www.washingtonmonthly.com/features/1999/ 9909.starr.gore.html (accessed February 11, 2006). For example, during

the 1995 Senate debate on S. 652 on June 8, McCain quoted from a Heritage Foundation report, a *Wall Street Journal* editorial, and cited a letter he received from Citizens for a Sound Economy. Debate on the "Telecommunications Competition and Deregulation Act," http://thomas.loc.gov/.

47. Mike Mills, "With the Bells on Their Toes," *Washington Post*, December 14, 1995, http://www.washingtonpost.com/wp-srv/politics/special/oncall/stories/oc121495.htm (accessed February 11, 2006).

48. Dole was promised that the digital TV issue would come up for later review. It didn't. In a telling statement reported in the *Washington Post*, Pressler told Dole that with every industry getting its fair share of the pickings, there would be "peace between these greedy, squabbling interests." Mike Mills, "A 'Camelot Moment' on Communications," *Washington Post*, February 4, 1996, http://www.washingtonpost.com/wp-srv/politics/special/oncall/stories/oc020496.htm (accessed February 11, 2006).

49. Quoted in Mike Mills, "Conferees, White House Agree on Telecommunications Reform," *Washington Post*, December 21, 1995, http://www.washingtonpost.com/wp-srv/politics/special/oncall/stories/oc122195.htm (accessed February 11, 2006).

50. Mike Mills, "Republicans Map out an Assault on FCC's Powers," *Washington Post*, April 13, 1995.

51. Neil Hickey, "So Big: The Telecommunications Act as Year One," *Columbia Journalism Review*, January–February 1997, http://archives.cjr.org/year/97/1/telecom.asp (accessed February 11, 2006).

52. "Public Interest Issues in the Telecommunications Act of 1996," *Technos Quarterly* 5, no. 3 (Fall 1996), http://www.ait.net/technos/tq_05/3vedrosb.php (accessed February 11, 2006); Michael W. Lynch, "The Good Soldier," *Reason*, January 1999, http://reason.com/9901/fe.ml.thegood.shtml (accessed February 11, 2006); Mills, "Conferees, White House Agree on Telecommunications Reform."

53. Mills, "A 'Camelot Moment' on Communications."

54. Federal Communications Commission, "In the Matter of Implementation of Sections 204(a) and 204(c) of the Telecommunications Act of 1996 (Broadcast License Renewal Procedures)," August 30, 2000, http://www.fcc.gov/Bureaus/Mass_Media/Orders/1996/fcc96172.txt (accessed February 11, 2006).

55. The ranking Democrat on the House Telecommunications Subcommittee, Edward Markey, helped frame the debate about what would be lost with the bill. Reacting to the lobbying from the telecom giants, he told *Time* that "consumers will wind up tipped upside down, with the money shaken out of their pockets to subsidize the deregulatory

dreams of the largest monopolies in the country. The fiber-optic barons are in control." John Greenwald, "Ready, Willing, Cable," *Time*, July 31, 1995, http://205.188.238.109/time/archive/preview/0,10987,134483,00.html (accessed February 11, 2006).

56. Alicia Mundy, "Put the Blame on Peggy, Boys," *Cableworld*, June 30, 2003, http://www.findarticles.com/p/articles/mi_m0DIZ/is_26_15/ai_104512683 (accessed May 31, 2006).

57. Section 202 of the Telecommunications Act of 1996, http://thomas.loc.gov/cgi-bin/query/z?c106:S.1577:.

58. Al Gore co-founded Current TV. Maria Saporta, "Gingrich Still Opining . . . as Tech Consultant," *Atlanta Journal-Constitution*, May 30, 2001. Fields helped establish the Twenty-First Century Group, which lobbies on telecom issues. "Congress Honors Former Congressman Jack Fields," press release, January 24, 2005, http://www.house.gov/brady/PressArchives/2005/JackFieldsPO.html (accessed February 11, 2006). Pressler serves on tech boards. Senator Pressler.com, http://www.larrypressler.com/boards.html (accessed February 11, 2006). Susan Crabtree, "Nixed by Tauzin, MPAA's Browsin'," *Variety*, January 23, 2004, http://www.variety.com/article/VR1117898961?categoryid=1064&cs=1 (accessed February 11, 2006).

3. The Federal Conglomeration Commission

1. The lobbying expenditures were tallied by the Center for Responsive Politics based on spending for communications and electronics. See "Lobbyist Spending: Communic/Electronics," Opensecrets.org, http://www.opensecrets.org/lobbyists/indus.asp?Ind=B&year=2000 (accessed February 5, 2006). The list of fifty most successful lobbying firms for 2004 was compiled by *Influence* magazine. "The Influence 50," *Influence*, March 16, 2005. See also Judy Sarasohn, "For Lobbyists, the $65 Million List," *Washington Post*, March 17, 2005, http://www.washingtonpost.com/wp-dyn/articles/A42041-2005Mar16.html (accessed March 13, 2006).

2. There was even some scandal involving political allies of former vice president Gore in how the FCC ended up at the Portals. See James Ridgeway, "The Veep and the Big Creep," *Village Voice*, September 23–29, 1998, http://www.villagevoice.com/news/9839,ridgeway,658,1.html (accessed February 5, 2006). Details about the Portals can be found at Republic Properties Corporation, http://www.republicpropertiescorp.com/the_portals.htm (accessed February 5, 2006).

3. Two former commissioners come to mind. Nicholas Johnson served from 1966 until 1973, and was an outspoken public-interest advocate

during his tenure. His book *How to Talk Back to Your Television Set* (New York: Bantam Books, 1970) was a primer for media reform advocacy. Johnson continued to advocate for change as a professor at the University of Iowa College of Law. Gloria Tristani, who served from 1997 to 2001 and was appointed by President Clinton, has been determined to work for public-interest-related efforts and has steadfastly avoided media industry employment.

4. For example, the Clinton administration and its FCC were fearful of taking on the powerful broadcast lobby. During the term of FCC Chair William E. Kennard, a number of media reform groups, including my own, urged the administration to support public-interest policies for digital TV. We were asked by a top communications policy aide to Vice President Al Gore "what was the low-hanging fruit" that could be asked of broadcasters in return for their gift of $470 billion in airwaves. A few weeks later, our group met with Kennard's chief of staff. She also asked us to tell her "what the low-hanging fruit was" that could be asked of the broadcasters. It was clear that the broadcast interests had so intimidated the administration and the FCC that nothing could be done to provide the public any kind of quid pro quo in return for one of the biggest government giveaways to corporate interests.

5. Center for Public Integrity, *Networks of Influence* (Washington, DC: Center for Public Integrity, 2005), 7–8.

6. Minow also did much nonprofit-related work, including at PBS and the Carnegie Corporation. But his principal employment remained with Sidley and Austin (now Sidley, Austin, Brown & Wood), which has a significant media and communications practice. See the profile of Newton Minow on the Museum of Broadcast Communications Web site, http://www.museum.tv/archives/etv/M/htmlM/minownewton/minownewton.htm (accessed February 5, 2006).

7. Henry Geller, former general counsel of the FCC, personal communication, 2004.

8. "Firm Overview," Wiley Rein & Fielding, http://www.wrf.com/about.cfm (accessed February 5, 2006).

9. Stephen Labaton, "Behind Media Rule and Its End, One Man," *New York Times*, June 2, 2003.

10. Labaton, "Behind Media Rule."

11. See, for example, Frank Ahrens, "FCC Sees Local Gain to Age of Max Media," *Washington Post*, May 15, 2003, http://www.washingtonpost.com/ac2/wp-dyn/A61585-2003May15 (accessed March 11, 2006).

12. For Ferris's biography, see http://www.mintz.com/about/directory/

biography/159/Charles_D_Ferris (accessed September 3, 2005). See also "Telecommunications and Media," Mintz Levin, http://www.mintz.com/expertise/industries/17/Telecom_and_ Media/ (accessed September 3, 2005); "Bush and Kerry Fundraisers: What Have they Gotten, and What Do They Want?" Common Cause, http://www.commoncause.org/site/pp.asp?c=dkLNK1MQIwG&b=196565 (accessed September 3, 2005).

13. For Cameron Kerry's biography, see http://www.mintz.com/about/directory/biography/262/Cameron_F_Kerry/ (accessed November 24, 2003).

14. For a list of lobbying clients and related expenditures, see "Well-Connected," Center for Public Integrity, http://www.publicintegrity.org/telecom/analysis/InfluenceTracker.aspx?MODE=LOBBY&LID=L002197 (accessed February 5, 2006).

15. For Fowler's biography, see https://www.talk.com/web.cgi/user/talkaboutboardofdirectors.htm (accessed September 4, 2005). See also Drew Clark, "Just Another Toaster," NationalJournal.com, October 3, 2005, http://www.drewclark.com/wiredinwashington/20051003.htm (accessed February 5, 2006).

16. For Patrick's biography, see "Three New Trustees Appointed to National Geographic Board," NationalGeographic.com, April 1999, http://www.nationalgeographic.com/events/releases/pr990406c.html (accessed November 24, 2003).

17. For Sikes's biography, see http://www.cymfony.com/abt_bdr.asp#acs (accessed February 5, 2006).

18. For Quello's biography, see http://www.radiohof.org/executive/jamesquello.html (accessed February 5, 2006). For a list of Quello Center donors, see http://quello.msu.edu/annualreports/2002Annual Report.pdf (accessed February 5, 2006). See also "Former FCC Commissioner James H. Quello Joins Wiley Rein & Fielding LLP as Government Affairs Consultant," press release, August 22, 2001, http://www.wrf.com/press_release.cfm?press_release_id=2059 (accessed February 5, 2006).

19. Stephen Labaton, "Is Antitrust No Longer the Issue?" *New York Times*, March 7, 2006; Arshad Mohammed, "The Titans of Telecom Face Off," *Washington Post*, March 7, 2006. For Hundt's biography, see http://www.intel.com/pressroom/kits/bios/bod_rehundt.htm (accessed March 7, 2006).

20. For Kennard's biography, see http://www.thecarlylegroup.com/eng/team/15-team1049.html (accessed February 5, 2006).

21. The author spoke to FCC staff during the agency's review of both

mergers. It was clear that they were not following the companies involved or industry developments.

22. Various FCBA events are organized to raise money for scholarships. But for a part of the legal industry that rakes in tens of millions of dollars for its firms, the FCBA provided a mere $150,000 to students in 2004. Major media and telecommunications companies supplied a great deal of that money, fixing their name to the academic bequest. This way, deserving high school students and their parents readily understood the largesse of BellSouth, Comcast, Microsoft, and Sprint. See the FCBA Web site at http://www.fcba.org (accessed February 5, 2006).

23. Ted Hearn, "Trade Group Seeks New Lobbyist," *Multichannel News*, January 15, 2001; "Wiley Rein & Fielding Announces Six New Partners," press release, December 29, 2003, http://www.wrf.com/press_release.cfm?press_release_id=1267 (accessed February 5, 2006).

24. Sara Miles, "Do YOU Know Tony Podesta?" *Wired*, December 1998, http://www.wired.com/wired/archive/6.12/podesta.html (accessed February 5, 2006).

25. Center for Public Integrity, *Networks of Influence*, 1–20.

26. Center for Responsive Politics, "TV/Movies/Music: PAC Contributions to Federal Candidates, 2003–2004," Opensecrets.org, http://www.crp.org/pacs/industry.asp?txt=B02&cycle=2004 (accessed February 5, 2006).

27. "Regulatory Resources," National Association of Broadcasters, http://www.nab.org/membership/regulres.asp (accessed February 5, 2006); "Your Voice on Capital Hill," National Association of Broadcasters, http://www.nab.org/membership/voiceonhill.asp (accessed February 5, 2006). See also Center for Responsive Politics, "TV/Movies/Music."

28. Bob Williams and Morgan Jindrich, "On the Road Again—and Again: FCC Officials Rack up $2.8 Million Travel Tab with Industries They Regulate," Center for Public Integrity, May 22, 2003, http://www.publicintegrity.org/telecom/report.aspx?aid=15 (accessed February 5, 2006).

29. David Hatch, "Hollywood Cash and Kerry," *Broadcasting and Cable*, February 9, 2004; Douglas McCollam, "Band in Boston," *Influence*, June 30, 2004.

30. On Mitchell and Disney, see http://corporate.disney.go.com/corporate/bios/george_mitchell.html (accessed March 12, 2006). On Nunn and General Electric, see http://www.ge.com/en/company/companyinfo/executivebios/nunn.htm (accessed March 12, 2006).

31. For Rodin's biography, see http://www.cmcsk.com/phoenix.zhtml ?c=118591&p=irol-govBoard (accessed February 5, 2006).
32. For Hills's biography, see http://www.timewarner.com/corp/corp _governance/board_directors/bio/hills_carla.html (accessed February 5, 2006).
33. For Tyson's biography, see http://www.newscorp.com/news/news _074.html (accessed February 5, 2006).

4. The Art of the Front

1. The PFF Web site (http://www.pff.org/) provides a good overview of the organization's past and current activities. See also "Issues and Publications," http://pff.org/issues%2Dpubs/ (accessed February 8, 2006).
2. Kyle D. Dixon, Raymond L. Gifford, Thomas M. Lenard, Randolph J. May, and Adam M. Peters, "A Digital Age Communications Act: Essays on the Need for Communications Policy Reform," Progress and Freedom Foundation, 2005, http://www.pff.org/daca/ 050201dacaessays.pdf (accessed February 2, 2005).
3. For a listing of PFF supporters, see http://www.pff.org/about/ supporters.html (accessed February 2, 2005). The PFF's self-described role in defense of "property rights" in "the age of the computer and the Internet" has also pleased its many technology supporters, including Apple, Amazon, Cisco, the Entertainment Software Association, Hewlett-Packard, Intel, BMG, EMI, Sony Music, and Vivendi Universal.
4. For Shelanski's bio, see http://www.pff.org/daca/workinggroups .html#shelanski (accessed February 8, 2006). For Shelanski's work with cable, see "NCTA Files Reply Comments with FCC regarding Cable Ownership Rules," National Cable & Telecommunications Association, press release, February 19, 2002, http://www.ncta.com/ press/press.cfm?PRid=232&showArticles=ok (accessed February 8, 2006).
5. For Wilkie's bio, see http://www.pff.org/daca/workinggroups .html#wilkie, http://www.ersgroup.com/Affiliate_ displayBio.asp?Bio ID=16 (both accessed February 8, 2006).
6. Progress and Freedom Foundation IRS Form 990, 2003.
7. For Keyworth's bio, see http://sciencepolicy.colorado.edu/science advisors/keyworth.html (accessed May 6, 2006).
8. For Miller's bio, see http://www.pff.org/about/board.html#miller (accessed February 8, 2006). For background on Howrey Simon Arnold & White, see http://www.vault.com/companies/whyus/

whyus_main.jsp?wu_page=2&ch_id=242&product_id=6806&tabnum
=6 (accessed February 8, 2006).

9. For Eisenach's bio, see http://www.pff.org/about/board.html#jeff
(accessed February 8, 2006).
10. For Dixon's bio, see http://www.pff.org/news/news/2004/072604
kyledixon.html (accessed February 8, 2006).
11. "The Federal Institute for Regulatory Law and Economics," Progress
and Freedom Foundation, http://www.pff.org/firle/ (accessed February
8, 2006).
12. For a list of Silicon Flatirons supporters, see http://www.silicon
flatirons.org/board.html (accessed February 8, 2006).
13. The Koch Foundation also sponsors work done by the conservative
State Policy Network (SPN). The PFF is a regular participant at SPN
briefings. See http://www.spn.org/events/eventID.12/event_detail.asp
and http://www.spn.org/directory/orgid.106/org_detail.asp (accessed
June 1, 2006).
14. See Progress and Freedom Foundation, "The Digital Age Communications Act Project," February 2005, http://www.pff.org/daca/ (accessed February 8, 2006).
15. For Cato's current board of directors, see http://www.Cato.org/
people/directors.html (accessed February 8, 2006).
16. Cato also has financial support from the conservative foundation universe that regularly underwrites pro–big business interests, including
the Scaife and Coors families. For a listing of Cato's corporate and
foundation supporters, see http://www.Cato.org/sponsors/sponsors
.html (accessed February 8, 2006).
17. For Corn-Revere's bio, see http://www.dwt.com/lawdir/attorneys/
CornRevereRobert.cfm (accessed February 8, 2006) and http://
www.cato.org/people/corn-revere.html (accessed June 1, 2006).
18. "About Us," Communications Industry Researchers, http://www.cir-
inc.com/info/about.cfm#clientele (accessed February 8, 2006), http://
www.cato.org/people/gasman.html (accessed June 1, 2006).
19. For Simon's bio, see http://www.idi.net/about/staff/simon.vtml (accessed February 8, 2006).
20. For a list of IDI's clients, see http://www.idi.net/about/clients.vtml
(accessed February 8, 2006).
21. For a description of IDI's Internet Monitoring, see http://www
.idi.net/research/monitoring.vtml (accessed February 8, 2006).
22. "About Us," Issue Dynamics, Inc., http://www.idi.net/about/ (accessed February 8, 2006).
23. For a listing of APT's supporters, see http://www.apt.org/about/
sponafflt.html (accessed February 8, 2006).

24. Alliance for Public Technology, IRS Form 990, 2002–3.
25. For a listing of the Black Leadership Forum's sponsors, see http://www.blackleadershipforum.org/sponsors.html; for a listing of the league's 2004 contributors, see http://www.lulac.org/publications/annualreport2004.pdf; for the American Association of People with Disabilities' funders, see http://www.aapd-dc.org/annualreport/annreport03.html (all accessed February 8, 2006).
26. Chris Stern, "WorldCom Opponents in Sync: D.C. Firm Helps Organize Protest," *Washington Post*, June 20, 2003.
27. Quoted in Russell Mokhiber and Robert Weissman, "Grannies and Baby Bells: The Gray Panthers' Corporate Connection," *Counterpunch*, June 20, 2003, http://www.counterpunch.org/mokhiber06202003.html (accessed March 12, 2006).
28. "About the NMRC," New Millennium Research Council, http://www.newmillenniumresearch.org/ (accessed February 8, 2006); Carol Ellision, "Municipal Wi-Fi: Let's Keep It Local," *eWeek*, February 3, 2005, http://www.eweek.com/article2/0,1759,1759677,00.asp (accessed February 8, 2006).
29. Diane Carol Best, "The Heartlander: October 2004," *Heartlander*, October 1, 2004, http://www.heartland.org/Article.cfm?artId=15759 (accessed June 1, 2006).
30. Joseph L. Bast, "Municipally Owned Broadband Networks: A Critical Evaluation," *Heartland Policy Study*, October 22, 2004, http://www.heartland.org/article.cfm?artId=15842 (accessed February 8, 2006).
31. For a list of members of the State Policy Network, see http://www.spn.org/newsite/main/organizations_search.php (accessed February 8, 2006).
32. Discovery Institute, IRS Form 990, 2002. Discovery has also long been associated with the Internet Law and Policy Forum. See http://www.ilpf.org/about/, http://www.ilpf.org/about/1998sep30.htm, and http://www.ilpf.org/about/1997jun23.htm (all accessed June 1, 2006).
33. "Armey Accused of Retaliating against Paper," UPI, October 7, 2002, http://www.upi.com/inc/view.php?StoryID=20021007-111802-8944r (accessed February 8, 2006).
34. "FreedomWorks Launches Kansas Campaign to Increase Cable Choice," press release, February 3, 2006, http://www.freedomworks.org/newsroom/press_template.php?press_id=1657 (accessed February 8, 2006); Drew Clark, "Franchising Issue Leads to Accusations of 'Front Groups,'" *National Journal*, November 10, 2006, http://64.233.179.104/search?q=cache:4y_6YmQeOfoJ:www.njtelecomupdate

.com/lenya/telco/live/tb-KHUU1132002307865.html+Freedomworks
,+corporate+sponsors&hl=en&gl=us&ct=clnk&cd=4 (accessed February 8, 2006).

35. The Media Institute had revenues in 2002 of more than $600,000, according to its IRS Form 990.

36. The Cornerstone Project, http://www.mediainstitute.org/cornerstone/ (accessed February 8, 2006).

37. For a list of the Media Institute's trustees and advisory councils, see http://www.mediainstitute.org/tac.html (accessed February 8, 2006).

38. For a listing of the institute's advocacy activities, see http://www.mediainstitute.org/broadcast.html (accessed February 8, 2006).

39. Brock N. Meeks, "Berman's Bailout," *Wired*, March 1995, http://www.wired.com/wired/archive/3.03/eword.html?pg=8 (accessed February 8, 2006). My organization is a tenant of the Electronic Privacy Information Center, a public-interest group that has often been at odds with the CDT over its policy positions. When I ran the Center for Media Education during the 1990s, I was also critical of the CDT's stance on issues, including online privacy. But my analysis here has nothing to do with my relationship as a tenant.

40. Foundations have also funded the CDT. But it could not operate without its corporate support. Foundation funding has been used to give the group the appearance of legitimacy. See the CDT's funding page at http://www.cdt.org/mission/funding.php (accessed February 8, 2006). Center for Democracy and Technology, IRS Form 990, 2002.

41. Internet Education Foundation, http://www.neted.org/ (accessed February 8, 2006).

42. See the Institute for Policy Innovation and Heartland link at http://www.heartland.org/Article.cfm?artId=16184 (accessed February 8, 2006). See also Philip Shenon, "On Opinion Page, Lobby's Hand Is Often Unseen," *New York Times*, December 23, 2005, http://www.commondreams.org/headlines05/1223-03.htm (accessed June 1, 2006).

43. For members of the IEF's Internet Caucus Advisory Committee, see http://www.netcaucus.org/advisory/ (accessed March 7, 2006). For the IEF's board, see http://www.neted.org/members/ (accessed March 7, 2006).

44. The Internet Education Foundation, IRS Form 990, 2003.

45. For congressional members of the Internet Caucus, see http://www.netcaucus.org/members/ (accessed February 8, 2006). For members of its Advisory Committee, see http://www.netcaucus.org/advisory/ (accessed February 8, 2006). For a schedule of Internet Caucus events, see http://www.netcaucus.org/events/ (accessed Feb-

ruary 8, 2006). See also the CDT's discussion of the creation of the caucus: "CDT Policy Post," March 29, 1996, http://www.cdt.org/ publications/pp_2.13.html (accessed February 8, 2006).

46. "New AOL Time Warner Foundation Established; Company Plans Initiatives for 21st Century Literacy, Digital Opportunity, the Arts and Community Engagement," press release, NIFL Technology, January 12, 2001, http://www.nifl.gov/nifl-technology/2001/0030.html (accessed February 8, 2006).

47. "Civilrights.org Puts the Power of the Internet behind the Civil Rights Community," press release, July 26, 2001, http://trace .wisc.edu:8080/mailarchive/techwatch/msg00145.shtml (accessed February 8, 2006). The Leadership Conference still lists the AOL Time Warner Foundation as its Web site sponsor at http://www.civil rights.org/about/civilrights/site_sponsors.html (accessed September 9, 2005). John Dunbar, "Anatomy of a Lobbying Blitz," Center for Public Integrity, October 8, 2004, http://www.publicintegrity.org/ telecom/report.aspx?aid=395 (accessed June 1, 2006).

48. "Microsoft and Co-Sponsor Dell and AOL Time Warner to Sponsor Technology Town Hall at NCLR Annual Conference," press release, National Conference of La Raza, July 9, 2003, http://www.nclr.org/ content/news/detail/2366 (accessed February 8, 2006). To further advance their interests with civil rights groups, the AOL foundation also hired a former official of the National Urban League as "Vice President of the AOL Time Warner Foundation and as senior director of Social Innovations for AOL Time Warner's Corporate Relations division." "One-on-One with AOL Time Warner Foundation's B. Keith Fulton," HUD's Neighborhood Networks, June 25, 2002, http:// www-domino4.hud.gov/NN/nn_news.nsf/0/8b6fd745b11dd7428 5256bf000553418?OpenDocument (accessed February 8, 2006).

49. "AOL Launches Philanthropy Portal," *E-Commerce Times*, October 20, 1999, http://www.ecommercetimes.com/story/1505.html (accessed February 8, 2006). "Supporters," Network for Good, http://www .networkforgood.org/about/ (accessed February 8, 2006). "Internet, Nonprofit Leaders Launch 'Network for Good' to Support Local and National Charities," press release, November 19, 2001, http://www .networkforgood.org/about/press/pressreleases/2001/11 -19.aspx (accessed February 8, 2006).

50. For a list of Independent Sector members, see http://www .independentsector.org/members/MemberbyType.asp?category=C (accessed September 11, 2005).

51. For architectural drawings of the proposed building for UCSB's Center for Film, Television, and New Media, see http://www

.cftnm.ucsb.edu/about.html (accessed February 8, 2006). For the advisory board, see http://www.cftnm.ucsb.edu/people/advisory _board.html (accessed February 8, 2006). The building project eventually received a number of major donations.

52. "About Us—Overview," MIT Media Lab, http://www.media.mit .edu/about/index.html (accessed February 8, 2006). For a list of Media Lab sponsors, see http://www.media.mit.edu/sponsors/sponsors .html (accessed February 8, 2006).

53. The Center eventually launched a series of media ownership-related lectures and meetings; see http://www.cftnm.ucsb.edu/conference/ index.html (accessed June 1, 2006). For a list of funders of USC's Center for the Digital Future, see http://www.digitalcenter.org/ pages/site_content.asp?intGlobalId=21 (accessed February 8, 2006). For a listing of USC Annenberg's Board of Councilors, see http:// ascweb.usc.edu/asc.php?pageID=141 (accessed February 8, 2006). UCLA's School of Theater, Film, and Television has a well-connected industry advisory group; see http://www.tft.ucla.edu/advisory_ab/ (accessed June 1, 2006).

54. Bruce M. Owen, Michael G. Baumann, and Kent W. Mikkelsen, "Affiliate Clearances, Retransmission Agreements, Bargaining Power, and the Media Ownership Rules," April 21, 2003, filed at the FCC on behalf of Fox, NBC/Telemundo, and Viacom. FCC Docket 02–277. For Owen's biography, see http://www.ei.com/bio_bruce_owen.html (accessed March 12, 2006). Owen's Economists, Inc. represents many media and telecom clients. See, for example, http://www.ei.com/ massmedia.html and http://www.ei.com/telecom.html (both accessed March 12, 2006).

55. For the New Millennium Research Council and its relationship to IDI, see http://newmillenniumresearch.org/about/ (accessed February 8, 2006). Compaine does have a Web site that lists such affiliations. But in his academic work, such relationships aren't well-defined. See http://www1.primushost.com/~bcompain/ (accessed February 8, 2006). For example, see "New Study Debunks U.S. 'Media Monopoly' Fears, Finds Choices for Consumers Are Growing, Not Shrinking," New Millennium Research Council press release, May 4, 2005, http://www.newmillenniumresearch.org/news/ (accessed June 1, 2006).

56. Ted Hearn, "Study Slams Cooper's Cable Research," *Multichannel News*, August 26, 2003. Ted Hearn, "Comcast Stakes a Counterclaim," *Multichannel News*, September 1, 2003. For Michael Katz's curriculum vitae, see http://www.haas.berkeley.edu/faculty/katz.html (accessed February 8, 2006).

57. Michael Katz, "An Economic Analysis of the Claims Made by Dr. Mark Cooper in 'Cable Mergers, Monopoly Power, and Price Increases,'" commissioned by Comcast Corporation, July 28, 2003. Haas School supporters at the time included the firms backing consolidation, including Morgan Stanley, SBC, Citicorp, General Electric, and Merrill Lynch. Annual Report of Private Giving, Haas School of Business, University of California at Berkeley, 2003–4, http://www.haas.berkeley.edu/alumni/giving/anreport.html (accessed February 8, 2006). Disclosure: Katz's hired report for Comcast criticized the methodology used by my colleague Mark Cooper of the Consumer Federation of America. My criticism of Katz and other academics concerns the process of taking money from media companies and not carefully explaining the full range of financial relationships.

58. Center for Telecommunications and Digital Convergence, http://groups.haas.berkeley.edu/fcsuit/ctdc.html (accessed February 8, 2006).

59. Advocates lobbying on an ongoing FCC proceeding who meet with commissioners or staff are required to file what are called ex parte comments about the substance of their conversations. Ex parte presentation of Victor B. Miller IV and Richard E. Wiley. Review of the FCC's Broadcast Ownership Rules, MB Docket No. 02–277, April 7, 2003, filed by Wiley Rein & Fielding. Ex parte presentation of Victor B. Miller IV. Review of the FCC's Broadcast Ownership Rules, MB Docket No. 02–277, May 2, 2003, filed by Wiley Rein & Fielding. Mark Wigfield, "Bear Stearns Analyst Helps FCC Reshape Ownership Rules," *Wall Street Journal*, June 2, 2003. Victor B. Miller, ex parte filings, Review of the FCC's Broadcast Ownership Rules, February 2, 2003, and May 28, 2003.

5. The Powell Doctrine

1. Eric Boehlert, "The Media Borg's Man in Washington," *Salon*, August 6, 2001, http://www.salon.com/tech/feature/2001/08/06/powell/?sid=1043664 (accessed February 16, 2006).

2. Seth Schiesel, "At F.C.C. Confirmation Hearings, Emphasis Will Be on Competition," *New York Times*, September 29, 1997.

3. James R. Dukart, "Powell Power: New FCC Commissioner Takes First Restrained Steps," Telephony Online, November 24, 1997, http://telephonyonline.com/mag/telecom_powell_power_new/index.html (accessed February 16, 2006).

4. "Separate Statement of Commissioner Michael K. Powell," June 20,

2000, http://www.fcc.gov/Speeches/Powell/Statements/2000/stmkp013 .html (accessed February 16, 2006).

5. Michael K. Powell, "The Great Digital Broadband Migration," remarks before the Progress and Freedom Foundation, December 8, 2000, http://www.fcc.gov/Speeches/Powell/2000/spmkp003.html (accessed February 16, 2006). Powell also favorably cited in the speech a market guru named Clayton Christensen, who spoke of "disrupting technologies." A small new company could easily eat a large competitor's market share, claimed Christensen, reflecting the mantra held then that start-up dot-coms could soon undermine major corporate empires. Such perspectives were soothing to the ears of the communications industry, which wanted the incoming Bush administration to do away with much of the commission's rules and regulations. See Christensen's Web site at www.disruptivetechnologies.com (accessed November 13, 2003).

6. Brendan I. Koerner, "Michael Powell, Our First Black President?" *Village Voice*, August 8, 2001, http://www.alternet.org/story/11305.

7. Pamela McClintock, "GOP Calls on Youth to Log On at FCC," *Variety*, May 20, 2001; "Senate Commerce Committee Holds Hearing on Powell Nomination," *Tech Law Journal*, May 17, 2001, http://www .techlawjournal.com/telecom/20010517.asp (accessed February 16, 2006).

8. "Statement of Senator John McCain, Chairman, Senate Committee on Commerce, Science, and Transportation, Nomination of Michael Powell to be FCC Chairman," May 17, 2001 (accessed February 16, 2006).

9. Jube Shiver Jr., "New Chairman Could Lead FCC on a Very Different Path," *Los Angeles Times*, January 8, 2001.

10. Shiver, "New Chairman Could Lead FCC on a Very Different Path"; Boehlert, "The Media Borg's Man in Washington"; Kevin Taglang, "The Trib Eats the Times, But Who Cares?" Headlines Extra, March 28, 2000, http://www.benton.org/news/extra/own032800.html (accessed 1 June 2006).

11. "The Powell and the Glory," *Guardian* (London), October 29, 2001, http://www.guardian.co.uk/waronterror/story/0,1361,582384,00.html (accessed February 16, 2006).

12. Shiver, "New Chairman Could Lead FCC on a Very Different Path"; Koerner, "Michael Powell, Our First Black President?"

13. Quoted in Stephen Labaton, "New F.C.C. Chief Would Curb Agency Reach," *New York Times*, February 7, 2001.

14. U.S. Department of Commerce, National Telecommunications and Information Administration, "A Nation Online: Entering the Broad-

band Age," executive summary, 2004, http://www.ntia.doc.gov/ntia home/digitaldivide/execsumfttn00.htm (accessed February 16, 2006). The report revealed that while 41.5 percent of all U.S. households enjoyed Internet access in August 2000, only 23.5 percent of black households and 23.6 percent of Hispanic households had Internet access.

15. To be fair, Powell's Democratic predecessor, Kennard—the agency's first African American chair—didn't pursue an agenda that would seriously redress such concerns either.

16. Boehlert, "The Media Borg's Man in Washington."

17. Stephen Labaton, "AT&T's Cable Deal: The Regulators; New Era in Washington Paves Way for This and Other Deals," *New York Times*, December 20, 2001. The one merger that the Bush FCC and Justice Department disapproved was the proposed Echostar takeover of DIRECTV. In that case, the only two competitors would have merged, a clear violation of antitrust principles even for the pro-business FCC. But a factor in the disapproval process was undoubtedly Murdoch, who launched a campaign to scuttle the merger so he could acquire DIRECTV for his News Corp. holdings.

18. The author's Center for Digital Democracy was one of the public-interest groups calling for open access rules for cable broadband. For Powell's statement, see "Separate Statement of Chairman Michael K. Powell," March 14, 2002, http://www.fcc.gov/Speeches/Powell/Statements/2002/stmkp204.html (accessed February 16, 2006).

19. Quoted in Jim Krane, "FCC's Powell Declares TiVo 'God's machine,'" Associated Press, January 10, 2003, http://www.sfgate.com/cgi-bin/article.cgi?file=/news/archive/2003/01/10/financial1802EST 0373.DTL (accessed March 12, 2006).

20. "FCC Chairman Michael Powell Announces Creation of Media Ownership Working Group," press release, October 29, 2001. This and other FCC media ownership documents are available at "Recent Actions," FCC, http://www.fcc.gov/ownership/documents.html (accessed February 16, 2006).

21. *Salon* cited the small number of media giants operating key online sites. Farhad Manjoo, "Can the Web Beat Big Media?" *Salon*, May 21, 2003, http://archive.salon.com/tech/feature/2003/05/21/web_vs_big _media/index_np.html (accessed February 16, 2006).

22. The Writers Guild of America had warned the FCC in January 2003 about the declining number of companies controlling both broadcast network and cable TV. Six controlled 70 percent of the total TV writing budget, for example. See "Writers Guild of America Calls on FCC to

Act on Behalf of TV Diversity and Creativity," Center for Digital Democracy, January 8, 2002, http://www.democraticmedia.org/news/ washingtonwatch/writersguild.html (accessed February 16, 2006).

23. *Associated Press v. United States*, 326 U.S. 1, 20 (1944). For a discussion of how the AP case framework influenced the creation of FCC safeguards, see Henry Geller, "Multiple Ownership Policies and the First Amendment," October 2002, http://www.democraticmedia.org/ issues/mediaownership/multipleOwnershipPolicies.html (accessed February 16, 2006).

24. Mark S. Fowler and Daniel L. Brenner, "A Marketplace Approach to Broadcast Regulation," *Texas Law Review* 60, no. 2 (1982).

6. Showdown at the FCC

1. Among the reasons that the reform movement disappeared was the loss of foundation funding. As the Reagan administration began slashing the federal budget that supported social programs, especially for low-income Americans, foundations spent more of their resources to address the impact of those cuts. Media policy advocacy, such as the funding of communications law programs, were understandably seen as less important than paying attention to the medical and economic needs of the public. Another reason for the cutbacks was the mistaken belief by some foundation officials that the so-called new technology at the time, specifically cable TV, would redress all media-related problems. These funders failed to understand that absent policy safeguards, new technology usually replicates the same old media problems. To the credit of their founders and leaders, groups such as Action for Children's Television and the Media Access Project survived and made critical, if lonely, efforts.

2. It's important to note that between 1981 and 1999, there were many public-interest victories. Despite meager resources, groups such as the Media Access Project, the Consumers Union, the Consumer Federation, and others were able to secure new safeguards, protect existing rules from evisceration, and the like. With each new media merger, these groups did what they could to ameliorate the worst proposals. But overall, the industry dominated the debate and policymaking. My own Center for Media Education helped play such a role, working to secure new policies for noncommercial satellite TV, online privacy, and children's educational broadcast programming.

3. Led by Andrew J. Schwartzman, the Media Access Project was the country's oldest public-interest law firm working on communications

issues. Its attorneys included Cheryl Leanza and Harold Feld.
Schwartzman and his colleagues were more knowledgeable about the
public-interest dimension of media policy than anyone in the country.
Gene Kimmelman, a legislative strategist as well as legal expert on
communications, ran the Washington, DC, office of the Consumers
Union (which publishes *Consumer Reports* magazine). Mark N.
Cooper, of the Consumer Federation of America, combined street-
smart advocacy with cutting-edge scholarship to provide research and
analysis. I played a role in helping reach out to other groups.

4. Michael J. Copps, "In Defense of the Public Interest," remarks of
commissioner Michael J. Copps before the Federal Communications
Bar Association, October 15, 2001, http://ftp.fcc.gov/Speeches/
Copps/2001/spmjc105.html (accessed February 17, 2006). Gloria
Tristani, a Democrat who served on the commission from 1997 to
2001, had also challenged Powell on media ownership and other issues. In a remarkable break from the corporate revolving door between the FCC and the media industry, Tristani sought out a
nonprofit public-interest job on leaving the commission. She eventually ran the Washington, DC, operations of one of the leading groups
concerned with media policy in the United States—the Office of
Communication of the United Church of Christ (http://www
.ucc.org/ocinc/).

5. "D.C. Circuit Decision Tips the Scale in Favor of Media Consolidation, against the Public," Media Access Project, February 19, 2002,
http://www.mediaaccess.org/press/foxownershippressrelease.html
(accessed February 17, 2006).

6. "FCC Initiates Third Biennial Review of Broadcast Ownership
Rules," press release, September 12, 2002, http://hraunfoss.fcc.gov/
edocs_public/attachmatch/DOC-226188A1.pdf (accessed February 17,
2006).

7. Ibid.

8. Comments of Kenneth Ferree, FCC, author's notes, June 2, 2003.

9. Federal Communications Commission, "Notice of Proposed Rulemaking, in the Matter of 2002 Biennial Regulatory Review—
Review of the Commission's Broadcast Ownership Rules and Other
Rules Adopted Pursuant to Section 202 of the Telecommunications
Act of 1996," MB Docket No. 02–277, September 23, 2002, http://
hraunfoss.fcc.gov/edocs_public/attachmatch/FCC-02-249A1.pdf (accessed February 17, 2006).

10. Ibid.

11. In the lone exception to its roster of market-friendly researchers, the

FCC did commission a research paper from scholar Joel Waldfogel of the Wharton School at the University of Pennsylvania.

12. George Williams, Keith Brown, and Peter Alexander, "Radio Market Structure and Music Diversity," FCC Media Bureau staff research paper, Media Ownership Working Group, September 2002, http://72.14.207.104/search?q=cache:dXVBhvF2wl4J:hraunfoss.fcc.gov/edocs_public/attachmatch/DOC-226838A18.c+%22listeners+in+local+radio+markets+may+have+experienced+increasing+song+diversity%22&hl=en&gl=us&ct=clnk&cd=1 (accessed February 17, 2006).

13. Professor Pritchard's work funded by Quebecor Media, Clear Channel, and others is listed at http://www.uwm.edu/Dept/JMC/facstaff/facresearch.html (accessed June 1, 2006).

14. For Einstein's bio, see http://qcpages.qc.edu/mediastudies/facutly%20pages/Einstein.html (accessed February 17, 2006).

15. "FCC Releases Twelve Studies on Current Media Marketplace," press release, October 1, 2005, http://hraunfoss.fcc.gov/edocs_public/attachmatch/DOC-226838A1.txt (accessed February 18, 2006).

16. "FCC'S Media Bureau Adopts Procedures for Public Access to Data Underlying Media Ownership Studies and Extends Comment Deadlines for 2002 Biennial Regulatory Review of Commission's Media Ownership Rules," press release, November 5, 2002, http://hraunfoss.fcc.gov/edocs_public/attachmatch/DA-02-2980A1.pdf (accessed February 18, 2006); "FCC Releases Twelve Studies on Current Media Marketplace." The Department for Professional Employees, AFL-CIO, issued a report by economist Dean Baker of the Center for Economic and Policy Research that critiqued the FCC studies. See Dean Baker, "Democracy Unhinged: More Media Concentration Means Less Public Discourse," n.d. [December 2002], http://www.dpeaflcio.org/pdf/FCC_Critique.pdf (accessed February 18, 2006). Advocates also had to petition that the FCC make the "underlying data" and the methodology of the publicly funded studies available, which the commission did only in part. In an illustration of how out of touch with its public responsibilities the Powell FCC was, the commission claimed that four out of the twelve researchers had used licensed "proprietary information." After pressure, the commission made that research available—but only to those who could come to the FCC's reference room. Those outside of the Washington, DC, area who wished to participate in the process were simply out of luck. Our overall criticism of the entire process did lead to some of the researchers actually having to revise their work. Ultimately, we helped undermine Powell's media marketplace "fact-finding mission."

17. "Clear Channel Communications," Wikipedia, http://en.wikipedia .org/wiki/Clear_Channel_Communications (accessed February 18, 2006).

18. "Commercial Radio Station Ownership Consolidation Shown to Harm Artists and the Public, Says FMC Study," press release, November 18, 2002, http://www.futureofmusic.org/news/PRradio study.cfm (accessed February 18, 2006); "Radio Deregulation: Has It Served Citizens and Musicians?" Future of Music Coalition, http:// www.futureofmusic.org/research/radiostudy.cfm (accessed February 18, 2006).

19. They included the Prometheus Radio Project, based in Philadelphia, which had transformed itself from a "pirate radio" guerrilla effort (broadcasting without an FCC license) into a major force promoting low-power community radio stations. There was Reclaim the Media and Media Tank, in Seattle and Philadelphia, respectively, which focused on media issues affecting their communities. They joined the San Francisco Bay Area Media Alliance, one of the oldest and most effective local media groups concerned about journalism and communications issues.

20. This group included both "guilds" representing all the writers for Hollywood film and TV (as well as many TV news personnel)—the Writers Guild of America, East and West. The American Federation of Television and Radio Artists, which represents many actors, was also active. The Caucus of Producers, Writers, and Directors, representing successful independent producers of Hollywood TV and film, played a major role. So did the principal union representing print journalists—the Newspaper Guild. Through the various guilds, the AFL-CIO (and its Department of Professional Employees) also became effectively engaged with the group. We were also joined by one of the last remaining major independent newspaper publishers, the Seattle Times Corporation. I played a leading role in organizing the coalition. This effort would not have been successful without the leadership of John Connolly of the American Federation of Television and Radio Artists, Linda Foley of the Newspaper Guild, Len Hill of the Caucus of Producers, Directors, and Writers, Mona Mangan (and Jesus Sanchez) of the Writers Guild of America, East, Jill Mackie and Frank Blethen of the Seattle Times Corporation, and Victoria Riskin and Jon Rintels of the Writers Guild of America, West. Rintels went on to create an important organization representing the interests of the creative community in public policy issues—the Center for Creative Voices in Media (http://www.creativevoices.us/).

21. Cooper has written a number of books on the subject, including *Me-*

dia Ownership and Democracy in the Digital Age (Stanford, CA: Center for Internet and Society, Stanford Law School, 2003).

22. Consumer Federation of America, "Public Opinion, Legal Principles, and Economic Analysis Support Media Ownership Rules," press release, December 16, 2002. This and other Cooper studies are at http://www.consumerfed.org/topics.cfm?section=Communications &Topic=Media%20Concentration (accessed February 18, 2006).

23. Copps had announced in November 2002 that he intended to conduct hearings. See Todd Shields, "Copps to Hold Panels on Media-Ownership Rules," *Editor and Publisher*, November 21, 2002, http://editorandpublisher.com/eandp/news/article_display. jsp?vnu_con tent_id =1766982 (accessed February 18, 2006).

24. The Richmond hearing was marked by bad weather. But that did not deter activists who opposed Powell's plans dressed as "Mad Scientists" from staging a photogenic protest. Wearing gleaming TV and radio headdresses as props, their message was, "You don't have to be a scientist to know that media concentration is bad for democracy!" They helped generate further press coverage, underscoring the message that Powell wasn't interested in facts. Among the groups helping organize the "scientists" were Prometheus Radio, the Media Alliance, the Free Press, Chicago Media Watch, and the Action Coalition for Media Education. See "Richmond Roundup," Reclaim the Media, March 4, 2003, http://www.reclaimthemedia.org/stories.php?story=03/03/04/ 8223856 (accessed February 18, 2006).

25. See the Writers Guild of America filing for an excellent analysis of concerns from writers and producers. "Comments of the Writers Guild of America regarding Harmful Vertical and Horizontal Integration of Television Industry," January 4, 2002, http://www.wga.org/ uploadedFiles/news_and_events/press_release/fcc/WGA-Comments .pdf (accessed February 18, 2006).

26. Quoted in Gal Beckerman, "Tripping up Big Media," *Columbia Journalism Review*, November–December 2003, http://www.cjr.org/ issues/2003/6/media-beckerman.asp (accessed February 18, 2006).

27. Stephen Labaton, "A Lone Voice for Regulation at the F.C.C.," *New York Times*, September 30, 2002. See also Writers Guild of America, "Statement from Guild President Victoria Riskin Expressing Concern over FCC's Dismissive Attitude toward Public Hearings," October 4, 2002, http://www.wga.org/subpage_newsevents.aspx?id=776 (accessed February 18, 2006); Beckerman, "Tripping up Big Media."

28. Mark Wigfield, "FCC Bombarded with Letters Opposing Media Consolidation," *Wall Street Journal*, January 3, 2003; Pamela McClintock, "FCC Opposition Tunes In," *Variety*, February 27, 2003.

29. Christopher Stern, "Deregulation Plans Assailed," *Washington Post*, January 15, 2003, http://www.mindfully.org/Industry/2003/Deregulation-FCC-Assailed15jan03.htm (accessed February 18, 2006); Yochi J. Dreazen, "Three Media Firms Ask FCC to Abandon Ownership Rules," *Wall Street Journal*, January 3, 2003.

30. Quoted in Stern, "Deregulation Plans Assailed."

31. Jennifer 8. Lee, "On Minot, N.D., Radio, a Single Corporate Voice," *New York Times*, March 29, 2003, http://faculty.msb.edu/homak/HomaHelpSite/WebHelp/Clear_Channel_-_Single_ Voice_in_Minot .htm (accessed February 18, 2006).

32. Jennifer 8. Lee, "Radio Giant Defends Its Size at Senate Panel Hearing," *New York Times*, January 30, 2003. "Coverage You Can('t) Count On," *On the Media*, February 7, 2003, http://www.onthemedia.org/transcripts/transcripts_020703_radio.html (accessed February 18, 2006); Brent Staples, "The Trouble with Corporate Radio: The Day the Protest Music Died," *New York Times*, February 20, 2003; Lee, "On Minot, N.D., Radio, a Single Corporate Voice"; interview with Senator Dorgan, *NewsHour with Jim Lehrer*, June 2, 2003, http://www.pbs.org/newshour/bb/media/jan-june03/dorgan_6-2.html (accessed February 18, 2006); Gloria Cooper, "The Censors," *Columbia Journalism Review*, July 2004, http://www.cjr.org/issues/2004/4/voices-cooper.asp (accessed February 18, 2006); Jennifer 8. Lee, "Musicians Protesting Monopoly in Media," *New York Times*, December 18, 2003.

33. As Safire wrote in a column he called "Media Giantism" (*New York Times*, January 20, 2003), "You won't find television magazine programs fearlessly exposing the broadcast lobby's pressure on Congress and the courts to allow station owners to gobble up more stations and cross-own local newspapers, thereby to determine what information residents of a local market receive. Nor will you find many newspaper chains assigning reporters to reveal the effects of media giantism on local coverage or cover the way publishers induce coverage-hungry politicians to loosen antitrust restraints. Should we totally deregulate the public airwaves and permit the dwindling of major media down to a precious few?"

34. Safire wrote about the broadcast spectrum giveaway in the 1996 Telecommunications Act. He continued to write on the issue and expanded his focus to include the FCC's media ownership proceedings. See, for example, "Essay: Spectrum Squatters," October 9, 2000, "On Media Giantism," January 20, 2003, "The Five Sisters," February 18, 2004, and "Regulate the F.C.C.," June 16, 2003, all written by Safire

for the *New York Times*. Safire was interested in the information provided by the advocates and open to learning more about the issue.

35. Pamela McClintock and Dave McNary, "FCC's Powell to Attend
Hearing," *Variety*, January 12, 2003, http://www.variety.com/index
.asp?layout=print_story&articleid=VR1117878558&categoryid=18 (accessed February 18, 2006).

36. Citing scheduling conflicts, Powell left early. Had he stayed, he would
have heard critiques of his position from an array of perspectives, including FCC commissioner Copps, Professor Robert W. McChesney,
Future of Music executive director Jenney Toomey, TV writer and
producer Tom Fontana (representing the Writer's Guild of America,
East), and *New York Daily News* columnist Juan Gonzalez. Charles
Lewis—the founder of the Center for Public Intregity, an independent investigative reporting organization—used the occasion to sum-
marize the center's research documenting the millions of dollars the
media companies had poured into Congress to help further their
agenda, including paying for junkets.

37. "Columbia Law School Kernochan Center for Law, Media, and the
Arts Announces a Forum on the FCC Media Ownership Rules," press
release, January 16, 2003, https://listserv.temple.edu/cgi-bin/wa?A2
=ind0301b&L=mmc&O=A&P=2282 (accessed February 18, 2006);
Charles Lewis, "Relaxing Media Ownership Rules Conflicts with
the Public's Right to Know," commentary delivered at the
Forum on Media Ownership, January 16, 2003, http://www
.publicintegrity.org/telecom/report.aspx?aid=96 (accessed February 18,
2006).

38. Since all the major newspaper companies (such as Tribune and the
New York Times Company) were also calling for favorable FCC policy changes, reporters and editors at those media outlets knew as well
what was at stake for their employers' future. The role that self-
censorship plays in journalism due to awareness of the political goals
of the owner is a factor to be reckoned with in assessing the quality of
coverage. For a discussion of self-censorship in the press, see, for example, Andrew Kohut, "Self-Censorship: Counting the Ways," *Columbia
Journalism Review*, May–June 2000, http://archives.cjr.org/year/00/2/
censorship.asp (accessed February 18, 2006).

39. Jeff Chester, "Strict Scrutiny: Why Journalists Should Be Concerned
about New Federal and Industry Media Deregulation Proposals," *Harvard International Journal of Press/Politics* 7, no. 2 (2002), http://hij.sagepub
.com/cgi/content/abstract/7/2/105 (accessed February 18, 2006).

40. See, for example, Alicia Mundy, "Rejected Antiwar Ad Stirs Consol-

idation Opponents," *CableWorld,* February 3, 2003, http://www
.broadband-accessintel.com/cgi/cw/show_mag.cgi?pub=cw&mon
=020303&file=rejected_antiwar_ad.inc (accessed February 18, 2006);
Nat Ives, "MTV Refuses Antiwar Commercial," *New York Times,*
May 13, 2004, http://www.commondreams.org/cgi-bin/print.cgi
?file=/headlines03/0313-04.htm (accessed February 18, 2006); John
Kamman, "Cox Rejects Anti-Tax Cut Ad, Citing Controversy," *Arizona Republic,* May 13, 2003, http://www.commondreams.org/
cgi-bin/print.cgi?file=/headlines03/0513-09.htm (accessed February 18,
2006).

41. Pamela McClintock, "FCC Opposition Tunes In," *Variety,* February 27,
2003, http://www.variety.com/article/VR1117881361?categoryid
=1236&cs=1 (accessed February 18, 2006); Bob Rayner and McGregor McCance, "FCC Gets an Earful in Richmond," *Richmond Times-Dispatch,* February 28, 2003; "Mad Scientists Descend on Richmond to
Oppose Media Concentration," Indy Media Richmond, February 27,
2003, http://richmond.indymedia.org/newswire/display/2756/index
.php (accessed February 18, 2006).

42. Organizations such as the Chicago Media Watch, the Media Alliance,
Media Tank, and Reclaim the Media organized hearings. See, for example, "The Future of Media: March 7, 2003," Reclaim the Media,
http://www.reclaimthemedia.org/pages.php?node=04/02/27/1968310
(accessed February 18, 2006); Jennifer Huang, "FCC Hearing Brings
Crowds and Controversy: Media Deregulation at Issue as Rules Come
under Review," Newsdesk.org, April 30, 2003, http://www.news
desk.org/archives/000046.php (accessed February 18, 2006); "A Public Forum on Media Ownership in Philadelphia," Media Tank, http://
www.mediatank.org/Events/fccforum.html (accessed February 18,
2006). I asked Haas to financially support these efforts. Other groups,
including the Benton Foundation, also supported hearings. See "The
Arizona Forum on Media Ownership," Benton Foundation, http://
www.benton.org/initiatives/ownership/azforum.html (accessed February 18, 2006).

43. Susan Crabtree, "FCC in NRA's Cross Hairs," *Variety,* May 14, 2003,
http://www.variety.com/index.asp?layout=story&articleid=VR111788
6238&categoryid=18&s=h&p=0&cs=1 (accessed February 18, 2006);
Beckerman, "Tripping up Big Media."

44. Emphasis in the original. The four-page alert, signed by NRA executive vice president Wayne LaPierre, explained that "the rules under
debate—known as 'Broadcast Ownership Rules'—have for decades
prevented the giant media conglomerates from gaining monopoly

control over what your fellow Americans can read in their newspapers, see on TV, and hear on the radio. *And they have prevented gun-hating media giants like AOL Time Warner, Viacom/CBS and Disney/ABC from silencing your NRA when we've needed to take our message directly to the American people in critical legislative and political battles*" (emphasis in the original). For a copy of the NRA letter, see "NRA Asks Members to Fight FCC Ownership Revisions," Center for Digital Democracy, http://www.democraticmedia.org/issues/mediaownership/nraLetter .html (accessed February 18, 2006). By accident, I was given a copy of this letter by a media advocate whose husband was an NRA member. I realized that the NRA's opposition to the FCC plan underscored how this wasn't just a Left-liberal issue but one that had truly aroused concern from across the political spectrum. Once given to reporters, it was clear that an unusually powerful alliance had emerged.

45. NRA letter, emphasis in the original. See also Frank Ahrens, "FCC Plan to Alter Media Rules Spurs Growing Debate," *Washington Post*, May 28, 2003.

46. Frank Ahrens, "Unlikely Alliances Forged in Fight over Media Rules," *Washington Post*, May 20, 2003.

47. Snowe's position was undoubtedly influenced by our ally, publisher Frank Blethen, who owns several Maine newspapers, including the *Portland Press Herald*. Lott's position reflected both his support for the NAB, which opposed a proposed FCC rule that would have enabled the four major TV networks to gain further control of the broadcasting business. He was also, in my organization's opinion, engaged in a form of media payback, helping thwart the interests of the networks that had contributed, in his view, to his loss of position as majority leader.

48. MoveOn.org partnered with Common Cause and the Free Press for the ad campaign. See, for example, David D. Kirkpatrick, "Media Deregulation Foes Make Murdoch Their Lightning Rod," *New York Times*, May 29, 2003; Ahrens, "FCC Plan to Alter Media Rules Spurs Growing Debate."

49. Quoted in Lucia Moses, "Powell to NAA: Expect Ownership Reform," *Editor and Publisher*, April 28, 2003. Powell's speeches are at http:// www.fcc.gov/commissioners/previous/powell/speeches.html (accessed February 18, 2006).

50. Moses, "Powell to NAA: Expect Ownership Reform." Among the publishers, only Frank Blethen of the Seattle Times Corporation spoke out against further media deregulation. In the same *Editor and Publisher* story, he said that "people ought to be scared to death when

you have a handful of big businesses that are getting bigger, that are going to control all the conduits of information."

51. Future of Music Coalition, "Citizens Urge FCC to Retain Current Media Ownership Rules," press release, May 14, 2003, http://www.futureofmusic.org/news/PRFCCdocket.cfm (accessed February 18, 2006). Undoubtedly adding insult to Powell's injury was the Future of Music's announcement that "over thirty high-profile musicians" had sent a letter to the FCC opposing changes. Among the co-signers were Jackson Browne, Jimmy Buffet, Neil Diamond, Billy Joel, Ellis L. Marsalis Jr., Pearl Jam, and Nancy Wilson.

52. Barry Diller, keynote speech, National Association of Broadcasters, April 7, 2003, http://www.creativevoices.us/php-bin/news/show Article.php?id=15 (accessed February 18, 2006); David Bloom, "Diller Disses Deregulation," *Variety*, April 7, 2003, http://www.variety.com/article/VR1117884264?categoryid=1064&cs=1 (accessed February 18, 2006).

53. Ted Turner, "Monopoly or Democracy?" *Washington Post*, May 30, 2003, http://www.creativevoices.us/php-bin/news/showArticle.php?id=17 (accessed February 18, 2006).

54. Turner ("Monopoly or Democracy?") went on, giving Powell and his allies a lesson in media industry realities, including what happens when independents and small media businesses disappear:

Large media corporations are far more profit-focused and risk-averse. They sometimes confuse short-term profits and long-term value. They kill local programming because it's expensive, and they push national programming because it's cheap—even if it runs counter to local interests and community values. For a corporation to launch a new idea, you have to get the backing of executives who are obsessed with quarterly earnings and afraid of being fired for an idea that fails. They often prefer to sit on the sidelines waiting to buy the businesses or imitate the models of the risk-takers who succeed. (Two large media corporations turned down my invitation to invest in the launch of CNN.)

That's an understandable approach for a corporation—but for a society, it's like over-fishing the oceans. When the smaller businesses are gone, where will the new ideas come from? Nor does this trend bode well for new ideas in our democracy—ideas that come only from diverse news and vigorous reporting. Under the new rules, there will be more consolidation and more news sharing. That means laying off reporters or, in other words, downsizing the workforce that helps us see our problems and makes us think about solutions. Even more troubling are the warning signs that large media corporations—with massive market power—could abuse that power by slanting news coverage in ways that serve their political or financial interests. There is always the danger that news organizations can push positive stories to gain friends in government, or unleash negative stories on artists, activists or politicians who cross them, or tell their audiences only the news that confirms entrenched views. But the danger is greater when there are no competitors to air the side of the story the corporation wants to ignore. A number of advocates urged Turner to weigh in on the debate. Former PBS president Pat Mitchell, a former Turner employee who was concerned about media consolidation, played a key role in encouraging Turner to speak out.

55. Bob Williams and Morgan Jindrich, "On the Road Again—and Again," Center for Public Integrity, May 22, 2003, http://www.publicintegrity.org/telecom/report.aspx?aid=15 (accessed February 18, 2006); John Nichols, "FCC Travels on Industry's Dime," *The Nation*, May 22, 2003, http://www.commondreams.org/cgi-bin/print.cgi?file=/views03/0522-10.htm (accessed February 18, 2006). All the then current commissioners also took trips on industry money, although to a far lesser degree than Powell.

56. Letter to FCC chair Michael Powell, sent by Sen. Wayne Allard, Sen. Olympia Snowe, and Sen. Susan Collins, March 19, 2003, http://www.consumersunion.org/images/0319SenateToPowell.jpg (accessed February 20, 2006).

57. For the correspondence between members of Congress and Powell, see "Chairman Michael K. Powell Responds to Members regarding Upcoming Biennial Review of Media Ownership," http://www.fcc.gov/commissioners/letters/media-ownership/ (accessed February 19, 2006).

58. Quoted in Norris Dickard, "Will Children Lose Out in Media Mergers?" Connect for Kids.org, July 2003, http://www.benton.org/publibrary/issuesinfocus/kids_media_merge.htm (accessed February 19, 2006).

59. Jeff Johnson, "Groups Warn FCC, about Media Ownership Changes," CNSNews.com, May 28, 2003, http://www.cnsnews.com/Politics/Archive/200305/POL20030528b.html (accessed February 19, 2006); Farhad Manjoo, "Can the Web Beat Big Media?" *Salon*, May 21, 2003, http://archive.salon.com/tech/feature/2003/05/21/web_vs_big_media/index_np.html (accessed February 19, 2006). Nearly two million people filed against the Powell plan. *Prometheus Radio Project v. FCC*, 373 F.3d 372, 386 (3d Cir. 2004).

60. Quoted in Matthew Benjamin, "Fewer Voices, Fewer Choices?" *U.S.*

News and World Report, June 9, 2003, http://www.usnews.com/
usnews/biztech/articles/030609/9fcc.htm (accessed February 19, 2006).

61. Quoted in "Online Focus: FCC Chairman Michael Powell," Online
NewsHour, June 2003, http://www.pbs.org/newshour/media/
conglomeration/powell_statement.html (accessed February 19, 2006).

62. "Consumer Groups Question FCC's Powell on Media Diversity Index: Index Will Lead to Concentrated Ownership Threatening Media Democracy," press release, Consumers Union, March 11, 2003,
http://www.consumersunion.org/telecom/media-d.htm   (accessed
February 19, 2006).

63. "Statement of Commissioner Jonathan S. Adelstein, Dissenting,"
FCC, June 2, 2003, http://hraunfoss.fcc.gov/edocs_public/
attachmatch/DOC-235047A8.pdf (accessed February 19, 2006).

64. "FCC Sets Limits on Media Concentration: Unprecedented Public
Record Results in Enforceable and Balanced Broadcast Ownership
Rules," June 2, 2003, http://hraunfoss.fcc.gov/edocs_public/
attachmatch/DOC-235047A1.pdf (accessed February 19, 2006).

65. Jill Goldsmith, "Dereg Buoys Media Stox; Some Underwhelmed," *Variety,* June 2, 2003, http://www.variety.com/article/VR1117887234
?categoryid=1064&cs=1 (accessed February 19, 2006).

66. Susan Crabtree, "FCC Regs on Hold," *Variety,* September 3, 2003,
http://www.variety.com/index.asp?layout=upsell_article&articleID=VR
1117891896&cs=1 (accessed February 19, 2006). Working against the
FCC was a growing fissure within the broadcast industry itself. The
NAB lobbying powerhouse was opposed to the new rule that permitted the broadcast networks to acquire more stations. Most NAB members didn't want to see the four networks gain additional negotiating
leverage with their "affiliates." By owning more stations, the networks
could further dictate the economic terms of their relationship, likely
reducing affiliate revenues. So the NAB, helped by the other opponents of media consolidation, worked to pass legislation.

67. Susan Crabtree, "House Panel Throws Curve at FCC Regs," *Variety,*
July 16, 2003, http://www.variety.com/article/VR1117889407
?categoryid=1064&cs=1 (accessed February 19, 2006); Elizabeth Guider,
"FCC's Cap Scrap Hits Speed Bump at House," *Variety,* July 27, 2003,
http://www.variety.com/article/VR1117889908?categoryid=1344&cs
=1 (accessed February 19, 2006).

68. Susan Crabtree, "Senate Shoots down Media Rules," *Variety,* September
16, 2003 http://www.variety.com/article/VR1117892547?categoryid
=1064&cs=1 (accessed February 19, 2006).

69. "Debating Media Ownership," *The Nation,* December 7, 2003,

http://www.thenation.com/blogs/actnow?pid=1114 (accessed February 19, 2003).

70. But the White House did come to the aid of Viacom and News Corp., cutting a deal with GOP congressional leaders that allowed the two media conglomerates to hold on to already-acquired TV stations, which they would have had to divest otherwise, as the FCC's "old" rules were still in effect. They had been counting on winning at the FCC so they could keep their extra stations.

71. Susan Crabtree, "Reps Pressure Speaker on FCC Vote," *Variety*, November 5, 2003, http://www.variety.com/article/VR1117895182 ?categoryid=1064&cs=1 (accessed February 19, 2006); "Nets Ride Omnibus," *Variety,* December 6, 2003, http://www.variety.com/article/VR1117896846?categoryid=18&cs=1 (accessed February 19, 2006); "Congress Delays FCC Vote," *Variety*, December 14, 2003, http://www.variety.com/article/VR1117897118?categoryid=1064&cs =1&s=h&p=0 (accessed February 19, 2006).

72. "Michael Powell's Thoughts on AO Innovation Summit and Silicon Valley Visit," July 16, 2004, http://www.alwayson-network.com/comments.php?id=4921_0_3_0_C (accessed February 19, 2006).

73. "Statement of FCC Chairman Michael K. Powell: On Leaving the Commission," January 21, 2005, http://hraunfoss.fcc.gov/edocs_public/attachmatch/DOC-256206A1.pdf (accessed February 19, 2006).

74. The final area (VII) in Powell's highlights covered his work "Restructuring the FCC," including having "built a university to keep FCC employees at cutting edge." See "Policy Highlights of Michael K. Powell's FCC Tenure," n.d. [January 21, 2005], http://hraunfoss .fcc.gov/edocs_public/attachmatch/DOC-256206A2.pdf (accessed February 19, 2006).

75. "FCC Chairman Michael K. Powell to Join Aspen Institute," press release, March 11, 2005, http://www.aspeninstitute.org/site/apps/nl/content2.asp?c=huLWJeMRKpH&b=696077&ct=778551 (accessed February 19, 2006); "Michael K. Powell's Golden Revolving Door," Center for Digital Democracy, August 11, 2005, http://www .democraticmedia.org/news/washingtonwatch/FCCrevolvingdoor.html (accessed February 19, 2006).

7. The Brandwashing of America

1. Advertising Research Foundation, "ARF, AAA, and ANA Are Getting Emotional about Engagement," September 27, 2005, http://www .democraticmedia.org/AdweekMRI.pdf (accessed February 20, 2006).

2. Ibid. The Association of National Advertisers (ANA) also has a new technology committee that works to advance interactive advertising. Among its members are representatives from Wachovia, Kraft, Merck, Burger King, and Phillip Morris. See "ANA Committees," ANA, http://www.ana.net/com/com.htm (accessed February 20, 2006).

3. "2006 Fact Pack," *Advertising Age*, February 27, 2006, 10, http://www.adage.com/images/random/FactPack06.pdf (accessed March 13, 2006).

4. Ibid.

5. As one major online advertising agency put it, despite the proliferation of more choices, "consumers are becoming . . . more insecure and vulnerable. . . . Media has the potential to become more powerful and influential than ever before." Lynette Webb, "The Emerging Changes in Media and Communications," executive summary, Carat International, http://www.carat.com/carat/IntranetDocViewer?wsDoc TypeId=0&wsScreenType=95&wsRow=1&wsCol=6&wsDepth=1 &wsBI=null (accessed October 28, 2005).

6. For a copy of Barlow's declaration, see http://homes.eff.org/~bar low/Declaration-Final.html (accessed February 20, 2006).

7. The Coalition for Advertising-Supported Information and Entertainment (CASIE), which is run by the ANA and the American Association of Advertising Agencies (AAAA), worked to prevent the passage of any federal privacy safeguards, contending that requirements for public disclosure on Internet data collection was "premature" and would "raise serious First Amendment concerns." Coalition for Advertising-Supported Information and Entertainment, "Comments on White Paper, 'Elements of Effective Self-Regulation for Protection of Privacy,'" National Information and Telecommunications Administration, U.S. Department of Commerce, July 6, 1998, and "Comments on the Federal Trade Commission's Interpretation of Rules and Guides for Electronic Media," Comment File No. P974102, July 7, 1998.

8. Peter Adams, "Just Add Cookies: Improving Your Understanding of Your Customers and E-Marketing Programs," *Advertiser*, May 2000.

9. Coalition for Advertising-Supported Information and Entertainment, "Comments on White Paper," and "Comments on the Federal Trade Commission's Interpretation of Rules and Guides for Electronic Media."

10. The Future of Advertising Stockholders eventually folded, but it stimulated the development of a more coherent research and advocacy effort on behalf on online advertising.

11. Martin Nisenholtz, "Media View: New Media Challenges the Cre-

ative Department," *AAAA Agency Magazine,* Fall 1996; Peter Lenz, Hesse Parelius, and John Ruluns, "Building Models of Ad Effect Using Data Mining," Advertising Research Foundation workshop, October 1998.

12. Nisenholtz, "Media View: New Media Challenges the Creative Department."

13. See, for example, "History," New York Times Digital, http://www. nytdigital.com/learn/timeline.html (accessed March 13, 2006).

14. See, for example, the marketing clusters of Prizm, "MyBestSegments," http://www.claritas.com/MyBestSegments/ (accessed February 20, 2006). AC Nielsen is typical of research companies that conduct panels to understand consumer behavior. See "Our Products," ACNielsen, http://www2.acnielsen.com/products/index.shtml (accessed February 20, 2006).

15. Pepper and Rogers have continued their work on "1 to 1." See their Web site at http://www.1to1.com/ (accessed February 20, 2006). Today, the concept of "one to one" has morphed into approaches called "Customer Relationship Management" or CRM. But the basic premise is still the same: through the use of data collection and other technologies, marketers will gain knowledge about your interests and behaviors. Companies can then engage you in what the industry calls a "lifelong branding" relationship.

16. Horst Stipp, vice president, primary and strategic research, NBC TV Network, presentation at ESOMAR, Excellence in International Research 2003. See also Michael Kubin, "The Internet: Out of the Ashes," *Admap,* May 2002, 29–31.

17. For an overview of ARF conferences, see http://www.thearf.org/conferences/past.html (accessed February 20, 2006). Among the ARF's members in 2005 were Coca-Cola, Frito-Lay, Kraft Foods, Miller Brewing Company, CBS, Fox, Disney, Time Warner, the New York Times Company, and Columbia University. For a full list of the ARF's members, see http://www.thearf.org/membership/members.html (accessed October 14, 2005). For a list of ARF councils, see http://www.thearf.org/councils/index.html (accessed February 20, 2006).

18. "ANA, AAAA, and ARF Are Getting Emotional about Engagement," 2005 Advertising Week conference proceedings, New York City, http://www.thearf.org/conferences/special.html (accessed February 20, 2006).

19. For Zaltman's bio, see http://dor.hbs.edu/fi_redirect.jhtml?facInfo =bio&facEmId=gzaltman (accessed February 20, 2006). The profes-

sor's "Zaltman Metaphor Elicitation Technique" (ZMET) helps identify the kind of "deep metaphors" that consumers will readily embrace about a brand or product.

20. Daniel H. Pink, "Metaphor Marketing," *Fast Company*, April 1998,
http://pf.fastcompany.com/magazine/14/zaltman.html (accessed February 20, 2006); "ARF Signs 10-Year Strategic Alliance with MSN to
Transform the Practice of Marketing," press release, Advertising Research Foundation, March 3, 2005, http://www.thearf.org/about/
pr_030305.html (accessed February 20, 2006). The ARF's *Journal of
Advertising Research*, published four times a year by Cambridge University Press, is filled with scholarly and more practical how-to articles.
Much of the research reported is on the role of advertising in shaping
the proper emotional and cognitive attitudes for brand awareness, including interactive marketing. There are dozens of other academic-
style journals on marketing and advertising, including *Interactive Marketing*; the *Journal of Consumer Behavior*; *Consumption, Markets, and Culture*; and the *International Journal of Advertising*, to name a few. Their
pages are filled with articles about how we are constantly being observed, focus grouped, anthropologically analyzed, and tested with
tools that pry into attitudes, behaviors, and lifestyles. For a list of advertising journals, see http://www.marketingpower.com/content15789
C4602.php (accessed February 20, 2006).

21. Worldwide Audience Measurement Conference, Los Angeles,
June 15–20, 2003.

22. For a list of IAB committees and task forces, see http://www.iab.net/
comm/index.asp (accessed October 15, 2005). Member companies
include Advertising.com (now owned by Time Warner), I/Pro, Atlas
DMT, Accipiter, and Overture (now owned by Yahoo!). For a list of
members, see http://www. iab.net/about/general_members.asp.

23. For "interactive marketing units" (banners, buttons, etc.), see http://
www.iab.net/standards/adunits.asp (accessed February 20, 2006). For
the IAB's "Broadband Ad Creative Guidelines," see http://www
.iab.net/standards/broadband/index.asp (accessed February 20, 2006).
To help demonstrate that online marketing really works (and to encourage advertisers to spend more of their ad budgets on the Internet), the IAB and the ARF have co-sponsored a series of research
studies. A variety of products have been tested to see how well they
sold on the Internet, including for McDonald's, Colgate, Ford, and
Dove soap. Not surprisingly, the studies demonstrated that online
marketing is a valuable tool. For example, in their report on McDonald's Grilled Chicken Flatbread Sandwich, researchers found online
marketing helped reach target audiences who were "not heavy televi-

sion users." Using the Internet, they noted, helped McDonald's improve the product's "image perception" and "emotive brand attributes." For the IAB's XMOS, see http://www.iab.net/xmos/case.asp (accessed February 20, 2006).

24. "When the Advertising Business Changed Forever," Jack Myers Report, July 24, 2002, http://www.ad-id.org/news/docs/jack_me.pdf (accessed February 21, 2006).

25. Quoted in ibid. Sealy predicted that marketers "will also be able to track the specific consumption behavior resulting from advertising exposure."

26. Users, comScore says, give "permission to confidentially monitor their online activities in return for valuable benefits such as server-based virus protection, sweepstakes prizes, and the opportunity to help shape the future of the Internet." See "Methodology and Technology," comScore Networks, http://www.comscore.com/method/ tech.asp (accessed February 21, 2006); "Nielsen to Offer Integrated, All-Electronic Television Measurement Across Multiple Media Platforms," Nielsen press release, June 14, 2006, http://www.nielsen media.com.

27. Brian Krebs, "Attack on Advertising Provider Jams High-Traffic Web Sites," *Washington Post*, July 28, 2004, http://www.washingtonpost .com/wp-dyn/articles/A19342-2004Jul27.html (accessed February 21, 2006); Matt Hicks, "DoS Attack Knocks Out DoubleClick Ads," *eWeek*, July 27, 2004; Kate Kaye, "DoubleClick Server Attack Halts Ads," *MediaPost*, July 28, 2004. There had been a similar attack on Akamai Technologies in June that harmed the operations of such online giants as Microsoft and its MSN.com as well as Yahoo.com. As one official who follows hacker attacks told the *Post*, "The hackers don't need to attack the Internet. If you attack Akamai or Double-Click you can take out 95 percent of what most people consider to be the Internet."

28. For more information about ad networks, see, for example, "Ad Networks," Accipiter, http://www.imediaconnection.com/resourcecon nection/adnetwork.asp (accessed February 21, 2006). There is an ad industry initiative on ad networks and data collection that allows one to opt out of cookies and other tracking efforts. See "Opt Out of NAI Member Ad Networks," National Advertising Initiative, http:// www.networkadvertising.org/optout_nonppii.asp (accessed February 21, 2006).

29. "Cookie's Marketing Score," DoubleClick, http://www.double click.com/us/about_doubleclick/privacy/marketing-scores/cookies.asp (accessed February 21, 2006).

30. "Marketing Score Categories," DoubleClick, http://www.doubleclick
.com/us/about_doubleclick/privacy/marketing-scores/categories
.asp? (accessed February 21, 2006).

31. "DoubleClick and Digital Envoy Partner to Offer Advanced Geo-
Targeting Solutions," press release, March 22, 2004, http://www
.doubleclick.com/us/about_DoubleClick/press_releases/default.asp
?p=424 (accessed February 21, 2006).

32. See DoubleClick Privacy Policy, especially "Cookie's Marketing Scores"
and "Information Used in Ad Serving," http://www.double
click.com/us/about_DoubleClick/privacy/internet-ads/information
.asp; "DART and Privacy," http://www.doubleclick.com/us/
about_DoubleClick/privacy/internet-ads/dart.asp; "Frequently Asked
Questions about DoubleClick and Privacy," http://www
.doubleclick.com/us/about_DoubleClick/privacy/faq.asp; "DART
for Advertisers," http://www.doubleclick.com/us/products/digital
_advertising/ dfa/; "DART Enterprise," http://www.doubleclick
.com/us/products/digital_advertising/dart_enterprise/; "Clear GIF's,"
http://www.doubleclick.com/us/about_DoubleClick/privacy/clear-gifs
.asp (all accessed October 18, 2005). See also Esther Dyson, "Spy vs.
Spy: The Accountable Web, Part 2," *Release 1.0*, April 2005; Jack
Myers, "DoubleClick Technology Delivering Early Online Promise,"
Jack Myers Report, October 22, 2003, http://www.media
village.com/pdf/10-22-03.pdf (accessed February 21, 2006); "Opti-
mizing the Online Business Channel with Web Analytics," Web
Analytics Association, July 6, 2005, http://www.webanalyticsassociation
.org/en/art/?9 (accessed February 21, 2006). For an industry defini-
tion of cookies and other online advertising terms, see Internet Advertising Bureau, http://www.iab.net/resources/glossary_c.asp (accessed
February 21, 2006). Just a few years ago, DoubleClick had planned to
merge its online data with off-line information when it acquired Abacus Direct in 1999. Groups such as EPIC and Junkbusters launched a
protest, concerned that Abacus's data on 2.4 billion consumer purchases from 1,100 catalogs "would have a surveillance database of Or-
wellian proportions." David Kleinbard, "Critics Aim at DoubleClick,"
CNNMoney, March 6, 2000, http://money.cnn.com/2000/03/06/
technology/privacy_doubleclick/ (accessed February 21, 2006). As a result of the pressure, DoubleClick backed off from a direct merger with
its Abacus database. But the information it collects, on so-called
anonymous users, is finely tuned, helping it to further segment and
target us.

33. See, for example, "Behavioral Targeting," Advertising.com, http://

www.advertising.com/BehavioralTargeting.html (accessed October 24, 2005).

34. The *New York Times* signed with TACODA Systems to help with its behavioral targeting. See "TACODA Signs NYTimes.com and Boston.com for Its Audience Management Service," TACODA press release, October 25, 2004, http://www.tacoda.com/mediaCenter_pressArchive.htm (accessed June 1, 2006). For the *Wall Street Journal* and *Business Week*, see Janis Mara, "Behavioral Targeting Heats Up," ClickZ News, March 12, 2004, http://www.clickz.com/news/article.php/3325541 (accessed June 1, 2006).

35. Many people rightfully consider this sort of data collection spyware. Some companies in the behavioral ad business claim that their users understand they are being targeted in this way. Among the companies involved in behavioral marketing are Claria (formerly the Gator Corporation), TACODA, and Revenue Science. Chang Yu, "Behavioral Marketing 101: Defining the Terminology," ClickZ Network, January 26, 2005, http://www.clickz.com/experts/media/behavioral_marketing/article.php/3463391 (accessed February 21, 2006).

36. Pamela Parker and Zachary Rodgers, "The Return of the Ad Network," ClickZ Insights, May 17, 2004, http://www.clickz.com/features/insight/print.php/3355051 (accessed February 21, 2006). Companies like DoubleClick provide services internationally. Since they know whether your browser is using English, Spanish, or another language, they can target accordingly. For a discussion of the capabilities of Advertising.com's AdLearn, see its SEC S-1 filing, April 2, 2004.

37. "Behavioral Segmentation Improves Advertising Campaign Performance," press release, Advertising.com, August 17, 2004, http://www.advertising.com/Press/04Aug17.html; "Behavioral Targeting," http://www.advertising.com/BehavioralTargeting.html (both accessed October 24, 2005).

38. Martin Nisenholtz, AAAA/ANA Marketing Conference and Trade Show presentation, July 15, 2002, http://www.nytco.com/investors-presentations-20020715.html (accessed February 21, 2006).

39. "Audience Targeting," NYTimes.com, http://www.nytimes.com/marketing/adinfo/audience/audiencetargeting.html (accessed February 21, 2006).

40. Kathryn Koegel, "Rich Media: What? Where? Why?" DoubleClick, July 2003, http://www.doubleclick.com/us/knowledge_central/documents/research/dc_richmedia_0307.pdf (accessed February 21, 2006).

41. Ibid.

42. Ironically, the increase in interactive ad technology has led to new forms of electronic con artistry. Note this claim from Google's initial public offering:

> If we fail to detect click-through fraud, we could lose the confidence of our advertisers, thereby causing our business to suffer. We are exposed to the risk of fraudulent clicks on our ads by persons seeking to increase the advertising fees paid to our Google Network members. We have regularly refunded revenue that our advertisers have paid to us and that was later attributed to click-through fraud, and we expect to do so in the future. Click-through fraud occurs when a person clicks on a Google AdWords ad displayed on a web site in order to generate the revenue share payment to the Google Network member rather than to view the underlying content. If we are unable to stop this fraudulent activity, these refunds may increase. If we find new evidence of past fraudulent clicks we may have to issue refunds retroactively of amounts previously paid to our Google Network members. This would negatively affect our profitability, and these types of fraudulent activities could hurt our brand.

Google, Inc., S-1/A filing, Securities and Exchange Commission, August 13, 2004, http://www.secinfo.com/d14D5a.148c8.htm (accessed February 21, 2006).

43. Quoted in "Google Advertising Patents for Behavioral Targeting, Personalization, and Profiling," *Search Engine Journal*, October 7, 2005, http://www.searchenginejournal.com/index.php?p=2311 (accessed February 21, 2006).

44. "Time Warner's AOL and Google to Expand Strategic Alliance," press release, December 20, 2005, http://www.google.com/press/pressrel/twaol_expanded.html (accessed February 21, 2006).

45. "Yahoo! to Acquire Overture," press release, July 14, 2003, http://docs.yahoo.com/docs/pr/release1102.html (accessed February 21, 2006).

46. Kris Oser, "MSN Links Keyword Search to Demographic Database," *Ad Age*, September 26, 2005.

47. Pamela Parker, "Interactive Ads Play Big Role in 'Minority Report,'" ClickZ.com, June 21, 2002, http://www.clickz.com/news/print.php/1369861 (accessed February 21, 2006).

48. Bryan Reeves, "The Benefits of Interactive Online Characters," n.d., http://www.eidoserve.com/eido_blue/docs/Stanford_Avatar_ Study.pdf (accessed February 21, 2006).

49. B.J. Fogg, *Persuasive Technology: Using Computers to Change What We Think and Do* (San Francisco: Morgan Kaufmann, 2002), 183.

50. Reeves, "The Benefits of Interactive Online Characters."

51. Oddcast, http://www.oddcast.com/home/ (accessed October 28, 2005).

52. See, for example, "Sponsorship," MIT Media Lab, http://www.media.mit.edu/sponsors/index.html (accessed February 21, 2006). Many of these universities are working with the Brand Experience Lab. See "Research Partners," Brand Experience Lab, http://www.brandexperiencelab.org/partners.html (accessed October 23, 2005). See also Stanford's Media X initiative, http://mediax.stanford.edu/about/index.html (accessed February 21, 2006); Yahoo! Research Berkeley, http://research.yahoo.com/berkeley/ (accessed October 23, 2005). For the USC Interactive Media Division, see http://interactive.usc.edu/about/.

53. "AdCenter Demo Fest Exhibits Leading-Edge Advertising Technology," press release, January 13, 2005, Microsoft, http://www.prnewswire.com/cgi-bin/stories.pl?ACCT=104&STORY=/www/story/01-13-2006/0004248428&EDATE= (accessed February 21, 2006).

54. See http://yahoo.client.shareholder.com/press/ReleaseDetail.cfm?ReleaseID=185028.

55. Quoted in Dawn Anfuso, "Emerging Platforms (Part 3)," iMedia Connection, August 4, 2005, http://www.imediaconnection.com/content/6446.asp (accessed November 7, 2005).

56. Much of U.S. TV, including cable and satellite providers, has already embraced on-demand TV. See Jean Bergantini Gallo, "Chasing Away the Clutter," *Multichannel News*, May 2, 2005.

57. A good overview can be found in "TV That Watches You: The Prying Eyes of Interactive Television," a 2001 report done by my organization, the Center for Digital Democracy, http://www.democraticmedia.org/privacyreport.pdf (accessed February 21, 2006).

58. "Interactive TV Will Revolutionize Mass Marketing," Claritas Europe, http://www.iburbiastudios.co.uk/studios/?home=i (accessed April 23, 2003).

59. See, for example, the ARF's Video Electronic Media Council, http://www.thearf.org/councils/ve.html; the ANA's TV Advertising and New Technologies committees, http://www.ana.net/com/com.htm. See also "ITA Pledges Support for Ad-ID Platform," *CED Daily*, September 4, 2003, http://www.cedmagazine.com/article/CA6271720.html; Interactive Television Alliance, http://www.itvalliance.org/; the AAAA's and the ANA's Ad-ID, https://www.ad-id.org/ (all accessed November 11, 2005).

60. Ad from nCube, "TV on Demand Summit" supplement, *Broadcasting and Cable*, November 2003; TiVo 8K filing, Securities and Exchange

Commission, March 15, 2005, http://investor.tivo.com/Edgar Detail.cfm?CIK=1088825&FID=1193125-05-195034&SID=05-00 (accessed February 21, 2006); Scientific Atlanta, "Take a Closer Look at IPTV from Scientific-Atlanta at SUPERCOMM 2005," June 6, 2005, http://www.scientificatlanta.com/newscenter/releases/05Jun06-1.htm (accessed November 9, 2005); Ken Kerschbaumer, "Who's Really Watching? How Cable's Digital Box Will Rock the Ratings World," *Broadcasting and Cable*, May 16, 2005, http://www.broadcasting cable.com/article/CA601520.html?display=Features&referral=SUPP (accessed February 21, 2006).

61. "Promoting the Development of the On-Demand Advertising Market," ID!A, http://www.idiaprogram.com/index.html (accessed November 5, 2005); "Innovations in Digital Advertising (ID!A) Unveils Groundbreaking Proposal to Define Ad Units across Digital Platforms at the AAA Media Conference and Trade Show," press release, March 1, 2005, www.idiaprogram.com/IDiA_at_AAAA_3_1_05.pdf (accessed February 21, 2006).

62. Joe Mandese, "Cable to Give Agencies the Data They Demand," Mediapost, March 3, 2005, http://www.idiaprogram.com/IDiA_Media Post_article_03_03_05.html.pdf (accessed February 21, 2006).

63. Open TV, "Interactive Advertising White Paper," http://www.actv .com/support/white_papers.html (accessed October 21, 2005). See also AAAA Advanced Television Committee, "On-Demand Television Metrics Guidelines," Version 1.6, February 2004, http://www .dimagroup.com/report/NR101_tvmetrics.pdf (accessed February 21, 2006); Digital Media and Advertising Group, "The DiMAS Report: An Analysis of Advertising Opportunities and Hurdles in Digital Media," April 2003, http://digitalgaragemedia.com/white_ papers/DiMASReportFinal.pdf (accessed February 21, 2006); CTAM On-Demand Consortium, http://www.ctamnetforum.com/ eweb/dynamicpage.aspx?site=ctampublic&webcode=GL0302_ODC (accessed February 21, 2006). For developments in the United Kingdom, see, for example, "Advertising: Sky Interactive Templates," Press Red, http://www.pressred.tv/pmwiki.php/Advertising/SkyInteractive Templates (accessed February 21, 2006). Many other organizations and groups have worked or are working on interactive TV and advertising, including the Worldwide Web Consortium, http://www.w3.org/; CableLabs, http://www.cablelabs.org/; TV Anytime, http://www.tv -anytime.org/; the Digital Video Broadcasting Project, http:// www.dvb.org/; and the American Television Systems Committee, http://www.atsc.org/aboutatsc.html (all accessed November 8, 2005).

64. "Delivering Dollars on Demand," TV on Demand Summit supplement, *Broadcasting and Cable*, November 2003; Kerschbaumer, "Who's Really Watching?"

65. See, for example, the data-collecting technologies from any number of interactive TV ventures, such as Murdoch's NDS (http://www.nds.com/conditional_access/audience_measurement.html), John Malone's Open TV (http://www.opentv.com/products/ent_measure.html), and Visible World (http://www.visibleworld.com/index_content.html) (all accessed March 14, 2006).

66. L. Sweeney, "Uniqueness of Simple Demographics in the U.S. Population," Carnegie Mellon University, Laboratory for International Data Privacy, 2000, http://privacy.cs.cmu.edu/dataprivacy/papers/LIDAP-WP4abstract.html (accessed February 21, 2006).

67. Comcast Spotlight, "Overview" and related material, including "Ad-tag and Adcopy Fact Sheet," http://www.comcastspotlight.com/sites/Default.aspx?pageid=2488&siteid=62&subnav=6 and http://www.comcastspotlight.com/sites/Default.aspx?pageid=7826&siteid=62&subnav=4. See also Adlink, http://www.adlink.com/resource_center/adtag/index.shtml and http://www.adlink.com/resource_center/adcopy/index.shtml; "Comcast Spotlight Selects SRC as Developer for Web-Based Demographic Analysis Mapping Platform," press release, November 15, 2004, http://www.comcastspotlight.com/sites/Default.aspx?hst=1&pageid=2486&display=1&pressreleaseid=92&siteid=62&subnav=5 (all accessed November 10, 2005).

68. For the Comcast-Liberate deal, see http://news.zdnet.com/2100-1035_22-5519600.html (accessed February 21, 2006); for the Comcast-MetaTV deal, see http://informitv.com/articles/2005/07/13/comcastandcox/ (accessed February 21, 2006). Cox is a partner in both deals.

69. Comcast Interactive, "Selected Investments," http://www.civentures.com/portfoliomain.htm (accessed February 21, 2006). "Comcast Spotlight Launches Industry's First Gigabit Ethernet Digital Program Insertion with C-Cor," press release, April 4, 2005, http://www.c-cor.com/about/PR/news_releases.cfm?action=view&ID=381 (accessed February 21, 2006). C-Cor, "Content Management—Advertising," http://www.c-cor.com/solutions/content_management/advertising.cfm?page=insertion (accessed February 21, 2006). "Comcast Spotlight to Offer Tools to Help Advertisers Customize Commercials in Top TV Markets," press release, April 9, 2004, http://www.comcastspotlight.com/sites/Default.aspx?hst=1&pageid=2486&display=1&pressreleaseid=94&siteid=62&subnav=5 (accessed February 21, 2006). Comcast has also gone into the electronic program guide

business, with partner Gemstar/TV Guide. The company is called Guideworks, LLC. Jean Bergantini Grillo, "Chasing Away the Clutter: Cable Networks Are Opening Doors to New Digital Advertising Opportunities," *Multichannel News*, May 2, 2005, http://www.multi channel.com/article/CA528745.html?display=Special+Report (accessed February 21, 2006).

70. "Advertisers," OpenTV, http://www.opentv.com/solutions/advertisers .html (accessed February 21, 2006).

71. "OpenTV Measure," OpenTV, http://www.opentv.com/products/ ent_measure.html (accessed February 21, 2006).

72. "NDS Audience Measurement System," NDS, http://www.nds.com/ conditional_access/audience_measurement.html (accessed February 21, 2006).

73. Stephen Johnson, "DVRs Offer a Gold Mine of Data for Advertisers," *Television Week*, July 26, 2004.

74. Sheree R. Curry, "PVR Threat Growing," *TV Week*, September 1, 2003.

75. Ibid.

76. *Time Warner Entertainment Co., et al, Plaintiffs, v. Replay TV, Inc.*, U.S. District Court, Central District of California, 2001, http://www.eff.org/ IP/Video/Paramount_v_ReplayTV/20011109_timewarner_complaint .pdf (accessed March 14, 2006).

77. While the loss of copyright value with Internet distribution was the primary concern, it was clear that Replay's posture on ad removal was also threatening. Ironically, one of the twenty-eight companies suing Replay was Sony, which owned Columbia Pictures. Sony had once fought Hollywood when it tried to prevent the use of VCRs (the Betamax case). The Electronic Frontier Foundation, among others, did fine work defending Replay users. See its archive at http://www .eff.org/IP/Video/Paramount_v_ReplayTV/. The Electronic Privacy Information Center also did important work, especially in defending the privacy rights of Replay users.

8. Cable Costra Nostra

1. "Cable TV: Long-Term Contribution Trends," Opensecrets.org, http://www.opensecrets.org/industries/indus.asp?cycle=2006&ind =C2200 (accessed February 22, 2006).

2. Kelly Robbins, "The Cable Center," *Advertising and Marketing Review*, n.d., http://www.ad-mkt-review.com/public_html/docs/fs041.html (accessed February 22, 2006).

3. Cable Center, letter to perspective donors, 2004.

4. Amy Bryer, "Cable Moguls Sponsoring Industry Museum," *Denver Business Journal*, April 27, 2001.

5. "The 400 Richest Americans," Forbes.com, September 22, 2005, http://www.forbes.com/400richest/ (accessed February 22, 2006).

6. National Cable and Telecommunications Association, "2005 Mid-Year Industry Overview," http://www.ncta.com/Docs/PageContent .cfm?pageID=46 (accessed February 22, 2006); Comcast, "Product Fact Sheet," http://www.cmcsk.com/phoenix.zhtml?c=147565&p =irol-factsheet (accessed February 22, 2006); "Overview: Time Warner Cable, Inc.," http://www.hoovers.com/time-warner-cable/ —ID__103276—/free-co-factsheet.xhtml (accessed February 22, 2006).

7. The major U.S. broadcast networks have been able to use their political power over Congress to gain leverage with cable for programming deals. Utilizing retransmission consent, broadcasters, as noted earlier, have forced cable to carry many new channels. Such is the broadcast lobby's power that it herded Congress to approve special-interest legislation in 1992 that enabled broadcasters to gain greater cable channel access. But Comcast has "the power to make or break a digital network." Shirley Brady, "Attention New Networks!" *CableWORLD*, June 21, 2004, http://www.cableworld.com/cgi/cw/show_mag.cgi ?pub=cw&mon=062104&file=attentionnewnetworks.htm (accessed February 22, 2006).

8. Charles Tate, "Community Control of Cable Television Systems," in *Cable Television in the Cities: Community Control, Public Access, and Minority Ownership*, ed. Charles Tate (Washington, DC: Urban Institute, 1972), 16–90. Local programming created by the public would facilitate a new kind of social cohesion. This would help address, advocates hoped, some of the serious racial and economic fissures roiling U.S. society at the time. As the FCC conducted two weeks of formal hearings in 1971 to discuss the future of cable, actor and activist Ossie Davis testified "to present minority demands and interests" on the then new medium. Tate, *Cable Television in the Cities*, 5. For example, communications scholar Ithiel de Sola Pool wrote that cable would help provide "citizens with increased participation in the running of their own communities. . . . Cable television may be the last communications frontier for the oppressed." Quoted in Tate, "Community Control of Cable Television Systems," 17. See also Ithiel de Sola Pool, ed., *Talking Back: Citizen Feedback and Cable Technology* (Cambridge, MA: MIT Press, 1973), especially Charles Tate, "Communications Technology and Community Control: Confrontation and Challenge,"

54–63. In his pioneering 1970 *Nation* article "The Wired Nation," Ralph Smith reflected on how "the elimination of channel scarcity and the sharp reduction of broadcasting cost can break the hold on the nation's television fare now exercised by a small commercial oligarchy. Television can become far more flexible in content, and far more responsive to the full range of pressing needs in today's cities, neighborhoods, towns and communities." Ralph Lee Smith, "The Wired Nation," *The Nation*, May 18, 1970, http://www.nationarchive.com/ Summaries/v210i0019_04.htm (accessed February 23, 2006).

9. While today the various cable companies and trade associations work mostly in tandem, a quarter century ago they actually competed with each other. As Gustave Hauser told the Cable Center's oral history project, "It was the only time that the otherwise brothers of the cable industry, who knew each other and were actually very fond of each other and today are still personal friends, went out and fought each other head to head. As a result, there was a lot of acrimony and a lot of backbiting and accusations. It was a bitter period. Once the franchising wars ended, everything went back to normal." Gustave Hauser, interview by Tom Southwick, August 1999, Cable Center Oral History Collection, http://www.cablecenter.org/education/ library/oralHistoryDetails.cfm?id=105#transcript (accessed March 13, 2006). The head of *Time* magazine's ATC cable operations, Richard Munro, recalled that "there was a feeding frenzy then. We were all running around like . . . chickens with their heads off trying to get any franchise that we could get our hands on. . . . The cable company wanted those franchises badly enough to promise anything that they were asked to promise and to compete viciously against each other. So, I think they made their own bed, and they had to sleep in it. But, we all kept chasing them knowing they were crazy, knowing that we would somehow or another have to renegotiate them." Richard Munro, interview, Cable Center Oral History Collection, http:// cablecenter.org/library/collections/oral_histories/history_detail.cfm ?SelectedHistory=229 (accessed July 11, 2003).

10. Nancy Jesuale with Ralph Lee Smith, *The Community Medium* (Arlington, VA: CTIC Cablebooks, 1982), 23, 32. Among the leading cable companies promoting cable's technological strengths were the Times Mirror (the newspaper chain of the *Los Angeles Times*), Cox, ATC (*Time* magazine), Comcast, and Warner-Amex (a joint venture of Warner Communications and American Express). Information partners for these trials included the Associated Press, Dow Jones, the *New York Times*, and the *World Book* encyclopedia. In dozens of communities, experiments and trials were underway to perfect the home

delivery of information. In the upscale neighborhood of Palos Verdes, California, for example, users of the Times Mirror's videotext system were to have access to twenty thousand pages of information. Trials in 1982 promised to deliver interactive capabilities to dozens of municipalities, including Louisville, San Diego, Orlando, Tucson, and Macon. Home retrieval of databases and connections to personal computers where part of the landscape during cable's gold rush days. In addition to national sources of information, some cable companies also promised "to deliver locally and community-oriented databases, with an opportunity for community input. . . . [S]ome companies have offered to place keyboards for community use in libraries, schools, government buildings, and other public places." Jesuale and Smith, *The Community Medium*, 24. More communities wanted such innovations as they learned about the financial and political benefits of a modern communications network. By the early 1980s, advocates for public-interest cable were better organized. There was the advocacy group representing public access producers, then called the National Federation of Local Cable Programmers (now the Alliance for Community Media). The Cable Television Information Center had been established in 1972 with foundation support to help local governments and other cable advocates with information and analysis. A series of booklets published in the early 1980s by this center focused on cable's role as "The Community Medium."

11. As the Museum of Broadcast Communications notes, "Nickelodeon came into being as a noncommercial program source created largely to serve as a goodwill tool through which cable system operators could win both franchise rights and subscribers." http://www.museum.tv/archives/etv/L/htmlL/laybournege/laybournege.htm (accessed June 1, 2006).

12. Laura Linder notes that cable "seized upon public access television as a service that had public relations appeal and could help them portray their industry as more responsive to local concerns than the networks. To demonstrate its capacity to provide an important public service, the cable industry promoted public access television to show it was a 'socially responsible medium.' . . . This commitment to public access television helped the cable industry differentiate itself from the network cartel and to legitimate it in the public mind." Laura R. Linder, *Public Access Television: America's Electronic Soapbox* (Westport, CT: Prager Publishers, 1999), 8. Ralph Engelman observes that "early support for public access by cable operators came at a time when an emerging cable television industry, vulnerable financially and politically, needed to establish its legitimacy vis-a-vis 'free' broadcast television. For a brief

moment, the interests of the cable industry and the video freaks of the radical video collectives coincided." Ralph Engelman, *Public Radio and Television in America* (Thousands Oaks, CA: Sage Publications, 1996), 293–94. In testimony before Congress in 1969, Irving B. Kahn, who then headed the TelePrompTer Corporation, told lawmakers that "there is one thing that cannot be ignored. And that is the great and growing body of competent, impartial opinion—from scientists, writers and journalists, members of the Government, businessmen, economists, and others—that stresses the great potential of [cable]." Quoted in Thomas Streeter, "Blue Skies and Strange Bedfellows: The Discourse of Cable Television," In *The Revolution Wasn't Televised: Sixties Television and Social Conflict*, ed. Lynn Spigel and Michael Curtain (Oxford, UK: Routledge, 1997). Some cable operators used a high-tech system known as Qube as bait to convince city officials and lawmakers that cable was a unique resource. Qube delivered many channels, including community information and interactive services. As L.J. Davis comments in *The Billionaire Shell Game*, there was the sense that "a city without Qube was a city that had turned its back on the television of the future." The cable industry used Qube's potential to convince the Nixon administration and congressional policymakers not to limit the industry's control over both programming and distribution. L.J. Davis, *The Billionaire Shell Game* (New York: Doubleday, 1998).

13. See Jesuale and Smith, *The Community Medium*, 24–38; Pool, *Talking Back*.

14. "The Gold Rush of 1980," *Broadcasting Magazine*, March 31, 1980.

15. Ralph Lee Smith, *The Wired Nation* (New York: Harper, 1972), 90–91.

16. Cable made new alliances and expanded its political operations. See, for example, the interview with John Malone that is part of the Cable Center's oral history project. Among the media giants that supported cable's plans for deregulation, according to Malone, were the Times Mirror, Tribune, Scripps Howard, the *Providence Journal*, Cox, and Taft. As he explained in his Cable Center interview, "We actually ended up, I think, winning the deregulation battle largely on the backs of the publishers who were invested in the cable industry." John Malone, interview by Trygve Mhyren, October 2001, Cable Center Oral History Collection, http://www.cablecenter.org/education/library/oralHistoryDetails.cfm?id=142#transcript (accessed March 13, 2006). See also how cable effectively organized in California—a model that became the blueprint for the industry's national deregulation effort. Oral history of Spencer Kaitz, interview by Marlowe Froke, December

1989, Cable Center Oral History Collection, http://www.cable
center.org/education/library/oralHistoryDetails.cfm?id=235#transcript
(accessed March 13, 2006).

17. The industry was able, for example, to organize an effective campaign
in the late 1950s to kill regulatory legislation in the U.S. Senate. See
Stephen Singular, "Relentless: Bill Daniels and the Triumph of Cable
TV," Bill Daniels Estate, 2003, 82–83. As early as 1960, California cable companies paid twenty cents a subscriber to the CCTA, providing
it "superior resources." Not surprisingly, California passed deregulatory
cable legislation in 1982, which became a model for cable's subsequent
federal campaign. By the early 1980s, the industry had powerful new
allies, including newspaper publishers like the Times Mirror and Tribune, that supported its political efforts. It could take advantage of the
conservative ideology of the Reagan administration. The GOP was
also in control of the Senate, with pro-business Republican Barry
Goldwater running the Subcommittee on Communications.

18. "Before the Subcommittee on Communications, U.S. Senate, Cable
Telecommunications Act of 1983 (S. 66), February 16–17, 1983." See
also Lucy Huffman, "Senate Opens Hearings on Cable Legislation,"
Multichannel News, February 21, 1983.

19. Singular, "Relentless," 219.

20. Tom Wheeler, interview by Tom Southwick, July 2000, Cable Center Oral History Collection, http://www.cablecenter.org/education/
library/oralHistoryDetails.cfm?id=184#transcript (accessed March 13,
2006). Malone also recalled that cable "had Tim Wirth." As Malone
remarked, "To this day I'll remember thinking all was lost and then at
the end he pulled it out in the Congressional session." As the official
biography of the cable industry's chief financial strategist Bill Daniels
explains, "Backed by money from local cable businesses . . . Wirth had
barely won the seat and would never forget who'd helped him. He
soon became a member of the House Telecommunications Subcommittee. From there, he would begin the long process of creating legislation that would eventually deregulate cable. Malone interview.

21. See the purposes section of the Cable Communications Act of 1984,
http://www.publicaccess.org/cableact.html (accessed February 23,
2006).

22. Engelman, *Public Radio and Television in America*, 294. Communications
law insiders like Max Paglin understood that the 1984 act was a victory for cable and a defeat for the public. Max D. Paglin, ed., *The
Communications Act: A Legislative History of the Major Amendments,
1934–1996* (Silver Spring, MD: Pike and Fisher, 1999), 253. See also
"'Bully-Boy Tactics and Strong-Arming' in the Cable Industry: Via-

com v. TCI et al, circa 1993," http://www.democraticmedia.org/issues/
cabletv/ViacomvTCI.html (accessed February 23, 2006).

23. As Tate wrote in 1971, "Blacks have little or no stake in the existing
radio and television enterprises in their communities." Tate, "Community Control of Cable Television Systems," 30.

24. R. Thomas Umstead, "TV One to Launch VOD," *Multichannel News*,
December 13, 2004; Steve Donahue, "BETS's Lee Search's for Viacom Synergies," *Multichannel News*, December 3, 2001.

25. "The Cable Industry's Lies about Programming Diversity and a la
Carte," Center for Digital Democracy, June 30, 2004, http://
www.democraticmedia.org/news/marketwatch/cablelies.html (accessed
February 23, 2006); "FCC Approves Merger of Spanish-Language
Media Companies," Online NewsHour, September 23, 2003, http://
www.pbs.org/newshour/media/media_watch/july-dec03/univision
merger_09-22-03.html (accessed February 23, 2006). The industry, as
part of its political public relations efforts, likes to claim it has promoted programming diversity. It's a lie, of course. There have been
limited programming and ownership opportunities on cable for minority interests. If one examines cable's Spanish-language lineup, for
example, one sees *Toon Disney in Spanish* (Disney/ABC), *WHUno*
(MTV-Viacom), *CNN en Espanol* (Time Warner), *Discovery Espanol*
(Liberty Media, Cox, and Advance/Newhouse), *Fox Sports en Espanol*
(News Corp./Fox), *HBO Latino* (Time Warner), *Mun2* (General
Electric/NBC), and *Si TV* (Time Warner). The dominant Spanish-
language network Univision is based on its ownership of broadcast
TV stations and run by longtime media entrepreneur Jerry Perenchio.
It also controls the Galavision and TeleFutura networks, and swal-
lowed up the country's largest Spanish broadcasting radio network in
2003. The Cisneros Group, a Venezuela-based media powerhouse,
owns about one-fifth of Univision. Most of its programming comes
from Cisneros productions. See also http://www.onetvworld.org/
?module=displaysection&section_id=200& format=html (accessed January 15, 2005). Cable giants saw African American and Hispanic audiences as a gold mine, too. They were an important demographic for
advertisers and considered loyal TV viewers. Cable's own research
showed in 2004 that African Americans, for instance, watch more TV
than other groups. They had a "buying power" of almost $688 billion
in 2003, according to the Cable Advertising Bureau, which predicted
this would grow to $921 billion by 2008. Hispanics by 2003 spent
more than $652 billion, expected to increase to more than a trillion
dollars five years later.

26. Comcast-controlled TV One, for example, features such shows as *Tan-*

gles and Locks, a program "exploring the world of black hair"; *Makeover Manor*, described as a "transformation series"; and various other "lifestyle" and cooking programs.

27. Kasowitz, Benson, Torres & Friedman LLP, in Re Adelphia Communications Corp., et al., a Delaware corporation, Debtors, Chapter 11 Cases, Case No. 02–41729 (REG), http://bankrupt.com/misc/ AdversaryProceeding_Wachovia.pdf (accessed February 23, 2006). As Rigas reflected on his first bank loan, "It was the beginning of a long history of signing bank notes all my life. I often said that if they ever put all my bank notes through a computer, it would choke it." Since 1970, banks would come knocking on cable's door to loan money, he noted. That's because cable was such a "cash cow," generating huge sums of money, for Rigas and every other owner. John Rigas, interview by E. Stratford Smith, October 2000, Cable Center Oral History Collection, http://www.cablecenter.org/education/library/oralHistory Details.cfm?id=253#transcript (accessed March 13, 2006).

28. Cable Center, "Pennsylvania Cable Pioneer and Wife Pledge $2 Million to Cable Center," press release, March 9, 1998, http://www.cable center.org/press/pressReleasesDetail.cfm?id=34 (accessed March 13, 2006). See also Cable Center, "The Cable Center Announces 2001 Inductees to Cable Television Hall of Fame," press release, http:// www.cablecenter.org/press/pressReleasesDetail.cfm?id=129 (accessed March 13, 2006); "John Rigas," Empire Sports Network, http:// www.empiresports.com/johnrigas.html (accessed March 13, 2006).

29. Rigas interview. The Cable Center, sponsor of the Fame awards, was undoubtedly grateful to Rigas. During its capital campaign to support the 74,000-square-foot museum and showcase for the industry, Rigas pledged $2 million for the John and Doris Rigas Theatre. Rigas was, in fact, chair of the capital campaign for the center. At the time of his Hall of Fame award, he was lauded by industry leaders, including John Hendricks of the Discovery Channel, for his leadership and vision. He wasn't the only Rigas honored by the industry. In 1996, son Michael had been named treasurer of the Cable Center board, where he served with fellow board members Ted Turner, Jerry Levin, and Comcast CEO Julian Brodsky, among many others.

30. Adelphia had financial relationships with most of the key cable television industry suppliers of programming. See Adelphia Communications Corporation bankruptcy petition, U.S. Bankruptcy Court, Southern District of New York, June 25, 2002.

31. SEC against Adelphia Communications Corp., John J. Rigas, Timothy J. Rigas, Michael J. Rigas, James P. Rigas, James R. Brown, and Michael C. Mulcahey, complaint filed in U.S. District Court, South-

ern District of New York, July 24, 2002; *Adelphia Communications Corporation et al. v. John J. Rigas, Timothy J. Rigas, et al.* U.S. Bankruptcy Court, Southern District of New York, July 24, 2002. Company funds purchased expensive real estate, including two apartments in New York City, a condo in Colorado, and one in Mexico. The family received a golf course, lavish Christmas trees, money to produce a feature film, and a hundred pairs of slippers for one of the sons. The family spent $150 million to run the Buffalo Sabres hockey team, where son Tim became president. One revealing transaction showed how the Rigas family mixed private and public-interests. In February 2000, the Rigases paid $464,930 for 3,656 acres of land in rural Pennsylvania. They then had the company pay $26.5 million for rights to the timber on that property, with language that the timber rights could convert back to the family under favorable conditions to them.

32. But to look closely would have dampened the spirits of the dot-com era that was benefiting high-tech-enmeshed cable companies. Wall Street and the press also praised Adelphia's high-flying ventures. When in April 1999 the company announced a billion dollar deal to buy another cable company with three hundred thousand subscribers, the *Wall Street Journal* reported that "Wall Street cheered the news." Leslie Cauley, "Adelphia Plans to Purchase Harron for $820 Million," *Wall Street Journal*, April 13, 1999. Yet just a month prior, Adelphia had acquired an even larger cable provider, spending $5.2 billion for Century Communications. Cable's number one banker, Daniels and Associates, had helped structure that deal. See Daniels's Cable Center biography, http://www.cablecenter.org/about/boardDetail.cfm?id=81 (accessed March 13, 2006). Leslie Cauley, "When It Comes to New Cable Contracts, Brokers Waller and Deevy Lead the Pack," *Wall Street Journal*, April 22, 1999.

33. These institutions included Goldman Sachs, Deutsche Bank, ABN Amro, Banc of America Securities, Barclays Capital, NNY Capital Corp., CIBC World Markets Corp., Citigroup Global Markets Holdings (Salomon Smith Barney Holdings, Inc.), Deutsche Banc Alex Brown, Fleet Securities, Morgan Stanley, PNC Capital Markets, Scotia Capital (USA), SunTrust Securities, and TD Securities. Letter from Lindsee P. Granfield, Cleary, Gottleib, Steen and Hamiltion, to Hon. Robert E. Gerber, U.S. Bankruptcy Court for the Southern District of New York, August 25, 2004. For the huge list of banks, see also http://bankrupt.com/TCR_Public/031029.mbx.

34. "Adelphia Founder Sentenced to 15 Years," CNN/Money, June 20, 2005, http://money.cnn.com/2005/06/20/news/newsmakers/rigas _sentencing/ (accessed February 23, 2006).

35. The publicity forced Bank of America, BMO, Wachovia, and Citigroup to prepare internal reports on the episode. As the suit acknowledges, "None of the status reports expressed any shock—let alone surprise—about the situation. . . . To the contrary, each of these institutions acknowledged they had always known all the material." The banks had known that they didn't have to worry about how the Rigas family would pay off those hefty interest payments or banking fees. They knew, as one lawsuit says, that "the cash flow generated from cable subscribers . . . would fulfill those payment obligations." *Adelphia Communications Corp. and its Affiliated Debtors and Debtors in Possession and Official Committee of Unsecured Creditors of Adelphia Communications Corp. v. Bank of America, N.A., et al.*, complaint, U.S. Bankruptcy Court, Southern District of New York, July 6, 2003. A hero here is a Merrill Lynch analyst named Oren Cohen, who raised the issue on a corporate call with investment firms. He actually asked where the money was coming from for the Rigas family to buy all the shares, and that's what opened up the story for the public and law enforcement. Roger Lowenstein, "The Company They Kept," *New York Times*, February 1, 2004.

36. "Adelphia Obtains $8.8 Billion Exit Financing Commitment from Four Global Financial Institutions. JPMorgan Chase & Co., Credit Suisse First Boston, Citigroup Inc. and Deutsche Bank AG Take the Lead; Financing Commitment—a Major Sign of Confidence for Adelphia," press release, February 25, 2004, http://www.adelphia.com/about/Adelphia_Obtains_$8.8_Billion_Exit_Financing.pdf (accessed February 23, 2006). In 2005, the SEC and the U.S. Attorney's Office for the Southern District of New York announced a settlement of the civil and criminal charges against Adelphia Communications, John Rigas, and Rigas's three sons. The Rigas family agreed to forfeit more than $1.5 billion in assets. "SEC and U.S. Attorney Settle Massive Financial Fraud Case Against Adelphia and Rigas Family for $715 Million," U.S. Securities and Exchange Commission press release, April 25, 2005, http://www.sec.gov/news/press/2005-63.htm (accessed June 1, 2006). As of June 1, 2006, Adelphia was still in bankruptcy, with a number of lawsuits against it from creditors still pending. In June 2005, John Rigas was sentenced to fifteen years in prison. Timothy Rigas received a twenty-year sentence. "Adelphia Founder Sentenced to 15 Years," CNNMoney.com, June 20, 2005, http://money.cnn.com/2005/06/20/news/newsmakers/rigas_sentencing/ (accessed June 1, 2006). Son Michael Rigas was sentenced to ten months of home confinement and two years' probation. Stephen Taub, "Probation for Adelphia's Michael Rigas," CFO.com, March 6,

2006, http://www.cfo.com/article.cfm/5598021/c_5591729 (accessed June 1, 2006).

37. Time Warner was forced to settle with the SEC on a number of financial improprieties. "SEC Charges Time Warner with Fraud, Aiding and Abetting Frauds by Others, and Violating a Prior Cease-and-Desist Order; CFO, Controller, and Deputy Controller Charged with Causing Reporting Violations," U.S. Securities and Exchange Commission press release, March 21, 2005, http://www.sec.gov/news/press/2005-38.htm (accessed June 1, 2005). The SEC conducted an inquiry into some of Cablevision's finances. Andrew Wallenstein, "Deadline for Dolan on Voom," *Hollywood Reporter*, March 4, 2005, http://www.hollywoodreporter.com/thr/article_display.jsp?vnu_content _id=1000827164 (accessed June 1, 2005). Charter Communications had to settle with the SEC over a charge that it had inflated its subscriber numbers. Stephen Taub, "SEC Settles with Charter Communications," CFO.com, August 3, 2004, http://www.cfo.com/article.cfm/3015611?f=related (accessed June 1, 2005). There have been a number of criticisms expressed about the governance structure of the Comcast board; see Allen Greenberg, "Comcast's Bad Governance," *Philadelphia Business Journal*, September 20, 2002, http://www.bizjournals.com/philadelphia/stories/2002/09/23/editorial1.html (accessed June 1, 2006).

38. Jeff Chester, "One Reason Why the FCC and FTC Should Reject the Takeover of Adelphia by Comcast and Time Warner: The ITV 'Tipping Point,'" Center for Digital Democracy, July 20, 2005, http://www.democraticmedia.org/news/Adelphiastatement.html (accessed March 13, 2006). One Comcast supercluster, for example, extends from New England to the Mid-Atlantic states, and includes Washington, DC.

39. The industry relied on a financial metric known as Earnings before Interest, Taxes, Debt, and Amortization (EBITDA) to show Wall Street that it was making lots of money. As Leo Hindery, one of cable's leading executives, told the Cable Center, "We're the kings and the queens of EBITDA. We're all about cash flow, pre-tax cash flow, and we try not to pay taxes." But such business practices really didn't provide accurate information to investors and the public about the financial health of cable companies. For example, when AOL merged with Time Warner, it used the EBITDA metric to help convince investors that the combined company was assured success. Nanette Byrnes and Tom Lowry, "A Different Yardstick for Cable: In Scandal's Wake, Many Say EBITDA is Too Lenient—and Fuzzy," *Business Week*, September 2, 2002.

40. John Wicklein, *Electronic Nightmare: The Home Communications Set and Your Freedom* (Boston: Beacon Press, 1982).

9. The Golden Wire

1. Groups such as Computer Professionals for Social Responsibility, the American Library Association, the Consumer Project on Technology, my own Center for Media Education, and many others were involved in advancing these and other proposals. Pressure from such advocates led to the creation of the E-Rate, which supports school and library Internet connections, as part of the Telecommunications Act of 1996, as noted earlier. Criticisms about how nonprofits were neglected in the Internet policy debate led the Clinton administration to respond with a half measure—its TIAPP funding program. This criticism was part of the public-interest principles developed by the Telecommunications Roundtable. See John Markoff, "New Coalition to Seek a Public Data Highway," *New York Times*, October 26, 1993.
2. Steve Case, National Press Club address, October 26, 1998.
3. AOL and others were also fighting policies that would regulate the Internet on so-called indecency concerns, as discussed earlier.
4. Case, National Press Club address.
5. Lawrence Lessig, *The Future of Ideas: The Fate of the Commons in a Connected World* (New York: Random House, 2001).
6. Most of us were wary of AOL. It was evident that AOL was more interested in securing access to cable for itself than ensuring that the U.S. communications system was governed democratically. Once AOL had its own access, we thought, what would happen to the other thousands of Internet service providers and the independence of online content in general?
7. Andrew Leonard, "Hands Off Whose Net?" *Salon*, July 19, 1999, http://www.salon.com/tech/log/1999/07/19/cable_regulation/print .html (accessed June 1, 2006).
8. Cisco Systems, "Controlling Your Network—A Must for Cable Operators," 1999, http://www.cptech.org/ecom/openaccess/cisco1.html (accessed February 24, 2006).
9. I discovered these documents as part of an annual industry fact-finding trip to the NCTA convention. I often find these events revealing, since the organizers don't expect anyone besides industry boosters and captured politicians to show up. See "What the Market Will Bear: Cisco's Vision for Broadband Internet," Center for Digital Democracy, http://www.democraticmedia.org/issues/openaccess/cisco.html (accessed February 24, 2006).

10. "The Road Not Taken: Building a Broadband Future for America," remarks of William E. Kennard, chair, Federal Communications Commission, before the National Cable Television Association, Chicago, June 15, 1999, http://www.techlawjournal.com/telecom/19990615ken.htm (accessed March 14, 2006). Broadband could, he said, "transform lives, rejuvenate communities and open up worlds of opportunities for millions of Americans." Kennard had faced intense criticism for his support of a Clinton administration plan to require free airtime for federal political candidates. Forced to beat a quick retreat after an attack by leaders from both parties, and not given political support by the administration, Kennard retreated into a defensive posture for most of his term as FCC chair.

11. Quoted in Jeff Chester, "The Threat to the Net," *The Nation*, October 9, 2000, http://www.thenation.com/doc/20001009/chester (accessed February 24, 2006).

12. Personal communication. Another reason for the merger was that both AOL and Time Warner needed to shore up growing problems with their businesses, as author and journalist Alec Klein notes in his book *Stealing Time: Steve Case, Jerry Levin, and the Collapse of AOL Time Warner* (New York: Simon & Schuster, 2003).

13. America Online and Time Warner Public Interest Statement, Federal Communications Commission, February 11, 2000, http://www.fcc.gov/mb/aoltw/aoltwap.doc (accessed February 24, 2006).

14. "Supplemental Information, America Online, Inc. and Time Warner, Inc.," submitted to the FCC March 21, 2000, CS Docket No. 00–30.

15. Ibid.

16. AOL and Time Warner, S-4 filing, Securities and Exchange Commission, 2000, http://www.shareholder.com/Common/Edgar/1105705/940180-00-646/00-00.pdf (accessed February 24, 2006).

17. "SEC Fact Sheet on Global Analyst Research Settlements," Securities and Exchange Commission, n.d., http://www.sec.gov/news/speech/factsheet.htm (accessed February 24, 2006).

18. The DOJ and FTC have developed their own formula for determining which agency gets to clear or approve a deal.

19. The DOJ has been notorious in supporting media mergers of any variety. Part of the problem is that the staff of the antitrust division is ultimately under the control of the attorney general and the White House. The FTC staff has shown more independence, although they are also too deferential to industry.

20. Quoted in Jeremy Pelofsky, "Networks Urge FCC to Condition AOL–Time Warner Deal," Reuters, July 25, 2000, http://www

.techtv.com/news/business/story/0,24195,1489,00.html (accessed February 24, 2006).

21. These public-interest safeguards were the work of many hands, including Lessig, FTC commissioner Mozelle Thompson, Portland city commissioner Erik Sten, the Media Access Project, the Consumers Union, and the Consumer Federation of America. I also played a role in enacting the interactive TV safeguards.

10. Supermedia Monopolies

1. See, for example, National Cable and Telecommunications Association, "Working Toward a Deregulated Video Marketplace," June 2005, http://www.democraticmedia.org/PDFs/NCTAVideoMarketplace.pdf (accessed February 27, 2006).

2. "TV/Movies/Music: Long-Term Contribution Trends," Opensecrets .org, http://www.opensecrets.org/industries/indus.asp?Ind=B02 (accessed February 27, 2006). See also John Dunbar, "Former Bells Dial-up Big Numbers in Statehouses," Center for Public Integrity, September 29, 2005, http://www.publicintegrity.org/telecom/report .aspx?aid=744 (accessed February 27, 2006). The talk of the need for a Telecom Act rewrite is so thick that you can hardly see money change hands from lobbyist to lawmaker. See, for example, David Hatch, "Ensign Expects '06 Action on Revised Telecom Bill," *National Journal*, October 18, 2005, http://www.njtelecomupdate.com/ lenya/telco/live/tb-AXTW1129666939921.html (accessed February 27, 2006); Chloe Albanesius, "Network Neutrality Provisions Unnecessary, BellSouth Says," *National Journal*, November 30, 2005, http:// www.njtelecomupdate.com/lenya/telco/live/tb-JEAV1133469048556 .html (accessed February 27, 2006); Jonathan Make, "U.S. Broadband Policies Needed to Boost Growth, Executives Say," *Communications Daily*, December 12, 2005.

3. Motorola, "Multiprotocol Label Switching Applications for Broadband Services," http://broadband.motorola.com/whitepaper/MPLSWP _web.pdf; "Carrier-Grade Deep Packet Inspection and Service Control Platform," Allot Communications, http://www.allot.com/pages/ product_content.asp?intGlobalId=1 (accessed February 27, 2006); "White Papers," Cisco Systems, http://www.cisco.com/en/US/ products/ps6135/products_white_ paper0900aecd80395c74.shtml (accessed February 27, 2006).

4. I certainly believe you can embrace commerce and financial gain. But it must be done in a manner that places democratic discourse needs

first, along with a social commitment to such issues as economic equity, community vitalization, and cultural and civic expression, especially of a noncommercial nature.

5. Cerf's letter is available at http://googleblog.blogspot.com/2005/11/vint-cerf-speaks-out-on-net-neutrality.html (accessed February 27, 2006). See also "Broadband Group Urges FCC to Ensure Consumer Freedom on the Internet," press release, Comptel, November 18, 2002, for letter to chair Michael Powell and the FCC from Amazon .com, Apple Computer, Microsoft, Yahoo!, Disney, and eBay, http://www.comptelascent.org/news/pr-archive/2002/111802.htm (accessed February 27, 2006).

6. Quoted in "At SBC, It's All about 'Scale and Scope,'" *Business Week,* November 7, 2005, http://www.businessweek.com/magazine/content/05_45/b3958092.htm (accessed February 27, 2006).

7. See, for example, "Creating Value from IPTV," *Global Telecoms Business,* November–December 2005, http://www.sun.com/solutions/documents/white-papers/te_iptv.pdf (accessed February 27, 2006).

8. Linda Haugsted, "Illinois Muni: Voted Down, Not Out," *Multichannel News,* May 5, 2003, http://www.multichannel.com/article/CA296518 .html?display=Top+Stories (accessed February 27, 2006). See also the Web site of the Fiber for Our Future citizens group, http://www .tricitybroadband.com/ (accessed June 2, 2006); Common Cause Education Fund, *Wolves in Sheep's Clothing: Telecom Industry Front Groups and Astroturf,* Common Cause special report, March 2006, http://www.commoncause.org/site/pp.asp?c=dkLNK1MQIwG&b=1499059 (accessed June 2, 2006).

9. Jim Barthold, "Verizon's Captain Charts Slow, Steady Course," *Telecommunications Online,* February 9, 2006, http://www.telecom magazine.com/archives/article.asp?HH_ID=AR_1713 (accessed June 1, 2006).

10. "ITU's New Broadband Statistics for 1 January 2005," International Telecommunications Union, April 13, 2005, http://www.itu.int/osg/spu/newslog/ITUs+New+Broadband+Statistics+For+1+January+2005 .aspx (accessed February 27, 2006); Thomas Bleha, "Down to the Wire," *Foreign Affairs,* May–June 2005, http://www.foreignaffairs .org/20050501faessay84311/thomas-bleha/down-to-the-wire.html (accessed February 27, 2006).

11. See http://www.itu.int/osg/spu/newslog/ITUs+New+Broadband +Statistics+For+1+January+2005.aspx; http://www.salon.com/tech/feature/2005/10/18/broadband/index.html.

12. Section 706 of the 1996 Telecom Act directed the FCC to make high-speed Internet service available to the public "on a reasonable and timely basis."

11. A Policy Agenda for the Broadband Era

1. See, for example, "Investment Funds Sign Net Pledge," p2pnet, http://p2pnet.net/index.php?page=reply&story=6912 (accessed March 8, 2006). Common Cause Education Fund, *Wolves in Sheep's Clothing: Telecom Industry Front Groups and Astroturf*, Common Cause special report, March 2006, http://www.commoncause.org/site/pp.asp?c=dkLNK1MQIwG&b=1499059 (accessed June 2, 2006).
2. Resources for community broadband include the Baller Herbst Law Group (http://www.baller.com/comm_broadband.html), Muni-Wireless (http://www.muniwireless.com/), and the Champaign-Urbana Community Wireless Network (http://cuwireless.net/whatis cuwin) (all accessed March 8, 2006).
3. "Necessary Knowledge for a Democratic Public Sphere: Connecting Media Research with Media Reform," Social Science Research Council, http://www.ssrc.org/programs/media/ (accessed March 14, 2006); "Social Science Research Council Receives $750,000 Ford Foundation Grant to Strengthen Connections between Media Research and Media Reform," press release, http://www.fordham.edu/images/undergraduate/communications/ssrc%20'necessary%20knowl edge'%20press%20release.pdf (accessed March 14, 2006).
4. Gilbert Cranberg, Randall Bezanson, and John Soloski, *Taking Stock: Journalism and the Publicly Traded Newspaper Company* (Ames: Iowa State Press, 2001). *Taking Stock* has a number of other recommendations that should be heeded.
5. We are, however, fortunate to have many journalists who have done precisely this, including Ken Auletta, Eric Boehlert, Frank Rich, and Bill Moyers. I have been privileged to work with each of them as a source. Moyers, who I consider a friend, has also provided generous financial support for my Center for Digital Democracy through the Schumann Center on Media and Democracy foundation.
6. Patrick Carney (personal communication, September 9, 2005), of the FCC explains the agency's lobbying policies in the following manner:

> The essential distinction is that the lifetime ban comes into play if I, as a federal employee, have personally participated in a covered proceeding, and the two-year ban applies if, although I was

not personally involved in the proceeding, it was pending under my official responsibility during my final year of federal service—which usually means that I was supervising someone who was participating in the matter.

For example, if one of our bureau chiefs personally participates in a license application (which would be a particular matter involving a specific party or parties, i.e., an adjudicatory-type proceeding), then he is barred for life by 18 USC 207(a)(1) from representing anyone other than the United States before any federal court, department, or agency in that same licensing proceeding. On the other hand, if he had no personal involvement in processing the application but it was being handled in his bureau during his final year at the commission, then 18 USC 207(a)(2) would prohibit him from representing anyone other than the United States for two years after he leaves federal service. The practical effect, as you can see, is that the two-year restriction in essence means that a bureau or office chief is going to be prohibited from lobbying back to the government on any adjudicatory-type matter that was pending in his bureau or office during his final year of federal service. (The same thing would apply as you go down the food chain: a division head couldn't come back and lobby on any adjudicatory-type proceeding that was pending in his division during his final year here. Going up the chain, the Office of Government Ethics has opined that everything pending at an agency is under the official responsibility of the head of that agency. Therefore, after leaving the commission a former chairman could not come back and lobby the federal government on any adjudicatory-type matter that was pending anywhere in the commission during his final year of service.) These two restrictions apply to all former employees of the commission (or any other executive branch or independent agency, for that matter) and are not confined to former senior personnel.

. . . [F]ormer "senior" officials (commissioners, bureau or office chiefs, and most members of the Senior Executive Service, for our purposes) are also subject to the 18 USC 207(c) one-year bar on coming back to the FCC representing anyone else on any matter, rule makings as well as adjudications, regardless of whether they participated in the matter or had it pending under their official responsibility. For former "senior" personnel there can obviously be some overlap between 207(c) and the two 207(a) restrictions during that first year's cooling-off period.

Index